The
ESSENTIAL
OUTDOOR GEAR
MANUAL

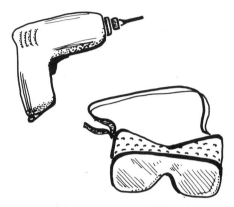

The
ESSENTIAL
OUTDOOR GEAR
MANUAL

Equipment Care & Repair for Outdoorspeople

Annie Getchell

Ragged Mountain Press
Camden, Maine

Published by Ragged Mountain Press

10 9 8 7 6 5 4 3 2 1

Copyright © 1995 Annie Getchell

Library of Congress Cataloging-in-Publication Data
Getchell, Annie.
    The essential outdoor gear manual : equipment care and repair for
outdoorspeople / Annie Getchell
        p.   cm
    Includes bibliographical references and index.
    ISBN 0-07-023169-9
    1.   Outdoor recreation—Equipment and supplies—Maintenance and
repair—Handbooks, manuals, etc.   I.Title.
GV191.76.G48
688.7'6028'8—dc20   95-7756
                                      CIP

Questions regarding the content of this book should
be addressed to:
Ragged Mountain Press
P.O. Box 220
Camden, ME 04843

Questions regarding the ordering of this book should
be addressed to:
McGraw-Hill, Inc.
Customer Service Department
P.O. Box 547
Blacklick, OH 43004
1-800-822-8158

♻ *The Essential Outdoor Gear Manual* is printed on
recycled paper containing a minimum of 50% total
recycled paper with 10% postconsumer de-inked fiber.

A percentage of the price of this book is donated to
the Access Fund, a national nonprofit climbers' organization
working exclusively to protect the natural resources used
by climbers and climbers' access to those resources.

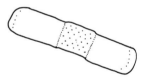

the ACCESS FUND
...*preserving America's diverse
climbing resources.*

Printed by R.R. Donnelley, Crawfordsville, IN

Design and Production by Dan Kirchoff

Illustrated by Annie Getchell

Edited by Jon Eaton, Dorcas S. Miller, Jerry Novesky,
Tom McCarthy

To Dorcas Miller, with her keen sense of direction.
Thanks for pointing me down the path.

Contents

Acknowledgments   x

Preface   xi

Part I: Soft Goods   1

1. Essential Techniques   4
Sewing Basics • Fabric Patching
Zippers: The Full Disclosure • Fasteners
Seams and Seamsealing

2. Fabrics & Insulations   26
Unraveling Fabric Mysteries • Insulations
Cleaning Methods • Patching • Seamsealing
Coating or Recoating Synthetics

3. Specialty Garments   38
Wetsuits and Neoprene Care • Drysuits
Shelled Gloves • Gaiters

4. Shelter   46
Tents • Sleeping Bags • Sleeping Pads

5. Packs   70
The Five-Point Pack Check • Packrats
Patching • External Frame Packs
The Tumpline

Part II: Footwear   78

6. Weatherproofing Boots   80
Keeping the Water Out • Boot Linings
Drying Boots

7. Custom Fitting   85
Breaking In • Boot-Fitting • Lacing Tips and Tricks

8. Boot Repairs   89
Typical Repairs • Ski Touring and Telemark Boots
Plastic Mountain Boots • Rock Shoes
Rubber Boots

Part III: Hardware   98

9. Stoves & Cookware   100
The Crankiest Item in your Pack • Stove Types
Pressurized Liquid-Fuel Stoves, Simplified
General Stove Maintenance • Fuel Conservation
Cold-Weather and High-Altitude Operation •
Small-Space Safety • Get the Most from Your
Cookware • Cast Iron Cookware

10. Water Filters   111
Filter Field Care • Bleach Flush

11. *Knives & Multitools*   114
   Cleaning • Storage • Gaining an Edge

12. *Optics & Lights*   119
   Binoculars • Cameras • Goggles and Glasses
   A Bit About Batteries • Headlamps and Flashlights

13. *Climbing Gear*   132
   Carabiners • SLCDs, Friends, and Assorted
   Springy-Thingys • Ropes • Slings and Kevlar Cord
   Harnesses • Ice Tools • Crampons

14. *Winter Gear*   142
   Touring Skis • Bindings • Poles • Skins
   Snowshoes • Collapsible Avalanche Shovels
   Sleds and Pulks

Part IV: Paddling   161

15. *Boats*   164
   Hull Materials at a Glance

16. *Rules of the Resin*   168
   Bad Juju • Thermoset Resins
   Resin Types • Safe Sets

17. *Hull Materials*   173
   ABS or Royalex • Aluminum
   Skin-over-Frame, a.k.a. Folding Boats
   Fiberglass and Kevlar • Gelcoat
   Polyethylene Hulls • Wood-and-Canvas

18. *Canoe Inspection*   201
   Gunwales • Furniture: Seats and Thwarts

19. *Kayak Inspection*   206
   Bulkheads • Rudder Assembly • Hatches
   Cockpit Coaming • Hanging Seats
   Footbraces • Sprayskirts • Hardware
   Seams • Deck Rigging • Storage Tips

20. *Paddles & PFDs*   216
   Wood Paddles • Composite Paddles • PFDs

21. *Dry Storage & Flotation*   221
   Patching • Dry Bag Tips • Flotation Bag Tips
   Dry Boxes

Appendices   225

A. *Adhesives*   225

B. *Low-Tox Cleaning Solutions*   229

C. *Kit Suggestions*   232

D. *Tools & Supplies for the Trail & Shop*   236

E. *Useful Knots*   239

F. *Directory of Repair Services*   242

G. *Materials Resources*   246

H. *Recommended Reading*   248

Index   250

Always in a pinch, when nothing else will do
It's the only thing that'll get your goofy ass through

When the tent rips, a pole breaks
Or someone's mouth keeps flappin'
Just pull it out, peel it off
And get yourself to strappin'

Blisters it will bandage, sunglasses it will bind
It'll downright save your ass
In most perils you will find

It ain't glue
It ain't paste
It ain't American Express

Think simple
Think clean
Allow your sorry self a guess

Feel its strength, sense its aura
Get yourself a roll tomorra'

Now you're set for any scrape
With your ol' friend . . . duct tape

—Mark Jenkins and Sue Ibarra

Acknowledgments

There's an old axiom, or should be one: something about how the more you know, the less you know you know. You know? My head started spinning the day this project began. Nearly every telephone call led me into some smart person's particular lair of expertise; several factory tours yielded enough material for as many books. The enthusiasm and willingness to educate from so many folks was heartening, occasionally overwhelming, and always appreciated. Thanks everyone for the interest, support, and patient guidance.

Dorcas Miller; Paul Hebert, Ascension Enterprises; Paul Ramer, Ramer Products; Audrey Sutherland; Win Ellis; Randy Burnett, Brunton USA; Jerry Lloyd, Kitty Graham, Pete Haggerty, and Diana Eken, Cascade Designs; Rob Center, Kay Henry, and Ken Beauchemin, Mad River Canoe; Amy Fischer; Dan Hammill, McNett Corporation; John Abbenhouse and crew, Northwest Kayaks; Stuart and Marianne Smith, Maine Sport Outfitters; David "The Doctor" Goodman; Dave van Kleeck, Nantahala Outdoor Center; Mark Jenkins; Tom McCarthy; the folks at Feathered Friends; Karen Peil, Five Ten; Jen Fuller, the cover girl; Chris Townsend; Mark Eckhart, Klepper Service Center; Phil Savignano, L.L. Bean Outdoor Discovery Program; John Harlin; Doug Simpson, Feathercraft; Cathi "Petal" Buni; Luke Hallman, Headwaters; Patrick Smith, Mountainsmith; the Cobblers: Steve Komito, Dave Page, David Yulan, and others; Greg Wozer, Leki Sport; Kenyon Consumer Products; Steve and Mary Gorman; Trondak/Aquaseal; Ted Dishner and Pendra Legasse, Moss Tents; Steve "Cupcake" Howe; Brad McAllister, Vista Recreation; Gordon Roe and Mike Ridout, MSR; Peter "Allah" Cole; Bob Upton, Rainy Pass Repair; Stowe Canoe and Snowshoe Company; Malcolm Daly, Trango USA; Paul Cleveland; Mike McCabe, ZRK Enterprises; Mike Curtis, Nikwax; Jerry Novesky; editors Jon Eaton and Tom McCarthy at Ragged Mountain Press; plus all the Grewes and Getchells, most especially my husband, Dave, savant of outdoor esoterica.

Further Note: This compendium of snippets, tips, and techniques spans myriad resources, including a zillion books and magazines. Those listed in Recommended Reading certainly guided the development of this project and are heartily recommended for a complete outdoor library. However, the real substance of research is contained in the countless product manuals, manufacturers' literature, and personal anecdotes from afield. Every attempt has been made to credit those contributions and make specific recommendations for further reading throughout the text.

Preface

Grow a Deeper Shade of Green

The cover says "Care & Repair," but this book is really about becoming a greener gearhead. While more and more outdoor equipment is marketed as "green," these lower-impact products amount to something of a mixed blessing that still promotes consumption. A better solution may be to look at what you already have in a new way. You can start by simply adopting a few new attitudes.

Use what you have. Outdoor gear can usually withstand a lot more abuse than weekend warriors dish out, and too many of us graduate to shinier, techier toys long before old ones wear out.

Maintain your equipment. Gear lasts longer and performs better given regular sessions of seam-sealing, waterproofing, cleaning, or tuning. Tinkering is fun, educational, and ensures reliable service from your equipment when you most need it. A little time spent puttering can be relaxing and meditative—a sort of mental half-step to some windy place you'd rather be, even if there's no time to actually go there.

Repair rather than replace. Fixing up rather than buying up can save enough to pay the airfare for a dream adventure. And just how big is that box of stuff you've been meaning to mend? My friend John moved his box from coast to coast

without ever opening it, but thinks the contents include torn rainpants, gored gaiters, bent ski bindings, a shorted-out headlamp, a bunch of tired boots, and assorted unknown stove parts. If you aren't going to fix stuff, give it to someone who will, or enlist a reputable repair center for a first-rate job.

Almost any gear is worth the effort to restore. Not long ago, I dropped off my battered rucksack at an outfitters for a repair estimate. Even though the shop offers a well-stocked preventive maintenance department, the salesperson quickly dismissed the idea, because major surgery would run nearly as much as a similar, new pack. The price, maybe, but not the cost—global cost of manufacturing, that is.

Keep old gear in circulation. The woods are crawling with incurable funhogs who windmill through equipment fads and trends. This accumulated, outmoded, outgrown stuff has more than sentimental value. Sell used hardware at an equipment swap or consignment shop; hold a cooperative gear sale with a gang of cronies, then take a trip with the ill-gotten cash. Churches, schools, and other charitable services do backflips for donations of warm, practical outerwear and usable sporting equipment. With just a few phone calls, we once assembled an entire family camping kit (packs, bags, tent, stove, boots, and more) for a neighbor whose home was destroyed by fire—all with stuff from the attic.

Replace your gear with pre-owned models. This book helps you profit from others' ignorance and unwillingness to care for their equipment. We recently acquired yet another canoe—a really nice one—on the cheap; all it needed was attention to the wood trim and minor patching at the stern. Buying used gear is like buying a used car: someone else takes the depreciation.

Modify and innovate. Recycle odd parts into functional inventions all your own. Consider this guide a primer of sorts that will teach the basics of materials, glues, and fasteners so you have the technical background to create custom gear.

Inquire about manufacturing practices and materials used in products you're considering buying. This book may enlighten you about the petrochemical nature of our leisure-time toys.

Learn to appreciate lasting quality. The more you repair, the more you'll value good design. One well-made backpack might outlast three el cheapos. If you're going to use plastic gear, you owe it to the planet to use less. Besides, the people who dream up and build the best outdoor gear deserve our support.

How to Navigate This Tome

In our golden age of sound bites and channel-surfing, the temptation to skim is nearly irresistible. Before barging straight into the table of contents in search of specific repair scenarios (like unclogging your stove), please take a moment to understand just how the book is organized.

First of all, I'm giving you credit for being familiar enough with gear to have wrecked it in the first place; for having a functional brain; for grasping the universal dharma of duct tape.

Given that all-purpose field repair is rarely more exotic than a roll of silver tape and a little red knife, this book focuses primarily on preventive maintenance. Each section starts with the building blocks of materials, design, and construction, followed by inherent weaknesses and typical failures. You'll find pertinent suggestions for field-fixes before going over the broad brushstrokes of effecting permanent repairs at home. You'll also learn when to cut your losses and send the mess off to a professional.

To best apprehend the contents, begin with Essential Techniques outlined in Chapter One, where you'll find the most generally useful and condensed information, like zipper repair, stain removal, or seamsealing tips. Then read the appendices. Otherwise, prepare to be sidetracked by cross-references to these sections throughout the text.

While looking for particulars, keep in mind that each section is designed to be read chronologically, so you first understand the materials at hand. This book is *not* designed to deliver the detailed beta, with exhaustive step-by-step repair directions for every conceivable broken widget. Rather, I'm offering a more conceptual treatment of techniques so you can apply what's needed to your unique situation.

By no means is this the last word on any of the topics discussed, but an opening to the world of outdoor equipment self-reliance. Like my novelist friend Marko says, "the book will never be finished, you just have to stop."

All puns are intentional.

—Annie Getchell,
Camden, Maine
April 1995

Part I

Soft Goods

*I cannot remember the number of needles I broke in
sewing the tent as I had to work in the quiet of the night
by the flickering light of an oil lamp, made from a
corned-beef tin. The thread I was compelled to use
proved to be so bad that I had to smear it with pitch.
Unlike thread and needles I did not need to "acquire" the
pitch, because we had it in plenty.*

—Felice Benuzzi, *No Picnic on Mount Kenya*

What More Could You Possibly Need?

When preparing for a wilderness adventure, there are two general packing methods. One is to pack hours before departure, wildly grabbing and stuffing, then stopping here and there en route to the put-in or trailhead to pick up last-minute or forgotten items. Followers of this school often wind up with too much gear, yet missing essential components like matches or a tent.

A second system advocated by the more disciplined is to carefully list and lay out every available manifestation of outdoor technology, accounting for plausible panhandling by practitioners of the first methodology. While this person may not have forgotten anything, he or she is certainly overburdened.

A happy medium? Consider the kit of our ancestors. Pioneers, trappers, and mountain men all carried less than an average woman does in her purse, yet they were ready for anything the wilderness could dish out. Called a "possibles" bag, an adventurer's 14-inch by 17-inch kit ensured comfort as well as survival. A possibles bag generally contained a knife and whetstone, tin cup for boiling water, tea, beeswax or lard for lubricating/waterproofing, awl, needle and waxed linen thread, several fish hooks and sinkers, and tinder, striker and flint. A little grain and dried meat supplemented each journey.

Patrick Smith, modern man and frequent traveler, also employs a possibles bag. Smith, better known as the founder and designer of Mountainsmith Packs, was once a teacher of wilderness survival and living skills in his home state of Colorado. Meticulous, Smith rarely leaves home without his signature lumbar pack that contains, among other things, his possibles bag. When asked, he'll enthusiastically review its contents, some of which have been in the kit for 20 years. "Someday I'll be in a plane wreck," he says, "and I'll be ready."

Patrick Smith's Possibles Bag

On his person:
- small notebook and mechanical pencil
- key chain with AAA Maglite
- wallet (which contains a spare AAA battery plus spare lead/eraser for his pencil)
- Swiss Army "Tinker" knife
- lip grease
- butane lighter

Possibles Bag Contents (in no particular order)
- compass
- lightweight gloves and hat
- Superglue
- wire saw
- nylon repair tape
- tiny tube of Urebond adhesive
- bandanna
- four spare AA batteries
- compact fluorescent light (uses AAs)
- several plastic Ziploc bags, large and small
- toilet paper and small package of baby wipes
- assorted rubber bands
- fiberglass strapping tape
- Power Bar
- toothbrush
- tiny headlamp (uses AAs)
- spare headlamp bulb
- fire-starting kit: Trioxane fire-starter, lighter, metal match
- insect repellent
- tape measure (Smith's a designer, remember?)
- custom sewing kit with nylon thread (*See Sewing Kits, this section, page 6*)
- slice of adhesive-backed Velcro
- first-aid bag: gauze, butterfly bandages, antihistamine, Tums, Kaopectate, aspirin, prescription pain killer and muscle relaxant, burn ointment, antibiotic
- antifog cloth for glasses
- fluorescent orange tape
- tiny stuffsack used for pillow
- baking-powder tin for melting snow/boiling water
- dental floss
- tiny whetstone
- tiny flask of baking powder for toothpaste
- ear plugs (for rushing streams and snoring companions)
- wire
- safety pins
- biodegradable soap
- tiny straw for sipping out of puddles or starting fires
- eyeglass screwdriver
- quarter-sized magnifying lens (for working with eyeglass screwdriver)
- bicycle valve core
- nail clippers
- tweezers
- tiny Peruvian worry doll

Patrick Smith never leaves home without his "Possibles" bag.

Chapter 1

Essential Techniques

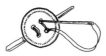

"Open thy bundle!"
It was the usual collection of small oddments: bits of
cloth, quack medicines, cheap fairings, twists of down-
country tobacco, tawdry pipe-stems and a packet of
curry-stuff all wrapped in a quilt.

—Rudyard Kipling, *Kim*

(See also Appendix A: Adhesives, *page 225.)*

Sewing Basics

Stitching a makeshift patch or reattaching a pack strap are pretty simple operations, requiring little skill with a needle. For those interested in more refined techniques (including replacing a zipper or creating a custom garment), check out the Materials Resources section for suppliers of notions and advice, or seek out a copy of Louise L. Sumner's *Sew & Repair Your Own Outdoor Gear.* Your local library houses many other books on this age-old craft. The methods discussed here are straightforward solutions to the most primitive sewing needs.

Needles and Thread

- For packcloth and multiple layers of rugged fabric, heavy-duty nylon thread, carpet thread, waxed linen, or dental floss are all suitable.
- For finer fabrics, including nylon taffeta, ripstop, laminates, or coated materials, use cotton-poly blend thread that is not overly strong. Thread that's too strong (like a thick nylon thread or monofilament line) will slice right through lightweight fabrics.
- Unless sewing on a button, don't double thread for stitching—you just make larger holes in the fabric.
- Use short lengths of thread—thread that is too long snarls easily and is weakened each time you tug it through the stitch hole.
- When removing stitches, use small scissors or tweezers to clip and pluck each thread. Don't be tempted to use a razor knife—you risk creating more of a repair than you started with.
- Carry several sizes of needles—they weigh next to nothing and are invaluable, particularly as gifts in remote villages.
- Use embroidery needles, which have bigger eyes for easy threading in the bush.

Always sew with a short thread. Long thread will tangle & weaken from being pulled repeatedly.

Techniques

Backstitching

Backstitching is a strong, simple stitch for closing seam tears.

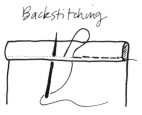

Backstitching

Hemming

Also called whipping or overhand stitch, the hem stitch is useful for attaching non-structural patches and repairing garments. The long, slanting stitches are visible on the working side; the finished side reveals little, since you catch just one or two fabric threads with each stitch.

Hemming or whipping stitch

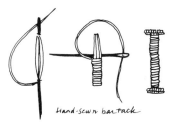

Handmade Bar Tack

A bar tack can prevent further ripping at the end of a fly or pocket, or can be used to reattach a belt loop or pack strap. Hand-sewing a bar tack is easy—make several long stitches to form the length of the bar tack. Small overhand stitches across the threads strengthen the bar. Finish with tiny bar stitches at each end.

Hand-sewn bar tack

Darning

Darning mitts is a pleasant, meditative task ideally suited to transcontinental flights or waiting out storms in your tent. Reinforcing socks or mitts requires little more than understanding the concept of weaving. The real trick is to work in new yarn or

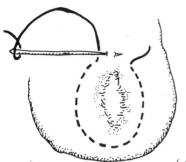

using thread or yarn to match original, run stitches around hole or worn area.

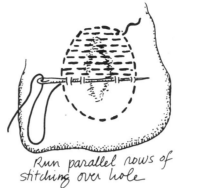

Run parallel rows of stitching over hole

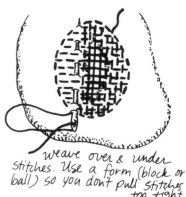

weave over & under stitches. Use a form (block or ball) so you don't pull stitches too tight.

Splicing socks; a.k.a. darning.

threads so there are no hard, blister-causing ridges. Thick yarn makes the job quick, but the repair won't be as long-lasting; try to match the diameter of the original fibers.

If you're beefing up a sock, employ a rock or tennis ball as your darning form (hardcore Yankees use a special darning ball that looks like something from a croquet set). Make a running-stitch perimeter around the worn area. Then run parallel rows of stitching across the hole. Work back-and-forth until the hole or worn spot is covered with parallel threads. Turn the work and run the thread or yarn through the stitch lines as if weaving—over, under, over. Don't draw the threads taut or the fabric will pucker.

Sailor's Palm

Basically a giant thimble, the palm protects the paws of salty dogs as they mend sails. The thick leather fits around your hand so you can stab away through multiple fabric layers with a heavy awl or needle and thread. Palms are convenient to carry in your pack

Sailmaker's Palm lets you hand-sew heavy fabrics or use an awl with ease.

Sewing Kits

A useful kit can be made by filling a 35-mm film canister with safety pins, needles, a few buttons, plus several colors and thicknesses of thread.

Make a tiny, self-contained kit with a matchbook. Cut matches out of the folder; notch sides and wrap with different threads. Staple or glue a piece of fabric to the top for holding needles and safety pins. (This is a great gift for kids to make.)

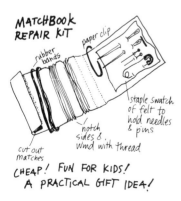

MATCHBOOK REPAIR KIT

paper clip

rubber bands

staple swatch of felt to hold needles & pins

notch sides & wind with thread

cut out matches

CHEAP! FUN FOR KIDS! A PRACTICAL GIFT IDEA!

Patrick Smith used a small section of an old aluminum tent pole to create a nifty sewing kit. Rubber caps on each end hold needles inside; the tube is wrapped with heavy-duty nylon thread.

The best kit, formerly distributed by Chouinard/Black Diamond Equipment, may still be found in outdoor stores or through Kenyon Consumer Products (*See Appendix G, page 246*). This tiny leather pouch includes the essentials plus the field lock-stitching assembly mentioned above.

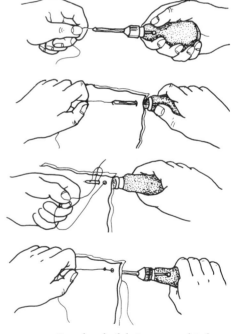

Tiny but tough

tent tubing wrapped with thread & filled with needles.

Sewing Awls and Lock-Stitchers

If you need an awl, you're working with rugged fabric or lots of layers, so be patient and focus so you don't punch a hole into a fingernail, as I've managed to do more than once. For leather, initiate holes before attempting to stitch—use the leather punch on your Swiss Army knife, hammer and finish nail, or ice pick.

Some field kits include a collapsible awl that combines a sewing machine needle, cotter pin, and plastic joint. Lock-stitchers, like the Speedy Stitcher (other brands are available), are a "machine" version of the basic awl and include a bobbin and tensioning post.

Lock-Stitching
- Draw out enough thread to cover the repair area plus about 4 inches for tolerance. If the repair is large, break up the stitching into several short sections so you're not encumbered with excess thread.
- Push the needle through the material, then draw the end of the thread through with your other hand. Pull the needle back out (leaving a long tail of thread).
- Push the needle through the material to make a stitch, then pull the needle halfway back, creating a loop of thread at the end of the needle.
- Thread the tail end of the thread through the loop, then fully withdraw the needle. Pull with equal tension on both awl and free thread, so the stitching appears the same on each side of the material. Don't pull so hard the material puckers.
- Repeat the procedure, taking care not to pucker the material, and finish the row by tying the two ends of the thread together on one side of the fabric.

Sew beefy fabrics or multiple layers with a lock-stitcher.

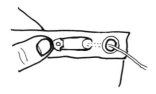

Rethreading Drawstrings

I thought everybody knew how to rethread a drawstring, so was astonished to stumble across my husband fumbling with his parka waistcord. Simply attach a cotter pin, paper clip or safety pin to one end of the string. Insert the pin into grommet or eyelet and begin threading the drawstring through the casing. Move the pin along through the channel by feeling with your fingers. Don't forget to knot the drawstring so it doesn't slip through again.

Fabric Patching

(See also: Seams and Seam Sealing, *page 21;*
Appendix A: Adhesives, *page 225.)*

Patches are badges of honor in two ways: They identify those who get out and really *use* their gear while at the same time revealing the sort of respect folks give to their possessions.

Prevention Patches

Regular inspection of all your gear alerts you to weaknesses and potential failures. Often you can reinforce a worn spot by sealing, taping, or patching, cover an abraded tent pole sleeve with matching nylon tape, or caulk tiny punctures in a gaiter with adhesive. Prevention patches *protect* the design integrity of any gear. Failure permanently weakens a structure, and a repair is often stronger than the material around it, causing further stress to the original (damaged and undamaged) areas.

Field Fix: The Duct Tape or Nylon Adhesive Patch

Considered a *temporary* repair, a taped patch may actually cling for years. I've longed to rip the dangling duct tape off a friend's tattered down vest but have so far managed to control this urge. Taped patches are best suited to puncture wounds in light nylon and other fabrics, or gear not often exposed to moisture. Taping does not work to hold stretched, stressed fabric together. The larger the tear, the less effective a taped patch will be.

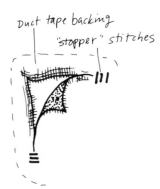

Ice axes & brambles often cause "L" shaped fabric tears. In the field, prevent further ripping by stitching tear terminus shut. Secure flapping fabric by backing with duct tape.

Just like any other glue or patch job, a successful taped patch depends on a clean, dry, prepped surface for best adhesion. In the field, these conditions are hard to control, so carry a foil-sealed alcohol swab in your repair kit. The alcohol will help your raingear or tent fly dry out enough for duct tape or nylon tape to stick.
- Clean and prep fabric.
- Cut patch at least ½ inch larger than the damaged area.
  Rounded edges on the patch are essential.

- Join two sides of tear together so they meet but don't overlap. Don't trim ragged edges.
- Place tape with adhesive facing inside and burnish patch edges with a blunt stick or spoon. Lay a paper barrier between the patch and your burnishing device so you don't agitate the edges of the patch and cause them to peel.
- Any straggling fibers can be burned back with a lighter or candle flame.

Urethane Adhesive Patches

Punctures in single layers of fabric lend themselves to adhesive patches. Small tears in low-stress areas are also adhesive patch candidates—sometimes a combination of nylon tape with adhesive works well. Since all adhesives shrink to some degree as they cure, and often cause fabrics to pucker, try to find an adhesive formulated to cure with minimal shrinkage, like those from McNett Corporation.

Urethane adhesive patches dry clear and are extremely flexible and waterproof. This type of patch is perfect for tent netting, wetsuit tears, holes in fabric/leather footwear, Hypalon boats, or snowshoe decking, and for just about any other patch that's smaller than a

there's a reason why Band-Aids have rounded edges -- they stick better, longer.

The Beauty and Perils of Duct Tape

As the heart of most repair kits and silver lining to many a catastrophe, duct tape certainly qualifies as the "eleventh essential." One day I asked everyone who called or dropped by to recall their most recent use for duct tape . . .

- Climbing skin
- Ski pole strap
- Heels ("Duct tape is much better than moleskin and sticks for many days," says outdoor writer/photographer Steve Howe. "The shiny surface doesn't catch on socks and peel off."
- Therm-a-Rest
- Windpants
- Gaiters
- Boots (along with some wire)
- Kayak crack
- Split canoe paddle

Despite its wonderful versatility, there's nothing a repair specialist hates more than duct

Silver solution

tape. In her years as a custom gear designer and "surgeon" at Needle Mountain Designs, Peggy Quinn has had to work around thousands of gummy blobs left by emergency duct tape applications. The silver solution may be terrific in the field, warns Quinn, but you may create a need for more extensive repair if tape is left to bake into the fabric indefinitely. Gray tape's tenacious adhesives are tough to remove even with solvents and abrasive cleaners (which can damage fabrics). Additionally, it's difficult to stitch through any residue—broken needles, gummed-up thread, and vile curses are guaranteed.

Similarly, those who rely on duct tape to patch a kayak hull should be forewarned that the stuff sticks just as determinedly to fiberglass. **Consider any tape a temporary fix.**

Shades of Glue

Throughout this guide you will encounter many references to urethane adhesive patches, whether for a wetsuit, fabric boot, or tent. While there are many urethane products available, those manufactured by McNett Corporation in Bellingham, Washington, are formulated especially for outdoor uses.

McNett offers shades of glue for various applications, and the biggest difference between them is their viscosity, or resistance to flow. For example, you'd need a stiff adhesive to patch a boot toe bumper so the glue won't flow away while hardening; conversely, a thinner mix will penetrate stitching better when seamsealing a rainfly.

The three main choices are:
- *Free Sole*—Engineered for high abrasion-resistance, this is the thickest, stickiest goop you'll find. Ideal for patching footwear, or filling gouges.
- *Aquaseal*—This medium-weight formula needs the support of a fabric to stay in place while hardening. Best use: wetsuit repair, general fabric patching.
- *Seam Grip*—McNett's thinnest adhesive is designed for maximum stick and flexibility; like the name says, use it for seamsealing or when you want to penetrate a material, as when patching a self-inflated sleeping pad.

quarter. This type of patch is really a home repair; the adhesive should cure undisturbed.
- Clean and prep both sides of fabric.
- Follow procedure for taped patch, except the tape should be placed on the back side of fabric (adhesive forms the outside patch).
- Turn over and apply urethane adhesive to exterior, covering tear plus ¼ inch.
- Lay flat and allow full cure time.

Sewn Patches

A sewn patch can be done with a patient hand in the field, but is most commonly performed at home with a machine. A sewn patch requires more finesse than most people realize, and it is commonly botched. Master gear-fixer Bob Upton at Rainy Pass Repair has rescued hundreds of failed home repairs and abandoned efforts to fix tents and garments. He recommends turning a patch job over to an expert whenever possible. "People think they'll save money doing a repair themselves and end up spending more because we have to *undo* everything they did," says Upton.

Part of the difficulty lies in the fact that a small patch often isn't effective—an entire panel of fabric may need replacement to ensure a successful repair, which involves meticulous de- and reconstruction of the damaged item. Knowledge of how a particular fabric stretches and accepts stress is also important. If you don't sew in the first place, save yourself time, money, and a big headache—send your damaged gear to its original manufacturer or to a specialist listed in

Bob Upton of Rainy Pass Repair in Seattle enjoys showing the difference between a typical home repair and a professional's approach to stitching outdoor gear.

Typical home patch job.

Pinch patch (bags, insulated garments).

Mock-felled patch (tents, other stressed fabrics).

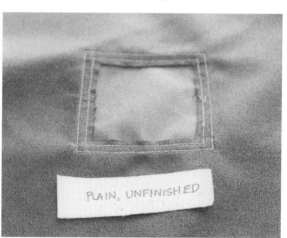

Unfinished patch with heat-sealed edges (heavy fabric bags and packs, mosquito netting).

Appendix G (page 246). Same goes if the garment or tent is new: Send the repair to the manufacturer or to a qualified repair center to assure a virtually invisible repair that will last at least as long as the manufacturer intended the gear to work in the first place.

Another point to consider when facing a big patch job is whether your repair will be too strong for the surrounding fabric. For instance, my friend Steve asked me to fix his tent fly, torn at a stake-out loop. While making the repair, I accidentally punctured another area of fabric a little too easily. I realized that the fly had succumbed to UV degradation and that further efforts to save it were moot.

Patching Tips for the Strong-Hearted

- Stop the tear in its tracks. Run a few stitches perpendicular to the rip to prevent further tearing. In vinyl or plastic, make a small round hole at the end of the tear to keep it from spreading.
- The best patch is sewn through existing seams, preserving the overall strength and waterproofness of the garment or shelter by minimizing the number of stitch holes.
- To open up an area larger than the patch, clip seam stitches individually with scissors. Never tempt fate by using a razor knife. You may have to remove a bar-tacked webbing loop—remember to mark its placement.
- Try to use repair material that matches the original fabric weight as closely as possible. Also try to match the weave when cutting the patch so patch threads lie along the same angle as the original material.
- Trace the angles onto your patch fabric, allowing extra fabric for turning edges under, if appropriate, and for splicing into a seam.
- Heat-seal patch edges. If you're turning edges under, press with a warm iron (on the uncoated side).

- Don't pin the patch to the fabric being repaired or you risk further tearing of fabric. If you need to stabilize the patch, tack it with a dot of quick-setting glue, like Superglue.
- Practice stitching on scraps to determine tension and stitch length (generally 10 to 12 stitches per inch in most light- and midweight nylons).
- Splice in patch, removing from the machine at regular intervals to smooth fabric; make sure the patch is lined up and the stitches are even. Before beginning the second line of stitching, remove from machine and review your work.
- For large patches, trim away original damaged fabric to within 1 inch of the patch stitching. Fold the cut edges of the fabric under and incorporate them into the second, inner line of stitching.
- Close up opened seams, replacing webbing with bar tacks if necessary.
- Seal along stitch lines. (*See Seams and Seamsealing, page 21.*)

Whether cut from tape or fabric, a round patch offers no snagging edges & will transmit/absorb an even load on stressed fabric.

Reinforcement Patches

If a snap, grommet, or webbing loop pulls out, it's because the strength of these fasteners surpasses that of the surrounding fabric; if a load is greater than seam strength, fabric will give way. Simply replacing the fastener does not cure the disease; you must create a reinforcement patch to evenly distribute load stress so the fabric will hold.

Use a heavier weight fabric than the original for a reinforcement patch. A round patch will evenly distribute stress on the fabric—if that's not possible, at least use rounded edges on the patch. Follow patching instructions above, then replace the fastener as needed. (*See Fasteners, page 17.*)

Zippers: The Full Disclosure

(See also Specialty Garments: Drysuit Zippers, *page 41.)*

Whatever you do
watch out for your lip
don't let it get bloodied
in the doggone zip.
Watch too for beards
scarves and hair
none of these
belong in there.
—Karen van Allsburg

Ever stop to count the zippers you're heading into the backcountry with? Your pack, tent, raingear, gaiters, and miscellaneous pouches all feature zipper closures—an average weekender will use about two dozen of the buggers. Despite their ubiquitousness, most people have never examined a zipper's anatomy and thus unnecessarily fall prey to the dreaded *Gaposis* on a cold winter's night.

The modern zipper is essentially similar to Whitcomb Judson's 1891 invention. Today's outdoor gear employs two general types of nylon zippers: *toothed* and *coil*. Both work with the same basic parts and are easy to troubleshoot once you identify them.

Toothed zippers have metal or molded nylon teeth, shaped like interlocking puzzle pieces, and generally operate more smoothly than coil types. Toothed zippers can take various forms: A **one-way separating zipper** has a stop at one end and is open at the other (this is the most common type, found on most clothing); a **two-way separating zipper** can be opened at both ends (like on parkas or sleeping bags).

Non-separating coil zippers utilize interlocking coils woven into the zipper tape; they're about twice as strong under stress as toothed zippers. Coil zippers have closure stops at both ends; the slider or sliders (there can be two) either open or close the teeth on each pass (this is the type of zipper commonly found on tents and packs). Non-separating zippers are self-healing—a pass with the slider will reunite the sides immediately.

Zipper Parts

Sliders have the onerous and underappreciated task of meshing two rows of zipper teeth or coils together into an integrated fastener. Inherently mechanical, a slider is usually the first part of a zipper to malfunction because it operates within very close tolerances.

Insert pins and retaining box are permanent, dovetailed parts of toothed zippers. The box, on one tape of a one-way zipper, receives

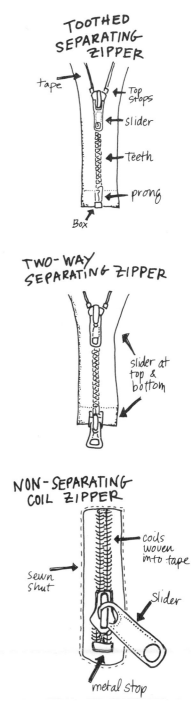

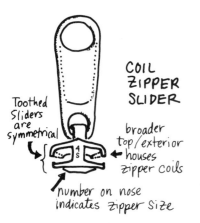

COIL ZIPPER SLIDER

Toothed Sliders are symmetrical

broader top/exterior ← houses zipper coils

number on nose indicates zipper size

the insert pin from the other side. On a two-way zipper, there are two pins, or prongs; the bottom slider serves as a box.

Stops are made of either metal or plastic, and can be removed and replaced (metal stops can be pried off and reused). Stops prevent the slider from coming off either end of the zipper. They are found at the bottom and both top ends of a separating zipper; one stop straddles both rows of a non-separating zipper at each end point.

Tape is the fabric to which the teeth and pins are molded. Tape on a toothed zipper has a reinforced area at box and pins. On a coil zipper, continuous nylon coil is woven directly into the tape; since coil zippers are cut to length, they have no reinforced areas of tape.

Zipper Size

Zipper size is designated by a number on the slider's nose; higher numbers indicate a more substantial zipper (No. 10 is strongest). Remember that a No. 5 coil zipper is nearly as strong as a No. 10 toothed zipper, but the larger zipper may withstand more use, dirt, and strain before failure. Consideration of their differing capabilities is just as important as the size.

Troubleshooting

Broken or Missing Element

A missing tooth, box, or pin will allow the slider to come off and disappear into space. While none of these parts is repairable as such, there are a few stopgap measures you can take to maximize your zipper mileage.

If a tooth is missing near the top or bottom of a separating zipper, you can insert a stop in place of the tooth to prevent losing the slider. This can be a regular zipper stop, a few turns of thread, or several drops of epoxy, seam sealer, or Superglue. If a tooth is missing in the middle of the zipper's track, place a stop across both rows or sew the rows shut at that point—you'll be able to zip halfway until you replace the zipper. Keep a spare stop in your kit.

Mashed Coils

Nylon coil zippers may be crushed in spots by fancy footwork or hardware abrasion. The slider will not be able to mesh this area properly, and the zipper will open at most inopportune moments. It's possible to realign coil loops with a straight pin: Slide the pin under damaged loops one at a time and tug very gently to pull them back into shape. Next, replace the slider to help to straighten the coils.

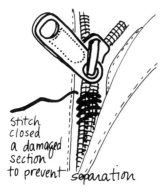

stitch closed a damaged section to prevent separation

Broken Slider Pull

Extremely common, with uncommon remedies, is the broken pull. Ribbon, a fishing swivel, paperclip, whistle, twine—you are limited only by your imagination. I find this an excellent use for leftover single earrings.

Worn Slider, a.k.a. Zipper Won't Stay Zipped
This is the most common coil zip failure. A slider gets worn from plain hard use, but it tires more quickly from grit trapped along the elements. Especially trying for a slider is the human when fabric gets jammed in the zipper. Rather than yanking on the pull, fetch your pliers and pull the fabric out. Otherwise you'll likely bend the slider.

If the zipper stays open after a pass with the slider, you can remedy the situation with a delicate pinching operation. First, open the zipper. This is sometimes difficult, so carefully align elements and feed them into the slider. (If the slider is truly stuck, pry it off with a screwdriver and replace as described below.)

When the zipper is open (separating zipper) or all the way to its start (non-separating), begin goosing with pliers. Squeeze just a little on one side, then on the other, with equal pressure. Try the zipper. Repeat the process two or three times until you have properly tightened the slider. Caution: Heavy-handed squeezing may overpinch the slider and it will refuse to work, or even worse, smash coils. If the slider sticks, pry off and replace.

NON-SEPARATING ZIPPER IN POSITION FOR PINCHING SLIDER

Replacing the Slider

Separating Zipper
Separate the zipper (you may need to pry off the old slider). Remove the stop on top of the slider (box) side of the zipper, and take the slider off. Check the size of the slider before tossing it aside. Replace the slider, then the stop.

Non-Separating Zipper
Remove stitching surrounding the bottom of the zipper. Be patient and clip the stitches one by one, or you'll end up doing a patch job, too. Remove the offending slider to separate the zipper. With the zipper facing you, insert one row of elements evenly into the larger (top) side of the slider; hold this side firmly while you insert the opposite row of elements into the slider an equal distance. Hold the inserted ends of the zipper tape securely, and push the slider to initiate meshing of coils. Whew! This tender operation accomplished, you will need to insert a stop at the open end. Do this with a metal stop across both rows or by restitching the placket shut.

Caution: Before zealously removing stitching on a down jacket or bag, check to see if the filling will leak out. Work the down away from the zipper area. Staple, pin, or run a line of stitching along the seam before clipping the zipper stitches. Be ready with a plant mister, and spritz water on any escaping plumes. This makes the down clump together rather than flying up your nose.

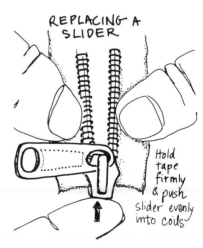

REPLACING A SLIDER

Hold tape firmly & push slider evenly into coils

Remember to quit while you're ahead. You can easily fix a zipper to death, which will require replacing the whole shebang.

Replacing a Zipper

The easiest way to remove the old zipper is simply to cut it off, trimming the zipper tape close to the fabric. Stitch in the new zipper behind the old one. This will save you a load of tedious stitch-plucking and is especially useful on down-filled products. Mental health tip: Have someone else replace your pack zipper (*See **Appendix F: Repair Services,** page 242*), or consult a sewing guide.

Preventive Practices: The Zen of Zipping

Practicing mindfulness is a good way to extend the life of any zipper. As you link the two sides (yin and yang), say "I am joining the zipper teeth now," and continue with this awareness as you pull the slider along the path to enlightenment.

Aside from this, the best thing you can do for your zipper is to keep it clean and free of sand and grit. Regularly irrigate your zippers with the pressure jet from a garden hose. Opinions vary regarding zipper lubricants like soap or wax; some folks believe lubricants simply attract more grime. A little dry graphite lubricant on the joined zipper may be an effective compromise. The best case for wax is as a protectant for zippers regularly exposed to salt water (wetsuit or drysuit) or on a rough patch of a coil zipper. Use solid wax like beeswax (or a candle stub in the field); liquids like TriFlow or spray silicones will spread and stain fabrics.

Seams inside packs and what-have-you will begin to fray and unravel over time. Loose threads cause untold frustration as they catch and bend a slider. Periodically check for these grabbers; trim, then burn back with a soldering iron, lighter, or candle. Alternatively, run a bead of seam sealer along the frayed fabric edge.

Maybe your zipper seems poorly suited to its task. If you're perpetually overstuffing a pack and the zipper bulges warningly, consider mounting some compression straps to ease the pressure.

(*See also **Appendix C: Kit Suggestions,** page 232, for the Zipper Rescue Kit, a terrific resource for zipper parts, trivia, and advice. In fact, much of the information shared here can be traced to zipper sage Mike McCabe, who developed the kit.*)

Fasteners

Fasteners have evolved just as dramatically as the rest of outdoor equipment. When was the last time you actually *buckled* a piece of outdoor gear? Gone are the wretched toothed hip-belt buckles that rusted and annoyed; they've been replaced by lightweight, molded nylon buckles that crack and annoy. Progress has also eliminated (for the most part) welded D-rings and substituted one-piece, synthetic versions. While notions are lighter, sleeker, and more efficient than earlier generations, outdoor gear closure systems still break. This very general listing of fasteners (there are zillions of super-specialized molded styles available) highlights the basic stuff you need to know. (*See **Appendix G: Resources,** page 246, for sources of notions by mail.*)

Place a toothpick between button & fabric, then stitch around it with doubled thread. Make about a half-dozen passes.

Buttons

My mother wouldn't let me wear any new sweater until she had "properly" resewn each button. Buttons illustrate a case where thread that's much stronger than the fabric will cause the fabric to tear; that is, don't sew cotton with heavy nylon thread, which may cut the softer cotton. Rather than dropping everything to sew on a button, use a wire twist-tie, scant in these Ziploc days, to secure the fastener in the field. For hardworking buttons, add a protective dot of seam sealer over the threads.

After removing toothpick wind thread around stitches, then fasten thread to fabric.

Guaranteed—durable button stitching.

Buttonholes

If buttonholes are frayed, stitch around them and create a perpendicular bar tack to ease stress on the fabric (you may need to back with a patch).

Snaps

Snaps are likely to crack and break if made of plastic, like those on some fleece and lightweight raingear. More often, a metal snap will stay snapped so tenaciously that it tears away surrounding fabric as you try to pop it apart. A reinforcing patch is required before a snap can be replaced—indeed, every snap should be backed by a stout scrap of packcloth or leather. A piece of nylon webbing is ideal.

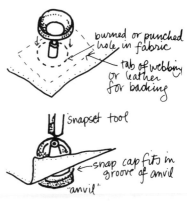

burned or punched hole in fabric

tab of webbing or leather for backing

snapset tool

snap cap fits in groove of anvil

"anvil"

Snapsetting

Snapset kits, which include snaps, setting tool, and positioning anvil, are available at some hardware and fabric stores or leather shops. Tap gently to properly set the male/female snap parts. Pounding forcefully will only bend the male part, and your snap will not be secure (though on big snaps, you may need to whale pretty hard). Practice on a scrap before you place the real thing.

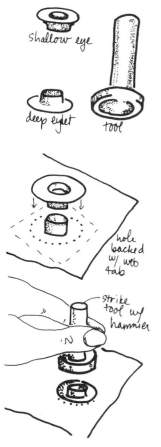

shallow eye

deep eyelet   tool

hole backed w/ web tab

strike tool w/ hammer

Grommets 101

Grommets

Grommets commonly pull away from surrounding fabric. Regular inspection lets you address the problem before a catastrophe strikes. Purchase a grommet-setter at a hardware, marine, or sewing shop. Size 0 is the size most often used for backpacks. When replacing a grommet, you'll need to reinforce the fabric, and every grommet requires a piece of backing fabric or leather as well. A scrap of nylon webbing works great for this. Grommets follow the same rules as snaps: Set gently with a wooden mallet; practice first.

Back snaps and grommets with a swatch of stout nylon webbing or leather.

Buckles

Buckles abound in a variety of shapes, sizes, and functions. The following molded types are available in bulk at most outdoor shops.

Ladderlock buckles give easy length adjustment on webbing. They may be metal or nylon and are most common on pack straps. There are a few tricks to threading them for their chosen purpose. Ladderlocks are closed, or sewn, near the webbing's attachment point. One terrific molded innovation: the ladderlock for field repair. This fastener allows you to instantly replace a broken buckle with no stitching required. These may be tough to find but are fabulous for backpacking and especially for winter traveling.

Friction-release buckles are nasty little metal units that work by sliding a bar with teeth into webbing. These are found primarily on accessory straps. Although they work well to hold, say, a cook kit together, friction-release buckles tend to stiffen and rust. Keep them operating well with a little TriFlow.

Threading a ladderlock, then "locking" the webbing

Cam-lock nylon buckles use eccentric cams to jam webbing into place. While more efficient to use in cold weather than friction-release buckles, cam-locks are not entirely trustworthy because slack web can easily become caught and open the buckle. Many people replace cam-locks with side-release versions.

Side-release buckles are everywhere, and for good reason. They're easy to use, adjust, and even to replace—a given, since they are prone to cracking after prolonged exposure to UV, cold, and general abuse. Nylon side-release buckles are available in several sizes, from ¾- to 2-inch, commensurate with webbing widths. Their only problem is that they originate from a bewildering array of manufacturers, and most are not interchangeable. So, if one part breaks (usually the female half), you'll likely have to replace both.

Sliders

Sliders, or Tri-Glides, are made of metal or nylon and are used as "keepers" to anchor floppy webbing (like on a pack waist belt) or to adjust the length of shoulder straps (like on a camera bag). These are available in many widths and shapes.

Properly threaded Tri-Glide slider.

D-Rings

D-rings are endlessly useful for modifying everything from packs to canoes, and are often doubled for use as a friction accessory strap.

Cord Locks

Cord locks have virtually replaced knots for fastening drawstrings. Spares are handy additions to any repair kit. Buy them by the handful at your favorite outdoor store.

Cord

Cording quality and function vary greatly with the materials used. Nylon is strongest; avoid cotton at all costs. We buy parachute cord in great spools and use it endlessly. The best cord, and naturally the most expensive, is climbing-type Perlon line in narrow diameters (2- or 3-mm), available at climbing shops.

Webbing

Flat nylon webbing is available by the foot in various widths at better outdoor shops with climbing or paddling departments. Flat webbing is easier to sew than tubular webbing and is commonly used for pack straps, compression straps, bag handles, reinforcing patches, dog leashes, and any number of other vital applications. Flat webbing works great in ladderlock or side-release buckles.

Tubular nylon webbing is available in ¾- and 1-inch widths by the foot. Although it has a silky smooth hand and is the strongest available, tubular webbing is difficult to sew and hard to thread through nylon buckles. It's popular for knotting up climbing runners, but do not attempt to sew your own—non-commercial tacks are unreliable, at best. Leave this to a shop or manufacturer.

Velcro

Hook-and-loop fastener tape (Velcro is one commercial brand) may be purchased in a fabric shop by the foot or in self-adhesive strips. The strips are useful in a repair kit to back up a failed zipper, but are difficult to sew through because the adhesive gums up needles and thread. Velcro is so strong in shear along its length that it often causes the other half to tear away from fabric. Sometimes the tape is sewn too close to an edge and pulls away from stitching. If this happens, add another row of stitches by hand or on a home sewing machine. Be careful and patient—this is thick, tough stuff. Another stopgap repair is to inject a little urethane seam sealer under peeling edges, then clamp to fabric. Don't close Velcro until adhesive has completely cured!

Velcro loses its oomph over time; the loops gradually pull apart, while the hook side becomes clogged by mitten fuzz, dirt, and cookie crumbs. Try combing out the hook side of the tape and gently scrubbing the fuzzy loop side with a toothbrush under water to pill up and extract these freeloaders and fluff-up any loops lying down on the job.

Seams and Seamsealing

(See also Appendix A: Adhesives, *page 225;* Shades of Glue *sidebar, page 10)*

Seams are the Achilles heel of tents, boots, rainwear, packs, and any exposed fabric. A seam is deliberately weaker than the material itself; if it's stronger, stressed fabric may pull away and tear along the stitching. But seams are a necessary evil, adding structure and shape and performance. Without them we'd be loping along in kilts and ponchos.

No matter what a fabric is made of, thousands of tiny stitches along seams amount to so many punctures—which become miniature gushers in foul weather. Most outdoor fabrics sport about 10 to 12 stitches per inch along each seam. Seamsealing gives you complete weatherproofing and also protects stitching in vulnerable locations, as on boots or gloves.

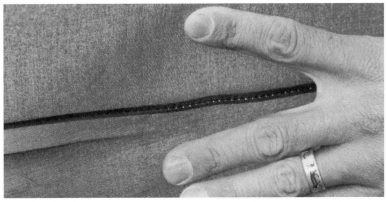

Hundreds of tiny punctures along every stitched seam must be sealed or taped if you expect to stay dry.

What Should I Seamseal?

- Hiking boots: external seams.
- Telemark boots: welt and toe seams, plus a layer over toe welt. (*See Ski Touring and Telemark Boots, page 91.*)
- Mitts and gloves: internal seams of shell layer on system gloves and mitts, plus an exterior coat to add texture to palms.
- Raingear: any untaped, internal seam.
- Tents: internal floor seams and hardware, all rainfly seams, external side of exposed taped seams. (Optional: all seams.)
- Packs and luggage. (Optional: unbound internal seams, exposed external seams when fabric is coated to repel water.)

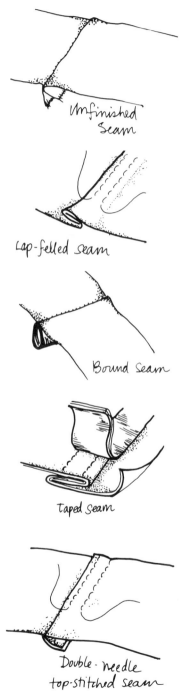

Typical seam types. When shopping, consider an unfinished seam a red flag.

Unfinished Seam

Lap-felled Seam

Bound Seam

Taped Seam

Double-needle top-stitched Seam

Unfinished Seams

Unfinished edges mean fraying fabric, which eventually allows the seams to pull apart. Dangling threads get caught in zippers (causing damage to the slider) and generally make a mess.
- Trim away any dangling strands of fabric.
- Place a soldering iron or wood-burning pencil in a vise.
- Skim raw fabric edge along heated rod to heat-seal the fabric.
  If you can't access fabric edge (such as a corner pocket on a tent) to heat finish, you can seal a raw edge with seam sealer in a syringe.

Finished Seams

Bound
Bound seams are found inside better-quality packs and luggage—gear made with rugged, coated packcloth or "ballistic" fabric. Nylon tape is folded and stitched over the seam to protect fabric edges—a sign of quality manufacturing. It's not a bad idea to seal the exterior line of stitching on bound seams, but this is overkill if the fabric has not been coated to repel water as well.

Taped
Factory taping is a process by which a waterproof or waterproof/breathable strip of fabric is heat-welded or laminated to the inner side of unfinished seams. You'll find taped seams on almost all raingear (if the garment is lined, you can still spot it through the outer shell), on all Gore-Tex raingear and tents (sealer won't stick to the breathable laminate), and on tents. Seams are taped and repaired by the manufacturer or a reputable repair center (*see **Appendix F: Repair Services**, page 242*).

Seam Sealers Differentiated

Seam sealers are essentially adhesives, formulated by suspending plastic or urethane material in a water or solvent base. Once applied to a seam (or exposed to air or moisture), the sealer base evaporates or reacts, leaving a film coating of cured, solid material stuck to the fabric. The favored coating, whether water- or solvent-based, is urethane, valued for its flexibility, resiliency, and abrasion-resistant properties.

Water-Based Sealers
If you are a fairweather camper and don't head out frequently in frigid temperatures, you are an excellent candidate for water-based seam sealer. Water-based products are made under more environmentally friendly circumstances and are somewhat less toxic to manufacture, use, and dispose of than solvent-based sealers. Water-based

sealers come in liquid form in sponge-tipped bottles and are easily applied to uncoated fabric.

The big drawback to water-based sealers is that they tend to have low abrasion resistance, become flaky, and must be reapplied every few seasons (or more often). Water-based adhesives simply float on the surface of any previous coating, making it paramount that you remove old coatings before applying seam sealer. Therefore, you must first use a solvent-based precleaner or alcohol to prepare seams.

Solvent-Based Sealers

Solvent-based sealants remain stretchy and flexible through temperature extremes and resist flaking and peeling, even in sub-zero weather. They are more viscous and less likely to spill than other liquid sealers, and are usually applied using a small artist's paintbrush or an irrigating syringe, which allows you to coat individual stitches.

Toluene is a solvent base for the most-often-recommended sealers on the market. Experts, manufacturers, and repair services tend to overlook toluene's less-redeeming qualities (it's banned for sale in some regions for its mind-altering capabilities) because the products work better than any others available. The solvent penetrates previously applied coatings and chemically bonds solid sealant to fabric, making it a permanent, one-time-only operation.

Sealer manufacturer McNett Corporation offers its views on toluene-based sealers: "As with any solvent product—from gasoline to MEK to kero—users should follow basic, commonsense safety precautions (work in a well-ventilated area, and avoid inhaling the fumes). The permanent nature of a single application of solvent-based sealer means there's less repetition and less packaging waste than with a water-based product."

Environmental regulations become more rigorous daily. While the development of effective, less-toxic alternatives to solvent-based adhesives is certainly imminent, the products and uses recommended here are state-of-the-industry.

Seamsealing Tips

- Work in a ventilated area, even if using water-based sealant.
- Keep kids and pets away from work area.
- Have a rag handy to wipe off drips or smears immediately. Paper towels tend to catch and make more of a mess. The best rag is a square cut from a PakTowl moistened with a bit of alcohol.
- Seams should be clean, dry, warm, and taut; erect the tent when preparing to seal it. Whenever possible, seamseal a new tent or garment before using.
- Prepare the surface to be sealed by buffing gently with a brush, then sponging a commercial pre-cleaner or alcohol along the

stitching. This removes any factory water-repellent finish that might interfere with a good sealer bond. (*See Fabrics & Insulations, page 26.*)

- Sealers bond best to the uncoated side of the fabric, and to the exterior shell of a waterproof/breathable laminate. Also seal the inside roll of a lap-felled or overlapping seam.
- Use a syringe to inject sealer along the folded edge of seams.
- Run a thin film of sealer along stitch lines, spreading any goopy spots with a fine brush.

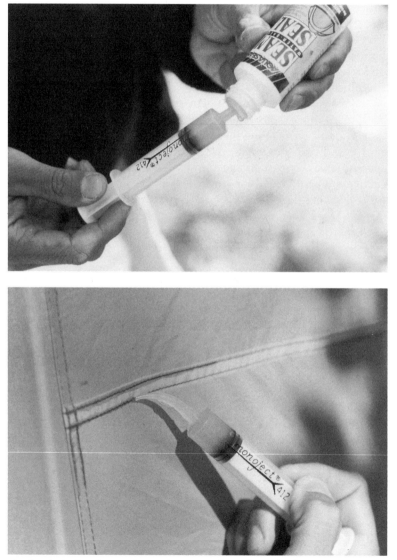

A plastic irrigating syringe gives you that clinical edge.

- Several thin coats of liquid sealant are better than one goopy coat; each successive coat is applied while the previous coat is still tacky. (Seam Grip brand sealant requires only one layer.)
- Pay attention to exposed snaps or bar tacks on webbing loops. Use a syringe to drop a bead of sealer into the center of the snap itself.
- Allow full cure time and then some before storing any freshly sealed gear. Otherwise, your new jacket or tent is likely to stick itself together. Some manufacturers suggest dusting newly sealed items with a very light layer of talcum, but if the adhesive has fully cured this is unnecessary.

Note: For ultimate protection, Bibler Tents recommends sealing exterior taped seams to prevent water from entering and channeling along the tape.

water enters at seam joint
⬇ (apply sealant here)
water channel
↖ laminated seam tape

Ultimate weatherproofing theory and practice by Bibler Tents.

Chapter 2

Fabrics & Insulations

Wool is by no stretch of the imagination an ideal invention, except perhaps for the sheep.

—Davidson & Rugge, *The Complete Wilderness Paddler*

Unraveling Fabric Mysteries

Outerwear is anything one might wear outside, though the fact that my mother takes the dog out each morning in flannel granny gown and sawed-off hip waders does blur distinctions somewhat. For outdoor enthusiasts, outerwear generally implies layers of garments that protect against the elements: next-to-skin, insulation, and shell. While these layers vary considerably, they are all made of fiber; identifying their composition will tell you how to care for them.

Natural versus Synthetic

There are two basic categories of fibers: natural (like cotton, wool, flax, hemp, or silk), and synthetic, or man-made. Natural fibers are inherently breathable. Synthetic fabrics may allow air transfer, but the fibers themselves do not. Natural fibers are absorbent and will shrink, while both factors are minimal in synthetics. Besides obvious rips and scuffs, any fiber's worst enemy is the sun, with mildew running a close second. No fiber or fabric will endure prolonged contact with salt water. Dried salt residue is a desiccant and attracts water, which invites mildew. Chemicals like battery acid and some insect repellents, and even harsh detergents, also damage fibers of any origin.

Cotton

Cotton has not been completely forgotten as a useful outdoor fabric. Nothing beats its breathability and comfort, but when it comes to water, cotton does exhibit some drawbacks. Once wet, cotton fabric swells, tightening the weave against drops of water. However, wet cotton does not withstand water pressure, and leaks. (Remember your dad's warning not to touch the tent wall?) This absorbent quality also means that cotton offers zero insulation once saturated. One solution is to coat cotton fabric with tent wax, available at well-stocked outdoor shops. Another is to spray the fabric with a water-repellent treatment—this works great on cotton and cotton blends, like your old favorite 60/40 parka.

Waxing Poetic. Re-waxing a waxed cotton anorak or tent is a lot like treating boots. Always apply wax to clean fabric. Look for "non-tack" wax, which provides a smooth, flexible surface without attracting dirt and grit. Figure about 3 ounces of wax per garment.

- Place clean and dry garments in a dryer (at "low" setting) or near a heat source to warm them before treating the outside of the fabric.
- Lay garment flat on a clean, protected surface (butcher paper is ideal).
- Use a warmed rag to apply wax generously to seams, joints and elbows (areas most likely to leak). Next, systematically coat the entire article. Some waxes are now available in pump sprays.
- Place garment on a hanger. Inspect for even coating and wipe away any excess wax. Hang to dry overnight in a warm, ventilated spot away from a direct heat source.

Treatment of cotton canvas tents follows the same procedure, with these variations:

Wait for a clear, dry weather forecast. Set up tent in full sun, then follow the rays as they warm wall surfaces, applying wax as recommended above. Heavy canvas tents are especially prone to mildew, either because they are not fully dry when stored, or because their storage location is a cool, damp cellar. Periodically air your cotton wall tent, especially if you never use it. Review *Appendix B: Low-Tox Cleaning Solutions* (*page 229*) for preventive care tips, or try Rainy Pass Repair's Mildew Removal Recipe offered here.

Silk

Silk is popular for use in socks and long underwear because of its fine wicking ability, soft hand, and elegant drape. It requires little care other than hand-washing with gentle soap and hanging to dry.

Rainy Pass Mildew Remover

Phase I: Mix ½ cup Lysol in 1 gallon hot water.
- Wash mixture into set-up tent with sponge and allow to dry completely.

Phase II: Mix 1 cup salt and 1 cup lemon juice in 1 gallon of hot water.
- Wash tent with this mixture and allow to dry.
- Rinse tent with fresh water and allow to dry before storing.

Wool

Wool takes on many tasks with equanimity: Durable and water-resistant as an outer layer, puffy and resilient as an insulating layer, stretchy and breathable next to skin. Each wool fiber bears its own protective lanolin coating and will shed dirt and water for years.

To care for any wool garment is to protect its wonderful natural qualities. Regular shakes, brushings, and spot-cleaning are better for the life of a wool garment than countless dry cleanings. Handwash with mild, non-detergent soap and block dry. Try a small vegetable brush (the wooden-back, yellow bristle type), Sweater Stone, or piece of pumice to remove pills. Don't shave with a razor or risk slicing the knit.

One oft-undervalued quality of wool is that it shrinks, something appreciated by herding cultures for centuries. Wet, agitated wool fibers cling to each other to form thick, lofty felt. If you've ever accidentally shrunk your favorite cardigan, you remember how tight the knit became. Boiled wool sweaters offer fabulous insulation that's both breathable and somewhat water-repellent. Make your own boiled wool layer by purchasing an oversized wool sweater (such as a Shetland crew), then carefully shrinking in the wash until it fits you.

Hemp

Hemp is making a comeback in the outdoor industry for many reasons. Requiring no pesticides for cultivation (a real problem with cotton), hemp is durable, naturally water-resistant, and non-polluting. Depending on the extent of refinement, hemp fibers are suitable for making coarse rope or fine clothing; its dirt-shedding luster is eminently hand-washable; and tighter weaves suffer little shrinkage.

So You Don't Want to Wear Fur

Creatures compressed in early
    Cretaceous
extracted, pumped and canned
by supertankers then poured
into refineries

Extruded as polymers
measured by diameter
per 9,000 meters of
    monofilament

Spun into yarn and
knitted into gray cloth
by a small gray town then

Agitated, stamped, rolled
dyed and clipped
teased, bonded, cooked then
    shipped

To Asia, or Mexico
for cutting and assembly
into garments specified by
earnest lifestylers and

Marketed bi-annually
in four-color catalogs with
environmental messages
mailed directly then

Closed-out by containers
last year's styles
half-price dinosaurs

            —A.G.

yo —

Wearing Dinosaurs

Synthetic fabrics roared into life during the 1920s as something for postwar petrochemical plants to manufacture. Many early man-made fabric names (like nylon) began as trade names of the same players who now bring us ripstop, fleece, and Gore-Tex. Petroleum-based fabrics have entered all aspects of 20th-century life, including my grandfather's hip.

Sadly, these miraculous fabrics are based entirely on a limited, extracted resource, and though affordable, we have yet to bear their price. While not quite ready to give up my wetsuit or cagoule or Lycra ski bibs, I am very conscious of "wearing dinosaurs."

High-tech synthetics beat natural fibers cold when it comes to their lightweight, quick-drying, elastic, and non-allergenic qualities. Synthetics are friendly—they bond easily in layers to outperform natural fibers, as in waterproof/breathable laminates. Requiring the same gentle care as natural fabrics, plastic fabrics can be periodically revitalized with a wide assortment of treatments and conditioners. One caution: Most synthetics are especially vulnerable to DEET (N,N-diethyl-meta-toluamide), a common insect repellent that also happens to be a fine plastics solvent.

Polypro

Synthetic underlayers quickly became *de rigueur* for mountaineers and other outdoor enthusiasts for their fabulous warmth-to-weight ratio and unsurpassed hydrophobia. Ever-popular polypropylene (or polyolefin) represented the first generation of these fabrics. The main care consideration with polypropylene is its low melting point (DO NOT put in dryer!) and odor-absorbing tendencies. Polyester underlayers (Thermax, Capilene, etc.) generally have a softer feel, less odor retention, and can be machine-dried.

Hang-drying is recommended for all underlayers, natural or synthetic. If you must use a machine, choose a low or delicate setting and don't use fabric softeners or dryer sheets, which can hamper the insulating and wicking power of many knits. Indeed, dryer sheets have been known to make a sort of greasy stain on garments if stuck to the fabric for any length of time.

Fleece

Fleece traces its origins to lowly acrylic or polyester griege (gray) goods that resemble jersey knit. After dying, fuzzing, trimming and other manipulations, fleece emerges as a lightweight, non-absorbent, colorful alternative to wool. Any parent will tell you that fleece is the best thing that's happened to kids' clothing since the snap. It follows, then, that fleece is virtually care-free. Cold-water machine wash, lift the lid, and remove a nearly spun-dry garment. If pilling is a problem, wash garments inside out, or try scraping the fabric with a vegetable brush, Sweater Stone, or piece of pumice while still damp.

Syntho-Green

Most garment manufacturers have switched to fleece reclaimed from plastic bottles. Not all fleece is made entirely from recycled bottles, but expect recycled content to increase. Other recycled woven synthetics are developing, like climbing webbing and packcloth; soon packs and outerwear will follow suit.

Believe it or not, recycled fibers are old news. Wellman, Inc., the largest supplier, has been turning out recycled polyester fiber (used primarily as insulative batting in textiles and furniture) since 1964. But while recycled synthetics technology has existed for a generation, consumer demand has not. Once consumers began seeking recycled products, it became a matter of adapting technology—and marketing hype—to fit the need.

Remember, though, that buying such "green" gear is still consumerism, and runaway consumption forms the core of our environmental rotten apple. Purchasing a new fleece sweater may keep 10 or 20 soda bottles out of a landfill, but this does little good if you continue to purchase beverages and foods in plastic containers, which, according to U.S. Food and Drug Administration mandate, must be made from virgin plastic, and are often not even recyclable at the local level.

Stinky Synthetics

Mark Jenkins, a minimalist traveler, once told me how, upon climbing Mount Everest, he wore the same polypro shirt for two weeks, then stuffed it away and donned a fresh polypro shirt. After another two weeks, he exchanged the second for the first, which smelled "fresh."

Most outdoorspeople have experienced the horrific odor-holding power of polypropylene, and often throw away perfectly serviceable garments in the name of sociability. Want to salvage a smelly synthetic? Try soaking it in a mixture of liquid soap and white vinegar or highly diluted citrus cleaner, then wash as normal. (*See Appendix B: Low-Tox Cleaning Solutions, page 229.*)

Waterproof Fabrics

A wade through your local outfitter's store will introduce you to the thoroughly confusing world of waterproof, waterproof/breathable, and water-repellent fabrics. Manufacturers' hangtags extol the singular virtues of their proprietary innovations, yet there are just three basic ways to add water-repellency to nylon or polyester fabric.

Coated, non-breathable fabrics bear a urethane-based water barrier on the inside of the garment. These fabrics are used primarily for foul-weather gear and are inherently waterproof, but do trap per-

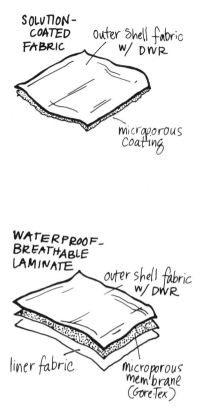

SOLUTION-
COATED
FABRIC

Outer Shell fabric
w/ DWR

microporous
Coating

WATERPROOF-
BREATHABLE
LAMINATE

outer shell fabric
w/ DWR

liner fabric

microporous
mem'brane
(Gore-Tex)

spiration. If the manufacturer has not sealed the seams with tape, you'll need to add seam sealer or periodically touch up the seams. (*See Seamsealing, page 37; and Seams and Seamsealing, page 21.*)

Coated, breathable fabrics often carry trade names like Ultrex, Helly-Tech, etc., but all employ a polyurethane coating that offers some breathability. Garments made with these fabrics may also benefit from seamsealing, but they are usually lined, denying access to the seams. Coated breathables typically sport factory seam tape.

Coated fabrics of either type (sometimes referred to as "solution-coated") can be revitalized by a spray or launder-in water-repellent treatment, described below. Do not machine dry unless the manufacturer suggests it. A peeling coating means your garment has seen better days, and there's little you can do to stop the flaking (*see Coating or Recoating Synthetic Weaves, page 37*). You can prevent flakes and peels by periodically rinsing both inside and out with clean water—especially if you sweat a lot—and letting the garment dry thoroughly before storing. If the garment is new and the coating peels, return it to the manufacturer.

Waterproof/Breathable Laminate

Waterproof/breathable laminate (typically Gore-Tex) implies a microporous Teflon membrane bonded to a tough outer fabric. Three-layer Gore-Tex is a sandwich of shell, membrane, and tricot liner, while two-layer Gore-Tex has a separate, free-hanging liner. This layered membrane allows water vapor (sweat) to pass through, but not large water droplets (rain). Highly stable, the membrane itself is damaged only by punctures or abrasion; myriad shell fabrics are employed to protect the membrane.

Gore-Tex does have different care requirements from other fabrics, and its performance greatly benefits from periodic maintenance. Machine-wash using non-detergent soap or a launder-in treatment (*see page 35*). Machine-drying restores water repellency to the shell fabric, as does a careful ironing of the outer fabric with a medium-temperature setting (amazing but true). You can further enhance repellency with a spray treatment. All Gore-Tex seams are factory-sealed with Gore-Tex tape; peeling seams should be returned to the manufacturer or authorized service center for warranted repair.

Restoring Water Repellency

Any waterproof garment is only as effective as its DWR—that's Durable Water Repellency—a synthetic outer fabric's water-phobic quality. Instead of cursing your expensive rainsuit after an unexpected soaking, revitalize it. Most DWRs are fluoropolymer coatings to the shell fibers, which make water bead up and run off the surface of the fabric. Time, dirt, wood smoke, abrasion, and laundering will hinder the DWR's function, allowing water to saturate outer fabric and make you feel clammy, even though the garment isn't really leaking.

The easiest way to restore factory DWR is to machine-dry the garment on medium heat (unless otherwise forewarned by the manufacturer). Next, ironing, as mentioned above, will reactivate DWR (again, read the label instructions—ironing is not a good idea for many coated fabrics). Before ironing, wipe the cool iron sole plate with denatured alcohol to make sure it's clean. As your garment ages and seems less responsive to these steps, consider a conditioning treatment.

CARDINAL RULE:
Do not store any fabric wet!

Water-Repellent Treatments. DWR treatments are available in two forms: liquid wash and spray. Look for fluoropolymer spray treatments like 3M Scotchguard or DuPont Teflon Fabric Protector. Silicone spray does work to shed water, but is not as long-lasting and will inhibit seam sealer adhesion. Wash-in DWR enhancers assure you of even coating and come in recyclable plastic containers. Look for Nikwax TX-Direct, which is a liquid version of the original DWR used by many manufacturers. The only case where a liquid is not the better choice is when the garment includes a free-hanging, wicking liner, the performance of which would be hampered by a DWR treatment.

Insulations

(See also: Sleeping Bags, *page 58.)*

Lacking fur or feathers, humans have trapped and skinned and plucked and emulated these organic insulators for centuries. Regardless of origin, insulation works by acting as a barrier against heat loss; generally, more volume means more insulation. Machine-laundering is known to be hard on all insulated garments, but most people simply don't take the time to hand wash (*see **Kinder, Gentler Machine Washing,** page 35*).

Down

Down's legendary compressibility gives it the greatest warmth-to-weight ratio of any insulation, including the latest synthetics. Down compresses to a very low volume, then springs back to fill as much space as allowed. Down is not feathers, but the soft underplumage of waterfowl, yet "leaking feathers" is a common complaint with down garments. Read the label carefully when purchasing and make sure you're looking at a down garment and not "down blend"—feathers have little insulating value and are nothing more than cheap filler.

The main drawback to down is its lack of insulating power when wet. There are many wash-in down conditioners available (Kenyon, Nikwax) that add a DWR coating to individual down plumes, enhancing the down's natural resiliency with a bit of water-repellent boost.

Down-filled garments or bags should not be stored tightly stuffed in their sacks, but hung or kept in a large, breathable cotton sack. When stitching a tear or zipper on a down garment, use the smallest needle possible to keep holes (a.k.a. down escape vents) to a minimum. If you're replacing a zipper, make sure the down is contained by a line of stitching before opening zipper stitches. Otherwise you'll be gasping for air in a room full of plumes. One trick recommended by Bob Upton at Rainy Pass Repair is to wet the down before attempting to work around it.

Synthetic Fill

Synthetic fill is every bit as delicate as down, despite what you read in the magazine ads. Most synthetic fills use polyester fibers held together in thin bats by a resinous bond, and this binder can be especially susceptible to heat damage—car trunks, hot water, and clothes dryers included. Hand-washing is recommended by manufacturers. Synthetic-filled items should be stored like their down counterparts—by hanging or in breathable cotton bags. Storing fiberfill garments fully compressed will ensure a chilling experience later.

Neoprene

(*See* Specialty Garments: Wetsuits, *page 38.*)

Cleaning Methods

Dry Cleaning—NOT!

Dry cleaning processes employ ethylene-based solvents that are harmful to down and synthetics. Even "Stoddard Process," often touted as better for down products, uses distilled kerosene. Most down garments and bags sport a "Dry Clean Only" label simply to prevent careless machine washing, even though the solvents are harmful to both down and synthetic fills (as well as to shell fibers). Spare your gear and the planet—limit your dry cleaning.

Kinder, Gentler Hand-Washing

While you shouldn't wash outerwear any more than absolutely necessary, hand-washing is recommended, especially for insulated products. About as much fun as bathing a dog, and more time-consuming, this process is definitely worth the effort. Remember to clean your pockets! Turn them inside-out and brush away lint, cookie crumbs, or anything likely to stain.

Use non-detergent, powdered soaps that do not employ surfactants (surfacing agents that will leave film or residue on fibers and reduce water repellency). Ivory Flakes and Dreft are recommended for hand- or machine-washing of outdoor gear. Dr. Bronner's Liquid Castile soap is also suitable for many applications. (*See **Appendix B: Low-Tox Cleaning Solutions**, page 229.*)

- Spot-clean any stains by scrubbing with a little cleaner and warm water (a toothbrush works great).
- Fill bathtub with lukewarm (not hot) water, then dissolve a small amount of cleaner in the water.
- Immerse items to be cleaned, and knead gently until thoroughly wet. Do not twist or wring the garment at any point.
- Allow to soak for about 30 minutes.
- Drain soapy water, then press water out of the garment by hand.
- Refill the tub with warm water, let garment soak for 15 minutes or so, then knead to remove soap. Drain the tub and compress water out of the garment.
- Repeat the rinsing process at least once more; several times is ideal.
- Lift the garment gently, then block dry on a towel or screen.
- Allow to air dry for a time before machine drying. Wool, silk, and synthetics should air dry; down products require the air and rotation of a machine dryer to redistribute and loft the filling.
- Machine-drying down: use low or delicate setting. Add a few clean, dry towels to absorb water. Skip the tennis ball or shoe. Check the dryer often and replace the towels when saturated.

"OUT, OUT DAMNED SPOT!"

Make a paste with your favorite powdered soap or stain remover & scrub with toothbrush

Kinder, Gentler Machine-Washing

Okay, so it's unrealistic to hand-wash your gear. If you're going to machine-wash, try to use a front-loading commercial washer rather than your home, top-loading spindle type, which twists, agitates, and damages insulating fibers and baffles, not to mention what it does to drawcords. A big commercial machine's tumbling action is also good if you're using a launder-in DWR treatment or down conditioner, because the fabric is less likely to crease and more likely to be evenly coated. Remember to use a non-detergent cleaner only.

Caution: Open zippers and Velcro tabs can wreak havoc in the wash cycle! Velcro is extremely abrasive to linings and coated fabric surfaces. Batten down your jacket thoroughly before washing. Securing opposite cuffs with Velcro or snaps is a good way to prevent the sleeves from turning inside-out or becoming hopelessly twisted.

Sticky Stuff

Pitch, chewing gum, wax, and weird gooey stuff lodged in a sweater or the seat of your pants is unpleasant, but easily removed. On the trail, try slathering the spot with peanut butter or cooking oil, which penetrates and loosens unwelcome bonds. At home, place the garment in the freezer. Once hard, at least some of the substance should crack off. Other solutions (after removing as much of the substance as possible): Rub the spot with egg white, then soak in vinegar before laundering, or apply citrus cleaner directly to the mess. Don't go overboard chemically trying to remove the substance or you may damage the fabric! Test a non-visible area of fabric for color-fastness before trying denatured alcohol or (as a last resort) nail polish remover on the sticky stain. (*See Appendix B: Low-Tox Cleaning Solutions, page 229.*)

Stain Removal

The best way to deal with stains is to prevent them with Scotchguard or other surface treatment that repels liquid. The sooner you attend to a spot, the easier it will be to remove. Commercial "stain sticks" are effective cleaners. Try making a paste with regular powdered soap and water, working it into the offending mark with a toothbrush. We stick to varying mixtures of borax, baking soda, lemon juice, egg white, or vinegar and hope for the best.

"I See You Have a Pet"

More than one person has remarked upon the state of our fleece garments. If you live with animals, the best way to remove their omnipresent hair is with a Sweater Stone, pumice, or stout clothes brush while the garment is still damp.

Animal lovers should consider pet hair color when purchasing fuzzy garments.

Patching

Duct tape is the most popular material for patching synthetic raingear, down vests, and just about everything else in the field. Kenyon K-Tape self-adhesive nylon repair tape is easy enough to carry in your field repair kit, though. Tenaciously sticky and available in both taffeta or ripstop, K-Tape is washable and comes in about two dozen colors to blend with any garment.

The trick for taping any tear is to clean and dry the fabric; a little alcohol swab from your repair kit will hasten drying and ensure a good bond. Rounded corners on the tape patch are also important. Another popular field and home repair is a urethane adhesive patch (see **Patching Techniques**, *page 8 and **The Beauty and Perils of Duct Tape**, page 9*). Remember that tape should be considered a temporary patch.

Seamsealing

Outerwear construction is so detailed these days it's difficult to find an untaped seam on any type of coated raingear. You can spot the outline of a taped seam through the outside of the garment. (*See Seams and Seamsealing, page 21.*)

Coating or Recoating Synthetics

If the waterproof coating on your favorite jacket is beginning to flake, you have a few options. Look for a liquid, water-based polymer like Aquaseal Poly Coat or Kenyon Recoat 3. However, a very economical option is Thompson's Water Seal (from the hardware store). Three ounces should cover about 10 square feet. Always apply to the uncoated side of the fabric (if you apply it to a flaky original coating, the new layer will just peel along with it, and probably exacerbate the problem).

handheld sprayer for sealants, gelcoat

- Thoroughly clean the surface to be coated. Hang the garment in an open, ventilated area or lay flat on a clean surface.
- Use a bristle brush or a Preval sprayer for consistent application.
- Thoroughly spread out any puddles or excess coating, which will blister and peel once dry.
- Fabric should be saturated.
- If applying a second coat, do so while the first coat is still tacky (within 30 minutes) to achieve secure bond.
- Allow to air dry for about three days before storing. When storing for the first time after coating, sprinkle a little talcum powder on the coated areas first.

Chapter 3

Specialty Garments

The Eskimos have discovered that for maximum protection against the cold the hair of the fur must be outside. Under the coat they wear birdskin shirts with the feathers inside. These are the only tight-fitting garments. Otherwise, the skin clothes are loose and do not overlap too much, so as to allow for ventilation.

–Peter Freuchen, *Book of the Eskimos*

(*See also:* Fabrics and Insulations, *page 26*; Essential Techniques, *page 4*; Appendix A: Adhesives, *page 225*.)

Wetsuits and Neoprene Care

Neoprene is the best wet insulator, bar none. Like other synthetics, neoprene has evolved from its first generation of sticky, bulky black rubber to the sleek, laminated forms we see today. Neoprene of varying thickness is now sandwiched between soft nylon fabric skins for comfort and ease of wear. Neoprene garments take many forms, from "Farmer John" wetsuits to socks, paddling gloves to ski pants, beanies to sprayskirts.

The finer points of wetsuit care have come from

my neighbor (who prefers the moniker "Neoprene Queen"), an avid diver and teacher of same. Neon costumes festoon our street during the summer months, because after each dive she carefully rinses and line-dries her wetsuit, whether she's been floating in the salt sea, local YMCA pool, or nearby lake.

"Few people realize," says the Neoprene Queen, "that fresh water is just as hard on synthetics as salt or chlorine—thanks to organic matter and pollutants. These contaminants are harbored in open cells of the neoprene." Sweat (body salt) also fatigues the fabric. Neoprene begins to deteriorate from the very day of manufacture, simply because of chemistry. Even if you treat your wetsuit with gentle reverence, its insulative value gradually decreases with time.

Maximize the life of your neoprene gear with a thorough rinse using a powerful water jet (hose or shower) both inside and out, paying special attention to zippers. Do this every time you wear the garment. Occasional conditioning by soaking in a tub with Aquaseal Wet Suit Shampoo (available at paddle or dive shops) is a good idea. Hang dry wetsuits inside-out on a stiff, shaped hanger to avoid creases, which will crack with age.

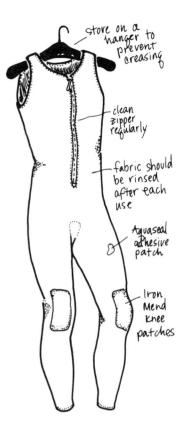

Punctures and Tears

Neoprene suffers primarily from abrasion and punctures. Small tears (usually in the outer skin) should be patched with Aquaseal or other polyurethane adhesive. One glance at a Maine coast urchin diver's gloves will tell you that Aquaseal is the goop favored by professionals.

Ruthless tugging of friction-prone suits or booties as you put them on can cause tears at seams. Neoprene is difficult to stitch on a home machine. It's better to hand-sew neoprene with nylon thread, but close inspection may reveal that you've torn through both the nylon outer skin and the neoprene itself, indicating that a structural patch is necessary.

Neoprene Patch

Patching neoprene requires a bridge to join intact areas of the nylon fabric. The simplest and most effective patching material is McNett's Iron Mend, a heat-activated nylon adhesive tape. Iron Mend comes in a precut knee-pad size (10 inches by 6 inches) in many colors—you can cut smaller patches from the sheet. Worn or abraded areas like knees and elbows, or stressed areas at crotch, zipper, or where a sprayskirt stretches over coaming, will benefit from an iron-on preventive patch. For just a preventive patch, skip the preliminary Aquaseal patching steps outlined below.

- Review patching techniques (see **Essential Techniques: Fabric Patching,** page 8).
- Make sure neoprene article is clean and dry. A little swab of

alcohol on the area to be repaired will also remove any lingering oils. Allow to dry.

- If the hole is larger than your fingerprint, plug the gouge with a piece of neoprene material.
- Join torn areas (and plug materials) together and apply a masking-tape backing.
- Create an adhesive patch using Aquaseal urethane repair material, and allow to cure.
- Remove masking-tape backing and clean area with alcohol. Allow to dry.
- Wipe off sole plate of a cool iron with a little denatured alcohol to remove any contaminants.
- Preheat iron to "acrylic," "low," or "delicate" setting, with no steam.
- Cut Iron Mend to cover area plus about 1 inch, remembering to round edges of patch.
- Place article on flat surface (ironing board, bench, counter).
- Position Iron Mend over damaged area, coated side down. Place silicone release paper (supplied with tape) over the area to be ironed.
- Hold iron on the patch with firm, steady pressure, about 10 seconds; make sure you heat the entire patch.
- Allow repair to cool before testing edges for security. You may need to apply more heat and pressure. If, after the second application of heat, the patch does not stick, start over with fresh tape.

Drysuits

The reason for owning and wearing a drysuit is to guarantee (as much as possible) against getting wet in very cold and exposed environments like windy, open waters or gnarly whitewater. Failure by way of leaking fabric or worn gaskets can be more than uncomfortable—the hazards of hypothermia become very real.

The two big reasons for taking good care of your drysuit: First, it's a very expensive, specialized toy; and second, this toy can literally save your life.

Fabric Care

Drysuits are usually made of coated nylon fabric with welded seams, but some employ Gore-Tex or other laminates. (*See Fabrics & Insulations, page 26, for specific care recommendations and tips on how to revitalize water-repellent fabric finishes.*)

Drysuits usually work so well that you'll crank out enough sweat to make you wet from the inside. The best way to keep your drysuit dry is to wear a liner of absorbent synthetic, which keeps moisture off you and prevents it from pooling.

Pollutants and dirt should be washed off the outside of the drysuit after each wearing. Salty condensation from your own body can cause mildew inside the suit. Turn the suit inside out and rinse with fresh water and allow to completely dry before rolling and storing in a cool, dry place. Placing the suit in a loose-weave cotton bag (as you would a sleeping bag) is also a good habit.

Finding an elusive leak in a drysuit may drive you to distraction. You might try hanging the suit in a darkened room, shining a flashlight inside it and looking for pinpoints of light. When you find such a spot, mark it, then patch with urethane adhesive or, better, with a fabric patch. Drysuit patches should be applied to the interior (coated side) of the fabric with urethane adhesive and allowed to fully cure before folding or wearing. Stitched patches are not recommended for obvious reasons.

Drysuit Zippers

When buying a drysuit, a lot of what you pay for is the watertight zipper, which is heat-seated or welded into position. Unlike your average coil or toothed zipper, these watertight versions are not repairable by normal humans, and must be returned to the factory for an expensive replacement.

When opening or closing a drysuit zipper, pull the zipper string at an angle (about 30 degrees) to minimize friction. Pulling directly at the slider will cause it to dig into the zipper teeth or coils. Get a friend to close or open the zipper for you. By doing it solo, you place pressure on the teeth in the wrong direction.

Always irrigate the zipper with clean, fresh water after wearing. Some people use wax to lubricate a metal zipper. Every other expert insists that the zipper must be stored fully closed or fully opened—never partway—or the delicate coils may kink. If you make a habit of zipping only to take the garment on or off, you'll conserve the zipper. Make sure that nothing heavy is placed on top of the zipper during storage, or it may become deformed.

Gaskets

Natural gum latex gaskets provide the ultimate moisture seal and are the most sensitive part of the drysuit. Gaskets may last anywhere from a few months to five years, but the average lifespan is about three years. Gaskets that are cared for definitely last longer.

The first line of defense is to put on your drysuit with tenderness—don't yank it on over your head, or you'll risk tearing the seals, especially if they are aging and weak.

Gaskets are especially vulnerable to damage by heat and petrochemicals, including most forms of water pollution and suntan lotions. DEET is absolutely lethal. The secret to gasket longevity is simple: Keep the rubber clean and cool.

As rubber stretches, its pores open to chemical contamination; when the gasket becomes slack, pores close around the entrapped dirt, salt, or pollutants, which go to work breaking down the rubber. Wash with gentle soap and water after each wear. After cleaning, apply a food-grade silicone or 303 Protectant to provide lubrication as well as a barrier against chemicals. Don't apply the lubricant without cleaning the gaskets first, though, since this will seal in any dirt. Storing your suit in a cotton bag will minimize air flow around the seals.

Protect the drysuit from heat. Even more damaging than UV, the heat inside a car trunk is enough to dry out rubber, or worse, turn it to tar-like goo. Keeping the rubber cool is extremely important.

When you first purchase a drysuit, the gaskets may be uncomfortably tight. Don't be tempted to pare them down without first giving them time to stretch. You can assist the breaking-in by prestretching the gaskets around neck-, wrist- or ankle-sized forms: coffee cans, juice cans, salad bowls, cook pots, or the subversive's solution, a traffic cone. Here's an actual use for your Lava Lamp.

If your neck gasket proves truly unbearable, you can trim it with very sharp scissors, but only ⅛ inch at a time. Make sure to trim evenly; leave no nicks, which will inevitably split on the first day of your next big trip. It's important to be patient, because the seals do stretch, and to a fault.

Many drysuits now come with overcuffs, which are designed to protect the seals from UV, dirt, and what-have-you. While they may be effective in prolonging gasket life, they are somewhat in the way when it comes time to replace the seals—and you will have to replace them. Do everything you can to delay that sorry day.

Patching Gaskets
Although rare, a punctured seal may be repaired with a bicycle tube patch kit.

Avoid the Black Plague
Nothing's more disappointing than pulling a drysuit out of storage to find the seals have disintegrated into a pulpy goo smeared all over the body fabric. The only way to get the stuff off the fabric is to scrape it away, then clean carefully with acetone—but don't scrub too hard or you risk damaging the fabric coating with the solvent. This ruinous black blight is a nightmare to remove, but it could have been avoided.

As you inspect the gaskets, if you notice the latex is losing its resiliency and is starting to feel a little tacky, remove them immediately, before goo sets in. Once the seals have lost their integrity, removal is very unpleasant and dependent upon the use of a solvent. Even if you don't plan to seat new gaskets until next season, remove the old ones, then clean and store the suit.

Replacing Neck Gaskets: Two Methods
Replacement neck gaskets are available at paddling, dive, or sail shops, or from the manufacturer. Gasket replacement is one of those potentially messy jobs you may wish to assign to someone else. Consider shipping your suit to its manufacturer, who will replace seals for a nominal fee (and you're guaranteed a professional-looking finish).

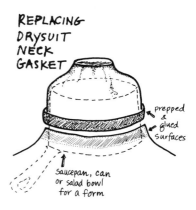

REPLACING DRYSUIT NECK GASKET

prepped & glued surfaces

saucepan, can or salad bowl for a form

Either method requires:
- A gasket "form" such as a kitchen pot, salad bowl, traffic cone, coffee can, or waxed paper container. The form is best wrapped with waxed paper to prevent adhesive mishaps.
- Prepare the gluing surface of the new gasket (the bottom 1 inch) by gently sanding with fine-grit sandpaper, then cleaning with denatured alcohol. Some manufacturers provide prepared seals that require only a quick wipe with solvent before adhesion.
- Place the form inside the suit neck and stretch a new (prepped) gasket into position as shown, peeling up the last inch for gluing.

Method One: Breakable Bond.   Use urethane adhesive such as Sta-Bond, popular for vinyl raft repair, or the proprietary adhesive recommended by your drysuit manufacturer (*see **Appendix G: Materials Resources**, page 246*). This method is very clean, neat, and professional-looking.
- Remove old gaskets by heating the bond with a hair dryer or heat lamp, which warms the glue enough that you can peel the rubber away easily. DO NOT use an open flame.
- If heat removal is not an option, resort to MEK, applied with an acid brush, to soften the glue. Keep the MEK away from any heat source. (MEK is available at auto parts stores and requires skin and eye protection.)
- Leave residue on the fabric—this provides a good adhesive base that requires no preparation. Remove any lumps of old adhesive, though.
- Attach parts to form as illustrated.
- Apply a thin coat of adhesive to each piece and allow to dry so it is not tacky. Apply a second coat of adhesive to the neck gasket and allow to dry. This method allows adjustment during positioning.
- Roll gasket into position.
- Use a hair dryer to heat the glued surface (the heat will activate the glue). Carefully burnish with your finger or corrugator to dispel any air bubbles.
- Allow to stand overnight to cure.

Method Two: Unbreakable Bond. Some adhesives chemically bond so completely that you must cut off the old gasket at the edge of the fabric. To replace, you must glue to the old gasket—a rubber-to-rubber surface. Aquaseal is normally recommended for this purpose.

- Prepare the gluing surface of the old gasket by sanding and cleaning with denatured alcohol.
- Use masking tape to protect the fabric, since Aquaseal is pretty goopy and stays wet for a long time.
- Attach both parts to form as illustrated.
- Apply a thin, even coat of Aquaseal to both surfaces.
- Gently roll the gasket into position.
- Use your fingers to carefully burnish the bond, working out any air bubbles or lumpy spots.
- Wrap the glued joint with a band of waxed paper, held tightly in place with a wrap of masking tape.
- Allow to set overnight in a warm—not cool—spot. Place a DO NOT DISTURB sign nearby.

Shelled Gloves

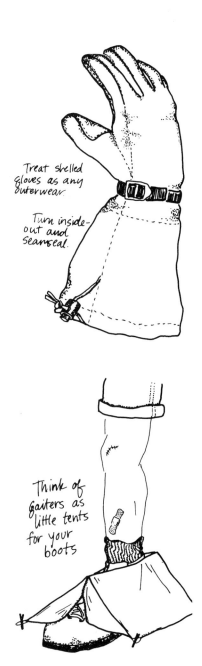

Treat shelled gloves as any outerwear.

Turn inside-out and seamseal.

Think of gaiters as little tents for your boots

Gauntlet-style overmitts and gloves should be treated like the rest of your outerwear. Ice climbing, sweat, and a season of skiing take their toll faster on gloves than on any other garment. Give your gloves a preseason tune-up.

- Wash gloves with non-detergent cleaner and dry thoroughly.
- Turn inside-out and seal all seams, preferably with Seam Grip, which is the most waterproof sealer. Allow to dry.
- Turn right-side-out and apply a DWR treatment.
- Increase the gripping potential of glove palms by putting them on, then dotting Aquaseal on the palm area. Spread fingers wide and allow to air-dry for at least 24 hours.

Gaiters

Think of gaiters as tents for your boots—their similar elements require similar care. Fabric and seams may be weatherproofed and cleaned, and fasteners maintained as needed. Other tips:

- Patch crampon lacerations immediately with duct tape or nylon tape. Once home, these are a great application for little urethane patches (my gaiters look like a crazy quilt).
- Puttee owners will find that Hypalon straps fray, tatter, or become unstitched. Melt-back frays with a flame. Inspect for abrasion and weakening around buckle holes. Protect and enhance stitch rows with a coating of urethane seam sealer. (*See*

Appendix G: Resources, page 246, for sources of replacement straps.)

- A lost strap or lace hook is quickly corrected in the field with baling wire, which doesn't ball up with snow.
- Give strap buckles, zippers, and snaps a pre-season rubdown with a silicone-saturated cloth. Prevent frozen-finger fumbling and frustration!
- Clean mitten lint out of Velcro. Accumulated wool fibers will mat together like felt, making closure difficult.

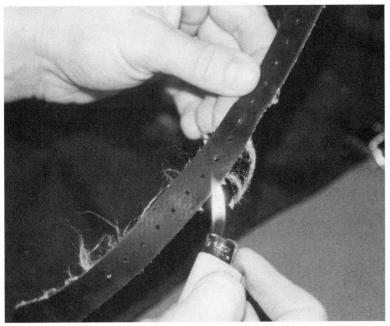

Burn-back fraying strands on Hypalon straps.

Chapter 4

Shelter

Small gnats that fly
In hot July
And lodge in sleeping ears
Can rouse therein
A trumpet's din
With Day of Judgement fears.

—Robert Graves, *One Hard Look*

Tents

Getting out in the wilderness wouldn't be nearly as much fun without a tent in which to hide from the elements. Your tent probably bears more exposure than any other piece of gear, so it should come as no surprise when you discover that your three-year-old shelter is looking a little worse for wear. Dirt, sand, leaves, sticks, salt, and stones are ground into the floor, zippers, and door panels, while sun, acid rain, pollen, pitch, and powerful gusts pummel the fly and canopy.

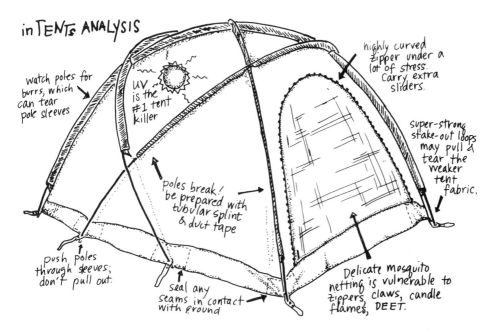

in TENTs ANALYSIS

watch poles for burrs, which can tear pole sleeves

UV is the #1 tent killer

highly curved zipper under a lot of stress. Carry extra sliders.

super-strong stake-out loops may pull & tear the weaker tent fabric.

poles break! be prepared with tubular splint & duct tape

push poles through sleeves; don't pull out.

seal any seams in contact with ground

Delicate mosquito netting is vulnerable to zippers, claws, candle flames, DEET.

UV radiation hastens the demise of most tents; direct sun can weaken both rainfly and tent body so dramatically that after just one season coatings peel, hardware pulls out, and the smallest scrape produces a nasty tear. Pitch your tent in the shade whenever possible; glacier and high-altitude campers might wish to pitch a tarp over the tent. Manufacturers all advise against leaving any nylon tent pitched for a long period. The worst thing you can do to your tent is to leave it standing in your backyard all summer.

Protect your guesthouse by pitching it under a tarp. One untried but certainly feasible way to avert UV damage is to coat your exterior tent fly with 303 Protectant. Normally recommended for boat hulls, this water-based "sunscreen" for petroleum-based materials works fine on fabrics, too.

Field Tips

Here are a few simple procedures for tent care in the field:

- Establish "house rules," such as no footwear to be worn inside the tent, and always roll up and secure door flaps so they don't lie in the mud. Meticulous campers might carry a scrap nylon "doormat" to curb tracking.
- Before packing up each morning, remove the fly and drape it upside down to dry the inside. Make sure the tent body is also dry. Pull up the stakes and lay the tent on its side to let the floor air. Before removing poles, open doors completely and shake out any debris.
- NEVER store a wet tent. If soaked when stuffed in your pack,

remove as soon as possible and set it up to dry. We've ruined more than one tent by neglecting to thoroughly dry the thing after a soggy trip. Even a little morning dew can cause mildew in a few days. Once mildew is established in dark, star-patterned splotches, coatings begin to delaminate.

- It's possible to "overpitch" a tent. Most tents have a series of grommets into which you plug pole tips. While the fabric should be taut, maxing the poles into the tightest grommet may unnecessarily stress the fabric. Save those last holes for damp weather and older, stretched-out tents.
- You can also "underpitch" a tent, which is a more certain formula for disaster. Indeed, many tent sagas are due to feeble pitch jobs. A floppy tent, poorly placed and staked, is extremely vulnerable to wind. A wall of snow or stone to windward isn't a bad idea in exposed, windswept terrain.
- A superb site is not so great if you can't get solid stakes in the ground. Imagine my chagrin after a day at the crags to find our tent tossed like tumbleweed into a barbed wire fence.
- Pay attention to signs of prevailing wind (leaning trees or snow drifts) when you're setting up camp. Pitch the low end of the tent into the wind, so the entrance is comfortably downwind.
- When pitching in a high wind, stake the upwind end first before inserting all poles and trying to erect the tent.
- In rough terrain or during extended trips, consider using a groundcloth to minimize abrasion to the tent floor. The cloth should never protrude from the perimeter of the tent or water will puddle under the floor. Sleeping out on just the groundcloth is also a nice option for clear nights under the stars, when a tent isn't really necessary.

To Roll or To Stuff? That Is the Question.
After measured consideration: One *rolls* a clean, dry tent around poles (always varying folds to avoid creasing fabric); one *stuffs* a soaking wet tent.

Cleaning

You say you stuffed soggy gear into the trunk, drove home, got caught up with work and didn't unpack until a week later? The easiest way to clean and dry a tent is to set it up. Once dry, you can shake out cooties, brush seams, and inspect stitching and seams for leaks. Notice any worn areas, and whether zipper sliders need attention. Like an aging pet, your tent should be treated gently.

Clean grubby tents with non-detergent soap (diluted Ivory Flakes or Dr. Bronner's) and a soft brush. If mildew has set in or there are sticky sap spots, scrub gently with a little borax or baking soda dissolved in water. Better to live with a stain than to damage the fabric

"My Tent Leaks"

Maybe. Water in your tent could be caused by:

Condensation. You crank out a lot of heat—and moisture—while you sleep. This moisture passes through the breathable, inner tent walls and condenses on the underside of the rainfly. Vent doors and keep rainfly tightly guyed away from tent body. If the rainfly sags and tent walls become saturated, you get evaporational cooling, which makes condensation worse. Try to vent an air intake down low and an air outlet up high.

Groundcloth seepage. If you use a groundcloth to protect your tent floor from abrasion, make sure it doesn't extend beyond the perimeter of the tent. Otherwise, the cloth will channel water into a pool directly beneath your sleeping bag.

Poor site selection. Are you camped in a drainage swale? Is the smallest area of tent upwind?

Seam leakage. If you're an all-season camper, seamsealing is a must—even the teensiest corner leak can soak a sleeping bag.

trying to eradicate it. (See *Appendix B: Low-Tox Cleaning Solutions*, page 229.)

The powerful jet from a garden hose is ideal for blasting out corners, irrigating zippers, and rinsing off pollen or sea salt.

Don't be tempted to wash your tent in a home washing machine, which can twist and wring fabric to death, cause delamination, and devastate netting panels.

Tent Sealing

(*See* Seams and Seamsealing, *page 21.*)

Surprisingly, even those enlightened enough to seamseal don't necessarily coat the right seams, or even the right side of the tent. Seam sealer should be applied to the coated, inside seams of the tent floor and the "bathtub ring" (where floor is attached to canopy). Pay special attention to corners and areas of tension, like sewn webbing loops—zillions of stitch holes wait there to become a showerhead. All rainfly seams should be sealed, as well as any exposed fasteners, such as snaps.

Bibler Tents also recommends sealing exterior seams, even if they've been factory taped. In wet conditions, moisture may enter stitching and track along the channel behind the seam tape. Seal exterior seams to prevent tracking and to get maximum waterproofness and durability. Some skeptics who've learned from hard use insist that all tent seams, inside and out, top and bottom, should be sealed. (*See Seamsealing illustration, page 50.*)

The best time to seal is when the tent is new, before any dirt contaminates seams. Always work in a ventilated but not breezy area (sheltered deck or barn). You don't want airborne detritus stuck to your tent.

Even if your tent is new, it's a good idea to prepare the seams by

Seal tent seams that are in contact with the ground.

buffing with alcohol or seam precleaner, which will remove any surfactants or water-repellent finishes so the sealer will stick. Otherwise, thoroughly clean the tent as recommended above, using a stiff brush on seams. Then use a precleaner or alcohol.

Erect your tent and let it warm up in the sun. Don't apply sealer in direct sun, though, or you may catch a nasty buzz. Consider using a syringe for deep corners. Put the rainfly on upside down and seal every seam.

Netting

Note: If you rely on no-see-um netting in the bush, you may also depend at times upon insect repellents. DEET, the active ingredient in many repellents, is extraordinarily hard on synthetics and fabric coatings. (If it melts nylon, how 'bout your skin?) Use caution storing and applying any repellent, and try not to handle the tent just after juicing up. Consider an herb-based "alternative" repellent or one with a reduced concentration of DEET.

Delicate mosquito-netting doors and panels should be treated with respect—especially if you live in blackfly country. Netting is the most likely part of your wigwam to rip, and is unfortunately positioned in vulnerable, high-traffic spots like doors. Practice zipper mindfulness when opening or venting your tent. Zippers, along with animal claws, are archenemies of mesh. Never store food in your tent, and teach Rover not to scratch at the door.

Patching Mosquito Netting
For smaller-than-a-dime-sized claw marks and snags, back the net with masking tape, then patch with Freesole or Seam Grip urethane adhesive. (*See **Fabric Patching**, page 8.*) Allow full cure time (up to 48 hours) before carefully removing tape and storing tent.

Larger tears are easily patched by hand- or machine-sewing. Since netting doesn't fray, there's no need to turn ends under. Simply double-needle stitch the patch with regular cotton-poly thread (nylon thread will tear netting), then carefully cut away damaged netting.

Fabric Tears

Tiny rips in a non-stress location are easily repaired: Apply adhesive-backed nylon repair tape to the uncoated side, with urethane adhesive on the opposite side. If the tear is too large to be effectively repaired with standard 3-inch tape, figure it's a sewing job.

Repair tape is also very useful reinforcing abraded areas, as on a well-used tent floor or pole sleeve. Maine Sport Outfitters puts their Moss demo tents through considerable torture during the course of a summer. Entire busloads of Vibram-clad, ice cream cone-eating tourists tromp through these shelters. Thanks to big sheets of nylon adhesive from a local sailmaker (used for numbers and graphics on big sails), the store can eke several seasons out of a tent before the floor disintegrates.

Pole sleeves can tear when a burred or cracked pole is pushed through the fabric channel. Avoid this type of tear by inspecting your poles for snags; always assemble the sections and thread poles gently and deliberately. In the field, use duct tape or nylon tape to patch a torn sleeve. Permanent repair means replacing the entire sleeve, which is best left to the manufacturer.

A tent may tear of its own volition at any point stronger than fabric, or where stress is concentrated: a bar-tacked seam, webbing loop or around a grommet. This is especially true of older, sun-weakened shelters. When this happens, tape doesn't cut it—reinforcement is in order.

Structural Reinforcement Patch

Remove stitching at seams and bar tacks. If seams are coated with sealer, use embroidery or nail scissors to clip each stitch, then pull threads through the uncoated side. Don't be tempted to take out stitches with an X-Acto knife—one slip and you'll have yet another repair. To work-in new fabric, you'll need to open an area at least three-times larger than the actual damage.

- Pay attention to construction order as you unfurl seams, joints, webbing, etc., so you remember how it all goes back together. Make a sketch if necessary.
- Skim the uncoated side of the area destined for repair with a warm iron to flatten out the fabric—never hold the iron in one place long enough for the fabric to get hot or the coating will delaminate.
- Cut a patch, carefully copying the shape and weave of the original fabric. Remember, patch edges must fold over at least

¼ inch. Turn edges under and iron as above.

- Before positioning patch on the inside, use nylon repair tape to hold original fabric together. This is the cosmetic part.
- Position the patch, coated side up. Use a little masking tape or a dot of Superglue to secure—*not* pins.
- Sew/splice in patch following the original stitching and construction order.
- Seal the outside stitch holes as well as the torn area with urethane sealer.

Sewn Patches

Patching your tent is a simple but tactical operation. If the reinforcement is not oriented properly, it will do little to alleviate stress on the weakened area. When cutting a patch, try to mirror the warp/weft orientation of the damaged panel, or try a circular patch, which can even-out load on the fabric (*see **Essential Techniques: Fabric Patching,** page 8*).

Flakey Coating

Flakes and peeling are signs of delamination and usually occur as a result of mildew, chemicals (like DEET or stove fuel), UV, and general old age. If your tent is new and begins to flake spontaneously, consult the manufacturer. Flaking is a sign that the fabric has deteriorated beyond its ability to perform in all conditions.

It's possible to prolong the life of your tent with a liquid polymer coating. While this process delays the inevitable, since coating

This webbing loop proved stronger than the tent fabric; a full-strength repair meant reinforcing the fabric panel before re-attaching the webbing—a time-consuming task of de- and reconstruction.

is applied to the opposite (noncoated) side, you're still faced with the original coat's dandruff problem.

Recoating solutions can be found at most outfitters and mail-order outlets. You might also try a water-repellent finish spray (not silicone), applied to the exterior fabric walls of the rainfly. We've also enjoyed good results with Thompson's Water Seal applied with a handheld sprayer—certainly the most economical option.

Applying Liquid Polymer Coating

Make sure the tent is clean. Rinse several times to remove any residue and dry completely. As with cleaning and sealing, coating is easily applied to an erect tent. Always apply new coating to the uncoated side of fabric—otherwise the new coating will bond to the old, flaky stuff, and simply fall away. Make sure to spread any pooled areas of coating, which will harden, blister, and peel away later.

Since a tent floor is the most likely place to peel, and since you're going to the trouble of recoating, do two layers. Apply the second coat while the first is still tacky. Let the coating dry completely according to manufacturer's instructions.

Waxing Cotton Wall Tents
(*See* Fabrics & Insulations: Cotton, *page 27, for recommended procedure.*)

Poles

Most pole difficulty starts on the ground—when you step on them. Treat poles as precision instruments and they'll last longer.

Shock-loaded, aluminum alloy poles are standard-issue with today's tents. Pole sections are usually straight when new, and take a bend over time as they are forced into the form of your tent. This is usually nothing to worry about, but a kink at or near a ferrule should be protected with a repair splint until you can have the section replaced.

The skeleton of your tent, like your own bones, suffers from stress concentrated at the joints—the most common point of injury. Always make sure you've completely fitted each ferrule to the next pole section or a crack will form at the joint, followed by a break. If you spot a crack, use the repair splint in your kit to prevent a more serious fracture.

Although it's fun to throw tent poles in the air and let them snap together like a spontaneously generated arachnid, this is really hard on the section ends, inflicting burrs and cracks. Instead, join the middle sections first, to allow maximum elasticity of the shock cord, then gently fit sections together. This way, you can inspect poles at the same

TENT POLE ANATOMY 101

end tip
end Section with insert
elastic cord
second section with insert
middle section with inserts
no insert (just tubing)
end Section with insert
end tip

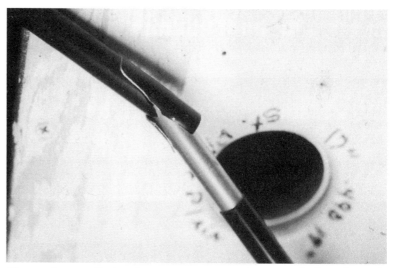

Tent poles usually break at section joints. Once cracked or sheared, tent pole sleeves are next to suffer.

time: Watch for too-tight joints, sand or salt inside the poles, worn shock cord, or cracks along the length of a section (usually at the end).

When breaking down your tent, push poles out of their channels. Pulling invites them to separate and snag fabric.

Rickety Joints

If poles feel gritty as you fit them together, clean with a blast from a garden hose, then dry thoroughly. If there's a lot of oxidation (black film that rubs off on your hands), wipe clean with a non-corrosive solvent like kerosene. Resist the urge to lubricate—that just attracts more dirt.

Really tight joints are often the source of a break and are bound to give you grief in cold weather when your fingers are fumbling. Check the connections for roundness. You can squeeze the poles back into shape with Vise-Grips or pliers, but go easy!

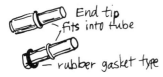

End tip fits into tube

rubber gasket type

Burrs can be toned down in the field with a stone or scrap of fine sandpaper, then filed off at home. Burred poles rip tent fabric and skin indiscriminately and are often harbingers of a fracture.

A ferrule may occasionally loosen and slip partway onto its pole section. You can usually pull a slipped ferrule back out by hand—compare it with another section to see how much to expose. This is a manufacturing defect and should be replaced. Superglue from your kit will work to secure the ferrule temporarily.

"old style" end plug

Loose Plugs

End plugs holding the shock cord can loosen, pull out, and cause cracks. This type of plug can be replaced with the solid "new style"

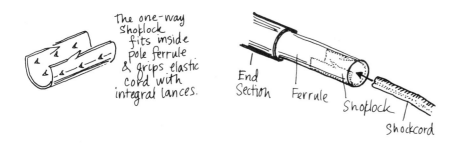

The one-way Shoklock fits inside pole ferrule & grips elastic cord with integral lances.

End Section   Ferrule   Shoklock   Shockcord

plug, which offers a tighter fit. With this type, cord is knotted, then stopped by the end ferrule fitted with a "Shoklock" rather than the plug itself. A loose solid plug can be ticked with a center punch to fit snugly into the pole. The notched variety is valuable for cinching-up tired cording in the field and is worth carrying in your stake bag. Ask the manufacturer for a few spares.

Some end plugs incorporate a rubber gasket, which makes the pole end less likely to slip out of the tent grommet during assembly, making setup much easier for a solo camper.

Stretched-Out or Broken Shock Cord

Severed cord is usually caused by a splintered pole section. Smooth or tape any rough spots to protect the cord from abrasion.

The rubber core of elastic shock cord does fatigue and lose its stretch—this usually happens in very cold weather. Join all but one end section, pull the cord snug, and tie off. Remove the plug from the end section—if it's the notched kind, you're in luck. Fit the last section, cinch-up cord (allowing about 2 inches extra per section), and cut off the excess. If you have a solid plug, follow instructions for replacement.

A stretched-out cord makes for the insanely tedious task of feeding poles through sleeves. If you're suffering this malady, take extra caution to be sure the ferrules are fully engaged, or you may splinter some pole segments.

Most manufacturers will happily restring your tent poles for little or no charge, using specially designed and formulated elastic. If you're in a time crunch or on a long trip, you may wish to rethread your own. Pull the end plug with pliers—if it's tight, tap the section end gently with a hammer to loosen. Cut the cord on the ferrule end of the section, then use a narrow rod or coat hanger to push the old cord out the open end. Follow the sequence shown to rethread the shock cord.

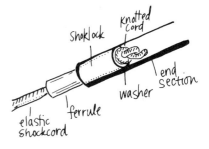

Shoklock   Knotted Cord   end section   washer   ferrule   elastic shockcord

Pole Splints

Pole fractures are easily splinted in the field, since most tents come with an alloy repair sleeve in the stakes bag. You will need duct

Splinting a cracked tent pole.

tape to hold the splint in place, however. Other pole splints include hose clamps, half-moon stakes, aluminum flashing (*see* **Winter Gear: Poles, *page 151***), or the Ramer pole patch. On long trips, you may want to bring two splints. Once home, send the broken part to the manufacturer—many offer unconditional guarantees on poles.

If your tent poles never made it back from Bolivia, or you require the services of a tent pole expert, try TA Enterprises. (*See* **Appendix F: Repair Services, *page 242***.)

Stakes

Whatever type stake you prefer, be sure to carry several spares. Consider using beefy nylon I-beam stakes for securing tent corners, especially in high winds. Use lighter-duty stakes for guys and secondary points. Half-moon stakes are great because they double as emergency splints for repairing poles of any type.

The Stake Bag
Besides stakes, here's where to stash extra widgets and spare whatnots for complete tent field repair:

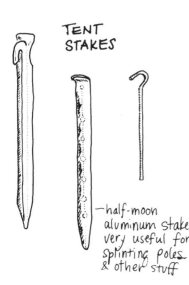

TENT STAKES

—half-moon aluminum stake very useful for splinting poles & other stuff

- spare guylines
- spare line tensioner
- roll of nylon repair tape
- pole splint
- extra zipper slider
- spare pole end plug—notched type

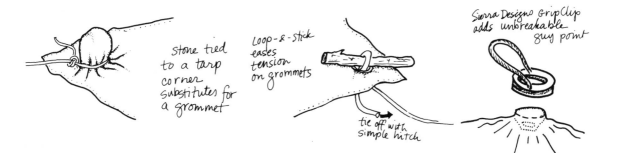

stone tied to a tarp corner substitutes for a grommet

Loop-&-stick eases tension on grommets

tie off with simple hitch

Sierra Designs GripClip adds unbreakable guy point

What a Great Guy!

On a correctly pitched tent, you can pluck a guyline like a banjo string and bounce pebbles off the stretched and shapely rainfly. Guys significantly enhance weatherproofness and durability of your tent. Tent guy-out loops and grommets are premounted on a rainfly by the manufacturer. If all guyline points are not prestrung, make a point of doing so. Coil up guys when storing and they'll be ready to roll when you're setting up camp in the face of big weather.

Aluminum or plastic line tensioners allow easy adjustment without fumbling with a knot. Buy a handful from any outfitter and slip a few spares in your stake bag.

If your guyline loop or grommet is damaged, you can easily create an alternative with a stone. Another nifty option is the Grip Clip from Sierra Designs, a secure, temporary guyline fastener that can also be attached to a pole.

line tensioner

Tent guys

WIND 10-20 mph

BIG WIND 30+ mph

unguyed tent walls distort & pinch poles to breaking point

WIND

BIG WIND

Guys too high, poles snap below guy anchor

WIND

BIG WIND

Guys 1/3 to 1/2 way up side support tent

Sleeping Bags

(*See also*: Sewing Basics, *page 4*; Fabrics & Insulations, *page 26*.)

Insulation

Unfortunately, sleeping bags do not provide warmth. Bag insulation simply slows the transfer of heat from your body to the air around it. This is the role of *loft*. The challenge of sleeping bag care is to sustain the insulation's ability to loft after countless compressions in a rucksack. Regardless of origin—fowl or crude—insulation should be treated delicately. As your final refuge from tempests and consciousness, your fleabag's filling is the most crucial element—everything else supports it. Equally crucial is how you store the bag (*see Storage: Safe Sacks, page 62*).

(*see Storage: Safe Sacks, page 62*)

. . . the men who had been relieved groped hurriedly among the soaking sleeping bags and tried to steal some of the warmth created by the last occupants . . .

—Antarctic explorer Sir Ernest Shackleton, after the wreck of *Endurance*

Down Fill

Down plumules have a natural oil coating that keeps each fiber supple and resilient. Heat, chemicals, dry cleaning, and even body oils will strip this protective coating and cause loss of loft. Good preventive maintenance means keeping a down bag's lining and shell as clean as possible.

Down may shift to one side of a sleeping bag; often this is a design feature so you can load the down to the top surface, depending on conditions. To redistribute down, lay the bag open on a flat surface, then pat, push, fluff, and cajole the fill where you want it to go.

Clumps—collected piles of down—result from compacting a wet bag, or from washing. If you've stuffed a wet bag in your pack, remove it as soon as possible. With your fingertips, work along the shell, baffle by baffle, and break up clumps by pulling them apart. You should do this several times during the drying process.

Are special, wash-in down treatments worth the bother? The jury is still out, but Nikwax offers water-based Down Proof, which coats fibers of down (and outer fabric) with a polymer/wax finish to repel moisture. While this may make sense for an older bag, consider that a treatment may make your bag shell less breathable, too. Better-quality down is carefully processed to ensure a proper acid/oil balance anyway, so the best treatment you can give your bag is gentle care. The best case for a wash-in treatment is if you know your down bag has been drycleaned. In that case, the down would benefit from some protective coating.

Synthetic Fill

Believe it or not, man has yet to develop an insulation as resilient as down. Synthetic fills lose their ability to spring back after compression much sooner than down, so the requirements of down care go double for synthetics. Most people choose a synthetic-filled bag for use in potentially wet conditions. When the bag does get wet, handle it tenderly to avoid tearing the batts (do not wring). NEVER dry clean a synthetic bag. Always keep synthetic bags away from intense heat—as in the trunk of your car—to which the fibers are most vulnerable. Use machine dryers only at the lowest heat (*see Cleaning, page 60*).

(*see Cleaning, page 60*)

Baffles and Shingles

Poor-quality bags have **sewn-through construction**, which parts the insulation so air can blast through the stitch holes onto your huddled

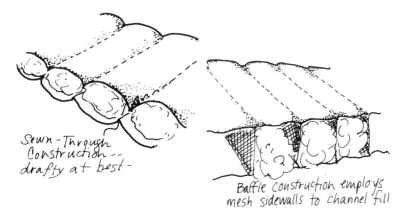

Sewn-Through Construction -- drafty at best -

Baffle construction employs mesh sidewalls to channel fill

Synthetic bags generally use shingle construction

form. The only thing you can do to improve this chilling situation is to seal the outer lines of stitching.

Most down bags employ a **baffling system** to regulate fill. Without them you'd have a cold heart and hot feet. Baffles are usually constructed of nylon mesh, which is strong and very light. These humble cells endure endless abuse as they are twisted and wrenched and yanked, and they deserve respect. Be mindful when removing your bag from its stuff sack. Inspect rows of stitching both inside and out; even a few pulled stitches should be caught early.

Synthetic batts are layered as **shingles**. Sheets of fibers are sewn directly to the shell and lining, and are as vulnerable to twisting as down baffles.

Shell and Lining

Among your sleeping bag's enemies are body and hair oils, salt, sunscreens, and insect repellents. All these acidic substances work through the shell to decompose down and reduce insulative performance of any fill. Your bag will work longer if you keep both shell and liner clean. Don't get naked in your bag! Even in summer, bring a light cotton shirt for sleeping.

Try a cotton, polypro, or silk liner between you and your bag. One terrific version is the Cocoon, a shimmery silk sleeve that weighs just a few ounces and feels fabulous. During summer, it's a cool, clean alternative to a hot, sticky bag; come winter, the silk adds insulation.

Winter campers or those on long alpine expeditions may want to consider a VBL—vapor barrier liner—to keep nightly body perspiration out of the down fill. As you sleep, your body heat and respiration (if you're a burrower) condense inside the bag, gradually penetrating the liner and dampening insulative capacity of the down.

Depending on quality, some down fills contain a certain volume of feathers. Poorer-quality fill can contain up to 18 percent feathers, the quills of which can poke maddeningly through shell fabric. Your best and most satisfying bet is to pull the offenders out (they offer no insulation) and make sure the hole heals itself. If a small puncture hole remains, add a drop of urethane adhesive or a nylon adhesive patch.

Zippers

The most common sleeping bag zipper is a No. 7 coil, which works well around bends and is unlikely to damage fabric caught under the slider. Usually there is an insulated draft tube to block airflow along the zipper's length. Watch to see this does not get stuck in the coils. (*See also*: ***Zippers: The Full Disclosure,*** *page 13.*)

If you've ruled out all possibility of zipper repair and have deemed replacement is in order, you can send your sleeping bag to the manufacturer or repair center for painless professional service, or you can replace it yourself. Before attacking the stitching, carefully determine if the zipper has been sewn into the seam—otherwise you'll have an instant roomful (or lung full) of down. If the zip is sewn into the seam, run a line of stitching behind the zipper to seal the down cells before removing the zipper stitching. Another tip: Fill a pump spray bottle with water and lightly mist the surface where you're opening baffles. The dampened down will stick to itself rather than to everything else in the room.

Cleaning

Attending to stains soon after they occur is an easy way to keep your bag clean and postpone the need for a complete washing. Use a vinegar/liquid soap or lemon/borax solution to scrub away any oil or food stains. (*See* ***Appendix B: Low-Tox Cleaning Solutions,*** *page 229, for cleaning recipes.*) For more tenacious tar or tree sap, you can employ a little kerosene—be sure to follow illustrated procedure, because the solvent may also harm insulative fibers. After scrubbing the spot, you might consider treating that area with a durable water-repellent spray.

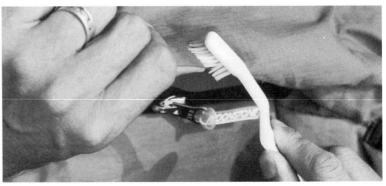

Spot-clean insulated bags or garments: lift fabric away from insulation before scrubbing.

Carefully lift the stained area of the shell away from the insulation (if it's a down bag, shift down away from the section you're treating). Fold in half through the stained area; gripping the fold, spritz cleaner or solvent on the spot and scrub with a soft brush. The cleaner will soak through to the other side of fabric without penetrating the filling. Clean opposite side of fold, then rinse with water.

No matter how you clean your sleeping bag, you'll break down some of the insulation. However, laundering restores loft; dry cleaning does not. Even if your bag says to dry clean, don't. Often a "dry clean only" label is placed there as a deterrent—a warning to treat the product gently—to prevent the bag from being washed carelessly at home. Dry cleaning solvents can destroy insulation (solvents strip natural oil from down and can distort synthetic fills). Beyond that, inhaling residual solvents has been known to cause allergic reactions, which cuts into the fun of your wilderness encounter.

No dry cleaning!

Air-Drying

Let your sleeping bag get fresh air and sunshine during trips to make sure it's dry before stuffing. (This is the only time you should expose your bag to UV radiation.) On a sunny day you can dry your just-laundered bag outdoors just as easily as you can in a machine, or use a combination of both methods. When hanging

hang-dry sleeping bags lengthwise

Machine-Washing

Once fabric starts to take a sheen, or if your bag is starting to lose loft, it is time for a wash. If you have a big investment in a high-quality, high-loft down sleeping bag, you might consider sending your bag for a professional groom by its manufacturer or a repair service center (*see* **Appendix F: Repair Services,** *page 242*). Otherwise you can wash your synthetic or down sleeping bag by hand (best) or locally using a commercial, front-loading washing machine only. (*See* **Fabrics and Insulations: Kinder, Gentler Hand-washing,** *page 35.*)

If you use a machine:
- Use a gentle, non-detergent soap. Feathered Friends, manufacturer of premium down products, recommends using a soap especially formulated for cleaning and restoring down.
- Apply soap directly to soiled areas.
- Soak 15 to 60 minutes (important).
- Wash on gentle cycle using cold water.
- Wash a second time using no soap.
- Lift the wet bag carefully to protect baffles.
- Dry as recommended.

from a clothesline, support the bag along its length, rather than hanging from one end.

Machine-Drying
"Under ideal conditions," says Bob Upton of Rainy Pass Repair, "drying a sleeping bag takes 1 hour, 40 minutes." So line up your quarters and plan to carefully monitor the drying process—as often as every 15 minutes. The bigger the dryer, the better. Drop directly affects drying time; if the dryer is too full, there's less drop, thus less drying. Inside an overpacked dryer, the air can reach temperatures higher than the assigned setting (hot enough to melt insulation or zippers). If the fabric is hot to the touch, remove the bag from the dryer to air.

If there's plenty of room, add a few dry towels in the dryer to absorb moisture from the bag. Remove wet towels at first check and replace with dry ones. Don't bother putting a tennis shoe or ball in the dryer, which will do more harm to the insulation than good.

Periodically remove the entire bag and check for clumping insulation. Down clumps should be worked apart so they'll dry evenly. Synthetic batts should not be broken apart; try to shift them without too much tension at stitch lines.

Storage: Safe Sacks
Compressing
Never store any sleeping bag in its nylon stuff sack—use that for short-term, on-the-road storage only. When storing under compression (in small stuff sack or pack) stuffing is better than rolling.

Step on a bottom corner of the stuff sack while you grasp the mouth in one hand. With your free hand begin stuffing the bag, starting with the bulky foot section. Press down often to compress the insulation as you stuff your way, accordion-like, to the hood section.

Long-term Storage
A bag should rest fully lofted. If you have closet space, suspend the bag from its end loop or else drape it over a hanger. The most popular method recommended by manufacturers is to store a bag in a large, breathable cotton storage sack, which allows the bag to breathe and loft.

Always store bags in a cool, dark, dry place, away from likely sources of mildew. Don't expose your sleeping bag to heat of any sort—even from sunlight—unless you're drying it.

Sleeping Pads

Sleeping pads provide more than comfort to your weary bones. A pad helps protect your sleeping bag insulation from being compacted excessively under your weight, so loft is maximized. A pad also provides insulation against the cold ground. Both functions help you sleep warmer.

There are basically two types of sleeping pads: closed-cell foam pads and self-inflating pads.

Closed-Cell Foam Pads

Evazote, Ensolite, and other polyurethane foam pads are superlight, bulky, and so inexpensive they're often considered "disposable," even though they last virtually forever. Indeed, old foam pads never die—they can become cup or bottle insulators, knee pads, back rests, or perform zillions of other custom functions. Closed-cell foam pads are ideal for outfitting canoes and kayaks, and should never be discarded lightly.

The big advantage of durable, closed-cell construction is that it doesn't absorb water like open-cell foams (a.k.a. sponges). However, the foam does compress over time and lose its insulative capacity. Store your closed-cell pad flat if possible, or loosely rolled. Storing bound by tight straps or bands will compress and deform the pad before its time.

Open-Cell, Self-Inflating Mattress

Foam
Open-cell foam works just like any other insulation, offering the most protection when expanded to its maximum capacity. Although naturally puffier than its closed-cell counterpart, open-cell foam

Old closed-cell foam pads may be reincarnated as knee pads, doll PFDs, or water bottle insulators.

requires inflation with air to sustain its loft under weight, and it must be protected from water. Therefore, open-cell foam is bonded to an air- and watertight envelope of urethane-coated nylon fabric with heat-welded seams, and inflated by means of a valve.

Mattress foam has a memory. If you store your mattress tightly rolled, the foam will forget everything it ever knew about loft, and hold the compressed, flattened shape. Always store your sleeping mat unrolled with valve open to facilitate maximum loft. Compacting the pad temporarily for trips does not damage the foam.

Preventive Tips from the Pros

While there are now several brands available, Cascade Designs' original Therm-a-Rest mattress irrevocably altered perceptions of backcountry comfort and remains today the most popular of all self-inflating mattresses. Innovative from the word go, Cascade Designs has been an industry leader in the quest for greener production standards, aggressively promoting warranty and repair policies, and constantly developing new repair techniques—the patching process described here is their very latest recommendation.

Diana Eken, Therm-a-Rest repair specialist, sees as many as 7,000 mattresses a year in her lab; about half are cheerfully replaced under warranty, despite the fact that many are battered, grimy veterans suffering from years of neglect. Diana laughingly assesses each mattress and efficiently effects hundreds of repairs per week. She has developed the patching process to a fine art and offers these commandments:

1. Always store your mattress clean, dry, and unrolled with the valve open.
2. Dry out your mattress between trips to prevent mildew.
3. Keep away from DEET, sun, and any heat source.
4. Keep away from pets.
5. Use Seam Grip or Urebond adhesives for repair.

Coated Fabric

Mattress fabric coating bears the dual tasks of holding air inside the mattress while keeping moisture and debris out. When your self-inflating mattress springs a leak, it's the fabric that's punctured, torn, abraded, or otherwise damaged. Keep the mattress clean and free from sand, dirt, and sharp objects such as crampons, sticks, and dry spiny things. Sparks from a campfire are common causes of leaks large and small. Direct heat from a stove can cause blistering and delamination of the fabric, too.

The seams of a self-inflating pad are heat-welded, bonding the urethane-coated fabric panels together. Damage to or near the seams usually spells factory repair.

As with any synthetic, the surface fabric (as well as foam underneath) is especially vulnerable to DEET, solvents, oils, and even sunscreens, which can melt, damage, and delaminate the coating. Never use any solvent to clean spots off your mattress. A quick scrub with soap and water, citrus or vinegar cleaning solution is your best bet. Close the valve when washing.

The slippery, coated fabric of a sleeping pad often causes dreaded *Gaposis*—your equally slippery nylon sleeping bag has no purchase on the surface of the pad, and you wake up shivering on the tent floor. This can be addressed with Cascade Design's Slip Fix, a urethane spray that gives a little textural resistance to the fabric. You can also try applying zig-zag beads of urethane seam sealer on the mattress surface.

Valve

Open-cell mattresses "self-inflate" because an opened valve allows passage of air into the mattress as the springy foam regains its loft. Once the valve is closed, air is trapped within foam cells to provide firm support and displacement when weight is applied to the mattress.

Valves are seated in a stiff, urethane-reinforced corner of the mattress using a urethane adhesive. On Therm-a-Rests, old-style metal valves occasionally bind and malfunction due to grit. These should be replaced with the newer nylon valve—available anyplace that carries the mattress. A very common problem is that puppies and other creatures will chew the valve and puncture the airtight mattress coating.

Valve replacement. Remove the old or damaged valve with pliers. Pull straight out—don't rock or twist or you may enlarge the molded valve seat. Apply a thin bead of urethane adhesive to the barbed end of the new valve, taking care not to let glue enter any part of the valve. Press or screw the valve into the molded hole, then wipe away excess adhesive.

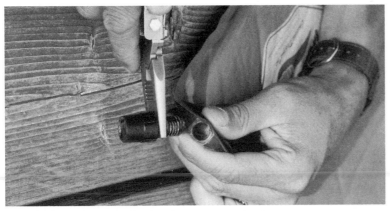

Pull faulty valve straight out from seat with pliers.

Deflation Technique

- Fold mattress twice with valve closed.
- Open valve and sit on mat to expel air.
- Close valve.
- Carefully roll the mattress—very tightly— forcing remaining air towards the closed valve.
- Open valve and roll out remaining air.
- Close valve.

Inflation: Breathing Lessons

The best way to inflate your mattress is to unfurl it, open the valve, and let it naturally loft while you go about setting up camp. Close the valve just before lying down. This is what self-inflating means. In very cold temperatures, the inflation process will be slower. Some people carry the pad against their body (inside a pack) to keep it warm for quick inflation.

A new mattress has been completely compressed for packaging purposes and requires an initial breath inflation to restore its loft. Blowing air into your mattress will provide firm support and increase its loft, especially in cold weather. However, if you do a lot of winter camping, breath inflation is not a good idea—moisture from your own hot air can accumulate, condense and freeze inside the mattress. Any residual moisture in warmer temperatures can cause mildew and hasten the demise of your sleeping pad.

Don't inflate your mattress with a high-pressure pump; this risks maxing out the seams. Likewise, don't leave an inflated mattress sitting in the hot confines of your car on a sunny day, or you may be taken for a terrorist.

Eew, Mildew

Mildew is caused by storing the pad in a damp, warm place, or by storing with the valve closed, or by storing a dirty pad. Moisture and dirt invite mildew to grow and deteriorate the fabric's airtight urethane coating from either inside or outside. Avoid mildew by keeping your mattress clean, and always store dry, with the valve open. If your mattress is wet, leave it in the sun for several days with the valve open before storing.

Field Repair

My first Therm-a-Rest was slashed by an ice axe. After a cold night, I gave it up for lost and sold it to a friend for a dollar. The second was skewered on my honeymoon by a porcupine-fish spine, dampening nuptial comfort. Both incidents could have been avoided with mindfulness. Punctures are easily field-repaired; lacerations can be surgically corrected at the factory.

Duct tape works fine temporarily, but tends to leak air slowly. The tape also leaves a nasty sticky residue that attracts dirt and renders a permanent repair almost impossible. If you enjoy your self-inflating pad, carry a patch of nylon repair tape—better yet, bring a repair kit containing a urethane-coated fabric patch and urethane adhesive, like Shoo Goo, or Free Sole. A regular bicycle tube patch kit sometimes works; Cascade Designs offers a compact repair kit.

I Think It's Leaking . . . But I'm Not Sure
Roll up the mattress according to the deflation technique above. Close the valve and leave the mat overnight. If your pad self-inflates, you have a leak.

Locate the leak.   Finding a slow leak in the field is difficult. If an inflated pad doesn't hiss, carefully roll it to increase pressure; listen with your face close to the pad to catch the sound of any emissions.

If that doesn't work, immerse the inflated pad (valve closed) in a bathtub or quiet pool and watch for a telltale stream of bubbles to lead you to the leak. If you know generally where the leak is, you can pinpoint it by misting that area of the inflated pad and watching for bubbles. The valve will typically emit a few bubbles, but if it's not a continuous flow, the valve is fine. Once you find the leak, mark it clearly. Don't forget to check for more than one hole!

If you know the pad leaks but are completely stymied as to its whereabouts, don't feel inept. Mere humans cannot breath-inflate a self-inflating mattress to more than 1 psi. At the factory service center, a special, precise machine will pump exactly 3.5 psi—the maximum pressure—into the offending mattress.

A leak within an inch of the edge of your pad is pretty difficult to patch effectively, and should be sent for factory repair. If that's not convenient, goop a bunch of urethane adhesive (Free Sole) to create a patch.

Patching in the Field or at Home
- Clean off any tape residue, sunscreen, or DEET with soap and water, then rinse thoroughly. Allow to dry. For best patch adhesion, clean with alcohol to remove any lingering soap or oils.
- Use the deflation technique to squeeze as much air out of the mattress as possible. Close the valve.
- A small puncture can be healed by working a small amount of urethane adhesive into the hole. Add a drop of glue to the top of the hole, too. Allow adhesive to cure completely before inflating.
- Large punctures and tears require a patch. Cut a patch at least ½ inch larger than the hole, making sure to round the edges. Position the patch on the deflated pad, then trace around it. Follow the field triage patching instructions, below, in order.
- If your patch is not a self-adhesive, coated material, you must

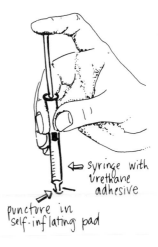

← syringe with
urethane
adhesive

puncture in
self-inflating pad

also apply a thin coat of adhesive directly to the patch. Do this before coating the damaged mattress so the patch surface is tacky but not wet when you apply it.

Air Mattresses

Punctured air mattresses can be treated as any inflatable. Most air mattresses are made of vinyl or plastic, so any glue you use should be formulated accordingly. Vynabond or PVC cement are popular options.

Pin-Sized Punctures

To fix a small puncture wound in your air mattress:

- Locate and mark the puncture as you would for a self-inflatable.
- Deflate the mattress.
- Prep the area with a swab of alcohol.
- Apply repair glue to the tip of a toothpick and insert into the puncture.
- Repeat.
- Apply a small bead of glue to the top of the puncture.
- Allow to cure completely (according to glue specifications).

Patches

Air mattress tears or punctures can be repaired by following the triage patching instructions, or try a bicycle tube patch kit.

Field Triage Patch

1. Thoroughly soak puncture area with clean water. Rub water into the fabric fibers briskly until area turns dark. Wipe off excess drops.
2. Boil a liter or so of water in a flat-bottomed metal pan.
3. While you wait for the water to boil, generously inject Seam Grip directly into the puncture.
4. Use the applicator nozzle to work Seam Grip thoroughly into the wet fibers and up to ½ inch away from the center of the puncture. Keep the coating even and about ¹⁄₁₆ inch (1.5 mm) thick.
5. Squeeze out an additional ¼ inch (6 mm) of Seam Grip onto the puncture to purge the nozzle of contaminated adhesive. Don't work into fabric—let this bead up on the fabric's surface.
6. When water boils, cut out patch, remove backing paper (if any) and place patch on top of puncture.
7. Set pan on the patch.
8. Lift pan from the patch. Check to make sure no Seam Grip has exuded from underneath the patch. Wipe off any excess.
9. Replace pan on mattress and allow to stand undisturbed for one hour. Mattress is now ready to use.
10. To check your repair, pressurize the mattress by folding with valve closed. Patch should not show bubbling leaks when wetted. If leaks occur, remove and discard patch. Repeat repair procedure and allow extra cure time.

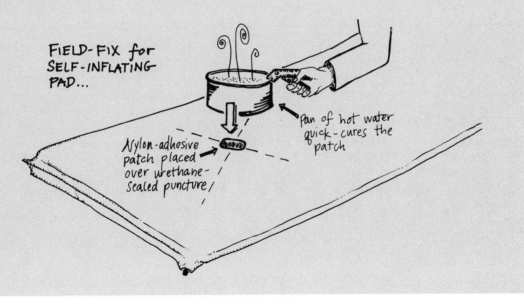

FIELD-FIX for SELF-INFLATING PAD...

Nylon-adhesive patch placed over urethane-sealed puncture

Pan of hot water quick-cures the patch

Chapter 5

Packs

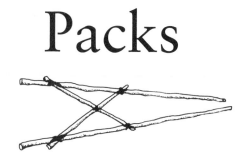

*It was an abortive climbing trip to Mount Louis in the Canadian Rockies,
the kind of trip you have nightmares about: bad rockfall, horrid weather, heinous bugs,
bushwhacking on the wrong side of a river. We mustered enough sense to admit defeat and started to
hike out. Finally, we found the trail and started feeling optimistic, fantasizing about overdue showers
and cheeseburgers. Then a key buckle in my pack suspension broke and the entire shoulder harness
came adrift. The only way I could carry the monster was bent over like Quasimodo. Seven miles of
staggering and snarling followed. People heading up the trail were gushing about the beautiful day
and rushing river; all I could do was sputter and swear. What really hurt was that the pack had
had the same failure before and I'd sent it to the factory for repair—just in time for our trip.
Once home, I attacked it with a Speedy Stitcher. That fix was still holding strong
when I yard-saled the pack 10 years later.*

—Dave Getchell, Equipment Editor, *Backpacker* magazine

The Five-Point Pack Check

Before you head out, take time to inspect and not neglect your pack.

1: Zippers

Modern pack zippers tend to be so huge you can't possibly break them, right? Well, most of the time. Usually zipper problems are slider-related (*see Zippers, page 13*); you should always have a spare slider if you use a panel-loading, zipper-dependent pack. This is less of an issue with top-loaders. If,

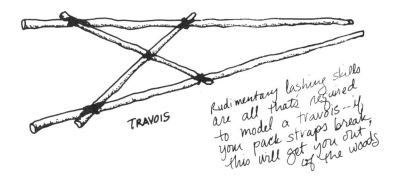

TRAVOIS

Rudimentary lashing skills are all that's required to model a travois -- if your pack straps break, this will get you out of the woods

after replacing the slider, you determine the zipper needs replacement, send the pack away! The tedious, technical task of replacing a pack zipper requires heavy-duty machinery and experience. If you insist on replacing the zipper yourself, consult Sumner's *Sew & Repair Your Own Outdoor Gear*.

Any snagging fabric threads? Clip back and heat-seal with a lighter or soldering iron as described later in this section. Use a garden hose with a powerjet attachment to clean out any grit, or try a stiff brushing in the tub or sink.

2: Straps

Straps rarely break; rather, they pull out from seams. Watch for any cuts or abrasions that may cause a failure. If an important strap does break, you can cannibalize another from your pack (a compression strap, for instance) and splice it in by stitching or with ladderlock fasteners from your repair kit.

Reattaching a Pack Strap

Use the sewing awl in your repair kit. Start from the outside to determine the correct placement. Pin the strap to secure the angle. Carefully turn the bag inside-out to expose the seam, then close with several lines of stitching. If there's enough length, anchor the pack strap tail to the body of the pack for added security.

3: Fasteners and Hardware

Polycarbonate buckles and sliders commonly fail—especially vulnerable is the female side of a 2-inch hipbelt buckle. Cold makes these plastic parts brittle, so if they get stepped on or tossed onto a rocky surface, *hasta la vista*, baby. Usually you can manage to keep the buckle functioning with a wrap of duct tape to hold the split together. For that matter, consider protecting the hollow half with a duct-tape jacket before it breaks. Always pack matching spares for crucial parts.

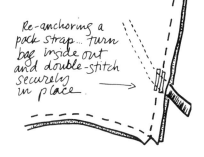

Re-anchoring a pack strap... turn bag inside out and double-stitch securely in place.

4: Fabric and Coating

Look for signs of abrasion, punctures, fading, stains, or mildew.

Abrasion usually occurs along the bottom of the pack or on climbing rucksacks that get hauled a lot. If there's wear in a specific location, you can add a patch of nylon tape to create a protective, slippery surface.

Punctures are the result of ice tools, slices from ski edges, or from an overstuffed pack getting dragged or shipped by air. Catch these when they're small and easy to patch with urethane adhesive.

Fading is due to excessive heat or UV exposure. This means the fabric is fatigued and you should be prepared to patch it at any time—expect to replace the pack before long.

Stains are inevitable and are part of the customized patina any pack develops. However, certain types of gunk can prematurely age the packcloth or damage the coating. Pack fuel carefully: Double-check the seal on the fuel bottle and store it in a sturdy stuffsack. Any sticky stuff on the outside of the pack (like klister wax from skis) should be removed as soon as possible or it will attract dirt and, ultimately, mildew.

Mildew destroys fabric and its coating. Always allow fabric to dry thoroughly and brush off dirt and grime before storing. A lot of pack damage starts from the inside when food or fuel spills are left unattended and cause deterioration of the coating. Food spills also attract nibbling creatures. Turn your pack inside out and clean it every now and then.

5: Seams and Stitching

Individual stitches stretch only so many times before they fatigue and break, especially if you typically stuff your pack to the gills. Look at all visible stitching on the main pack body to check for any broken stitch lines—touch these up immediately by hand with an awl. If there's a spot of stitching that's getting abraded for some reason, run a bead of urethane seam sealer along the stitches to protect them.

Turn your pack inside out, brush grime from the seams, and check for frays. Any loose threads should be clipped and heat-sealed. This is more of a problem with older packs. New packs of good quality usually have taped or bound seams.

It's really not worth the time and effort to seamseal your pack when a $10 pack cover will keep water out much better. Pack your gear (especially food) in waterproof stuffsacks, or carry a few extra plastic trash bags for weatherproofing gear (the pack cover is a more durable choice).

Quik-Attach Tensionlock w/ slotted bar for field use

A terrific recent innovation is the Quik-Attach Tensionlock. This has a slotted bar that allows you to replace any tensioning fastener without having to unsew the webbing loop it's attached to. No field repair kit should be without one.

Pack Rats

Public Pack Enemy No. 1

Infamous bugaboo packrats and Columbia ground squirrels taught me the single most important preventive maintenance tip for packs: Never employ your pack for overnight food storage! Use something relatively expendable, since conniving creatures will outwit even the most ingenious rigger.

On one particular trip, the rodents perforated my 5,000-cube hauler, suspended from an overhanging boulder with thin cord. Ravenous packrats then munched their way through one side and crunched out the opposite, leaving crumbs and two substantial holes in my trusty Gregory. Our rigging system became increasingly elaborate until finally the food bag hung between large swiveling foils 30 feet from anything. Still, a succession of holes marked the path of hungry visitors through another stout little rucksack. Our serene Buddhist friend was seen trying to skewer a bold little varmint with his ice axe, so great became his frustration.

Use a heavy stuff bag (bring plastic garbage bags to waterproof if necessary) for hanging food. If rain is likely, consider a paddling dry bag for food storage. These PVC or urethane-coated bags have a watertight seal which keeps animal-attracting smells in and rain and rodents out. Animals are also attracted to sweat and body salts that accumulate on pack straps and on the back panel; discourage this by regularly rinsing your pack with fresh water.

Public Pack Enemy No. 2

There's a reason why airline ticket agents make you sign a waiver when you check your backpack—something about these rugged carryalls brings out aggressive handling. Between check-in and the time you pull your bedraggled pack from the carousel, any number of goons have grabbed, hurled, lurched, wrenched, and wrestled with whatever strap dangled near. After two or three broken pack straps, we developed a surefire binding technique that leaves only one handle available—the one designed to lift the pack.

Breakable and hard-edged items like tent poles or cook kits should be packed deep within the beast and generously padded with soft stuff. If you don't feel comfortable sitting on the pack from any angle, start over. Do not load anything on the exterior. Cinch down all compression straps, and carefully weave dangling ends out of sight. Tighten shoulder straps to their shortest length, also tucking any loose ends away. Wrap the hip belt forward around the pack body to achieve a smooth, round profile. Run the belt through ice-axe loops, too, so it stays wrapped. String your claim ticket

Have You Spotted these Public Pack Enemies?

1-900-PACWATCH

This rucksack is battened down and ready for travel; note hip belt is fastened forward around pack body.

around the handle—a little flag that means "lift me here."

Of course, the simplest way to avoid mistreatment of your pack is to envelop it within a big duffel bag lined with a foam sleeping pad. If you're shipping ice tools, definitely use foam pads—or risk multiple puncture wounds to all your fabric gear.

Patching

(See also: Essential Techniques: Fabric Patching, *page 8.)*

The holes you're most likely to experience are due to animals: *Ursidae*, *Canidae*, *Rodentia*. The type of patch you'll need depends on the hole size and level of damage to the pack. Most chewed-up packs come out of the woods with duct tape or adhesive nylon patches affixed, but these are almost certainly temporary, since they are neither structural nor waterproof.

Small, bite-sized holes or punctures can be cured either with urethane adhesive or by heavily overstitching the area with a packcloth swatch for backing.

A fist-size or larger patch requires deconstructing seams and splicing in new fabric. Most home machines can't handle layers of heavy packcloth; for a really strong, durable patch I strongly recommend sending the job to the manufacturer or a repair center (*see **Appendix F: Repair Services**, page 242*). If you're heading on a long trip, be sure to bring an awl, heavy-duty thread, and a few squares of pack cloth so you can effect a rudimentary repair.

External Frame Packs

Externals require the same Five-Point Pack Check, with a few other considerations. Shoulder straps are connected to the frame (rather than the pack body) by a grommet, clevis pin, and retaining ring. If your external's shoulder strap goes, it's usually caused by the fabric tearing away from the grommet. You can repair this in the field by heating up your knife awl and punching it or a red-hot stick through the strap about an inch away from the original grommet. Make sure the new hole's edges are heat-sealed to prevent tearing, then insert the pin/ring. Carry a spare pin and ring, too. Once home, order a replacement strap from the manufacturer.

The other problem specific to an external frame pack is failure of the frame. This is usually due to Public Pack Enemy No. 2, or by sitting or falling on a frame in such a way that it bends the tubing and substantially weakens the structure.

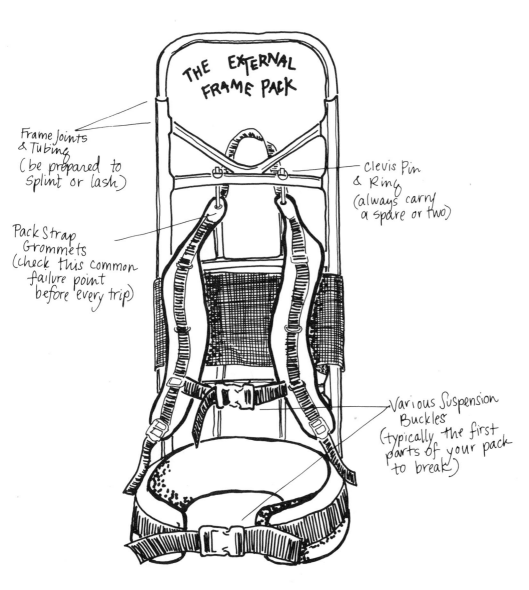

THE EXTERNAL FRAME PACK

Frame Joints & Tubing
(be prepared to splint or lash)

Pack Strap Grommets
(check this common failure point before every trip)

Clevis Pin & Ring
(always carry a spare or two)

Various Suspension Buckles
(typically the first parts of your pack to break)

Correct the bend with a splint from parts in your repair kit—a section of split tubing, soda can, or aluminum flashing can be bound with hose clamps. Of course, a stick and bootlace is an equally suitable splint. (*See* **Winter Gear: Poles,** *page 152, for an illustration of this repair.*)

Pack tubes rarely shear, but if they do, plug the tubes with a green stick, then splint as suggested above.

If the frame is welded, it may well break at a joint. If that's the case, splint and lash the frame as best you can and evacuate!

Revitalizing an Aging Duluth Pack

A few weeks before setting out on a Canadian river trip, I decided to give our well-used Duluth pack a makeover. The packcloth's interior coating had been disintegrating for some time, leaving bits and pieces of cruddy brown gunk on whatever was stored in the bag. Turning the pack inside out, I used a stiff brush with warm water to scour away any lingering coating.

Next step was to trim away all the frayed fabric edges along interior seams, which tended to catch in the zippers. I sealed the raw edges by running them along a heated soldering iron held stationary in a vise.

Turning the pack right-side out, I waterproofed the clean and dry cloth using Thompson's Water Seal in a handheld sprayer, beginning by tracing all the seams, then saturating the pack body. Proving the treatment was as easy as tossing the pack out into a rainstorm—drops of water beaded up reassuringly on the fabric surface.

All this preparation was worthwhile, since it rained for most of the trip. However, my attention was so focused on re-waterproofing that I forgot to check a very basic, essential element: the pack straps' attachment points! The stitching held just until the last mile of the last (and longest) portage. A simple enough field repair, but better avoided had I done the Five-Point Pack Check.

Cut away fraying threads along seams and zipper track.

Heat-seal raw seam edges with a wood-burning pencil or soldering iron.

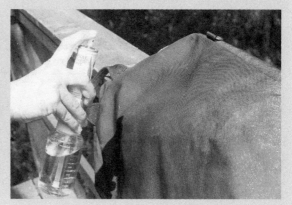

Use a Preval sprayer with Thompson's Water Seal to re-waterproof fabric, paying special attention to seams.

The Tumpline

If you find your pack straps straining under a full load, or if they suffer suspension failure, try a tumpline to relieve the stress. This primitive technique has yet to be improved upon: A single strap serves to correctly balance a load over your skeleton so you have more energy to walk and chew gorp at the same time. The headpiece fits at the junction of your forehead and crown, thereby lining up your vertebrae into proper load-carrying position.

For some reason, anyone who ever writes about the tumpline spends most of the time talking about the pain of maladjustment, but I leave that to individual experience. Most Duluth-style packs come with a tumpline, or at least with attachment points, but one can be rigged to any pack or odd-sized load with practice. Try to affix ends at or near shoulder height, using whatever attachment points are available, i.e., compression straps, frame stay, what-have-you. Knowing how to rig a tumpline can prove invaluable if you blow a packstrap on a long trip.

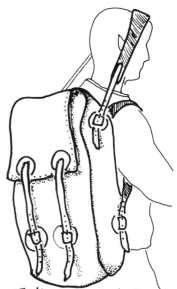

Traditional Duluth Pack rigged with a Tumpline

Part II

Footwear

There's man all over for you,
blaming on his boots the faults of his feet.

—Samuel Beckett, *Waiting for Godot*

A Tale of Two Cobblers

How the '80s Nearly Claimed Komito

If any one person awakened me to the idea of repair as an honorable profession it was Steve Komito in Estes Park, Colorado. His shop served as a sort of climbers' bistro during the heroic days of free-climbing, and Komito himself is a classic climbing character. His vocation as cobbler the perfect complement to his avocation as skier and climber, Komito delivers pithy wisdom and goodhearted gossip with every resole. Just about everyone knows somebody who's bivouacked on his deck, yet despite his generosity and enthusiasm Steve nearly called it quits a few years back.

What almost killed his business was the disposable '80s, when people started buying lightweight, inexpensive "sneaker boots." In the good old days, climbing and hiking boots were expensive—an investment that required reverential care.

Enter the recent surge in rock climbing and telemark popularity, and a new generation of footwear once again worthy of repair. "Hundred-and-fifty-dollar rock shoes were the best thing that ever happened to me," he says. Now his shop even has an 800 number.

Net Fit

"Since Jesus's sandals, footwear was all made the same way," waxes Dave Page, cobbler, during a visit at his Seattle neighborhood hangout, Still Life with Coffee. "An upper was stitched to a slab of sole, then trimmed to fit. Now the trend is for *net fit*, where a finished sole is pressed on with adhesives—no stitching, no trimming, no smoothing. We no longer resole, we *re-bottom*."

This trend toward adhesion of molded, cemented soles rather than an externally stitched welt can be traced back to the first lightweight fabric-and-leather hiking boots, which employed running shoe construction methods to create a lightweight boot that required virtually no break-in. Unfortunately, like other conveniences of our time—diapers, lighters, and dinner out—those first-generation fabric boots became disposable.

Happily, bootmakers responded to pleas for more substance and drier feet without reverting entirely to the heavy clunkers of yore. Today's hybrids combine leather uppers with molded footbed, and are not only more durable and weatherproof, but can be re-bottomed by select cobblers like Page, whose Italian deep-cavity press is literally *deus ex machina*. Both cobblers celebrate better boots; we celebrate their craft. (*See* **Appendix F: Directory of Repair Services**, *page 242, for a listing of specialty cobbler shops.*)

> ### Dave Page's Mantra for Footwear Longevity
>
> 1. Clean after use.
> 2. Waterproof in moderation.
> 3. Keep away from heat.

Chapter 6

Weatherproofing Boots

...no use dodging puddles when your feet are soaked...
—Gary Snyder, *Wind Has Blown*

(See also: Essential Techniques: Seams and Seamsealing,
page 21; Appendix A: Adhesives, *page 225.)*

Keeping the Water Out

Boot maintenance centers on one thing: keeping water out. The less water absorbed by your footwear, the longer it will last. You can accomplish this in several ways: by treating the leather, carefully drying after use, wearing vapor barrier liners, and by using gaiters whenever possible. Think of gaiters as little tents for your boots, protecting both leather and your efforts at leather treatment. (*See Specialty Garments, page 44, for more information about gaiter care.*)

Seamsealing Boots

Generally, fewer seams equal a dryer boot, and less likelihood of a catastrophic blowout. Improve wearability and weatherproofness by caulking all external seams—especially where the boot upper meets the sole. A thin application of urethane sealant on clean, dry seams *before* weatherproofing does the trick.

First, clean along the seams with water and a stiff brush (an old toothbrush is ideal). Once dry, buff the seam with denatured alcohol to remove any residual oils and ensure a successful bond. The best way to achieve a clean, consistent bead of sealer is with a syringe. Allow full cure time before applying leather treatment.

Use a syringe to apply seamsealer along stitch lines -- neat & precise

Beeswax

> Sweet milk and gratitude
> as fingers by the fire
> rub warmth and glow
> into cracked leather toes
>
> They had traveled far
> to bathe in honey
>   —AG

Treating Leather

Leather is hydrophilic; it will absorb most any wet stuff like a sponge. Once leather becomes wet, moisture quickly travels from pore to pore by pumping action (as the boot flexes) and from fiber to fiber by wicking, or capillary action. Wet leather is extremely conductive—your body heat passes through faster than you can gobble a Power Bar.

Even though leather is one of the most durable and resilient materials known, once wet it stretches and weakens; as leather dries, it shrinks and becomes brittle. Leather is skin, plain and simple. Unlike skin, however, natural lubricants and protective coatings are no longer in steady service—unless *you* supply them, that is. The key to long life for your leather boots is to maintain the leather's natural equilibrium with lubricants that provide water repellency.

Boot Goops

While difficult to differentiate among the zillions of leather products available, Komito insists that as long as you use *something*—anything, even basil-infused olive oil—to waterproof your footwear, you're on the right track. However, since most boot treatments fall into the following general categories, you can make an educated choice.

Fats or Greases

Fats or greases such as tallow—historical standbys—offer only the shortest-term protection against moisture. These coatings also contain contaminants that will invite mildew and other cooties to roost inside the leather, and may also attract nibbling varmints.

Oils

Oils quickly penetrate pores to soften leather and are a good choice if you're faced with stiff, beastly boots that chew your feet to shreds while you're out trying to have a good time. Oil provides breathable weatherproofing because it coats individual leather fibers; however, oil also permits the fibers to stretch, thereby weakening the overall strength of your footgear. Oil treatments are best reserved for breaking in new boots, softening the odd hotspot, or reconditioning old, brittle leathers. Use any penetrating oil, including mink oil, very infrequently because such dramatic softening capabilities will result in premature loss of fit.

Waxes

Waxes by themselves have a hard time penetrating leather; they work by clogging pores to create a waterproof, non-breathable barrier. Slathered-on wax tends to float on the leather surface, forming a thick skim coat that abrades or cracks off. However, several very thin coats of wax applied to warm (not hot) leather and allowed to cure thoroughly between applications will form a tough, flexible, weatherproof shield. There's no need to heat wax before applying it; adequate heat is generated by applying with your fingers.

Silicone Treatments

Silicone treatments—especially spray types for fabric and leather boots—are popular for their super-hydrophobic, lubricating qualities. Breathable silicones also repel stains and soils, but don't offer much durability. As with adhesives, silicone leather treatments don't form a chemical bond with leather fibers, and tend to dissipate quickly. There is also the argument that a silicone treatment may penetrate existing adhesive bonds and inhibit future adhesives. The best use for silicone or polymer spray treatments is on suede or nubuck leather uppers.

Dave Page warns that waterproofing can actually speed up deterioration of your boot's construction; treatments can migrate into the seam between upper and sole, penetrating and damaging adhesive bonds.

Water-based Polymer Coatings

These coatings carry a certain proprietary mystique—no manufacturer will tell you *exactly* what's in his brand—but they function somewhat like durable water-repellent (DWR) textile treatments by bonding to individual leather fibers without softening or altering integrity. Water-based polymer coatings are excellent for field use

The waterproofing Caveat: Treatments may penetrate adhesive bond between upper & sole.

Boot Treatment Tips

The type of leather conditioner you choose is less important than how you apply it. Simply slathering on boot goop won't protect your boots. A great amount of damage occurs when wax is applied over dirt, which gets worked into pores and weakens the leather. **Thorough leather treatment begins with a clean boot.** A stiff brushing under the faucet will remove old wax and dirt. Jeff Grissom, a cobbler at Page's shop who apprenticed with Morin Custom Boots in Colorado, contends that Woolite is the best boot cleaner available. "Wash both inside and out before conditioning," he says.

- Break in new boots slightly before treatment (*see* Breaking in, below)
- Boots should be very dry before conditioning (unless you're applying a water-based treatment).
- If you plan to seamseal boots, do so *before* waterproofing the leather and allow the sealer to fully cure before treatment.

- Remove boot laces and meticulously work in the dressing with your fingers, paying special attention to overlapping seams and folds around tongue gussets, where most water penetrates.
- Allow dressing to fully cure, preferably overnight, before wiping off excess with a lint-free cloth (chamois or PakTowl). At this point you may wish to apply a second, thin coat of goop, depending on the condition of your boots.
- Set freshly treated boots in a sunny window or apply moderate heat (from a woodstove or hair dryer) to warm and soften the conditioner. Then polish or buff the boots to seal the dressing—that is, to create a hard, smooth finish.
- If the boots feel sticky even after 24 hours, the dressing has not cured and will pick up dirt rather than protect the boot against it. Rewarm and buff the boots until any excess conditioner is removed.

(as on a long trek) because they can be applied to a wet boot; as the water evaporates, polymer residue clings to leather fibers, forming a thin, breathable, waterproof coating.

Fabric-and-Leather Considerations

Fabric-and-leather boots require just as much treatment as leather boots do if you want them to last very long. Follow guidelines for leather boot care, with an occasional application of a spray water-repellent treatment (*see* **Fabrics & Insulations**, *page 26*). Apply the treatment to clean, dry fabric *before* waterproofing the leather.

Boot Linings

Your feet crank out pint-loads of moisture during a hike or ski tour, which transfers from socks to boot linings and may result in mildew and a less-than-subtle fragrance. Since the bulk of foot perspiration is through the bottoms of your feet, the most expedient drying method involves removing innersoles or innerboots after wearing and allowing the linings to air. On a trip, take a minute before turning in to *wring* the moisture out of your innersoles—you'll be amazed at the volume! Hang-dry the liners in your tent, and both boot and footbed will feel drier in the morning.

VBLs

Vapor barrier liners—VBLs—will do a lot to preserve the integrity of your leather boots and make them considerably more comfortable during a long trip. Vapor barrier socks are like coated nylon foot jackets: Worn over your socks, they keep moisture from penetrating outward into boot linings. Feet have their own nifty little thermostats to regulate perspiration, so you won't overheat.

This "closed system" created by the VBL actually reduces body heat loss. Your socks get wet, but you can easily dry them overnight or change them and eliminate the discomfort and danger of donning frozen, saturated boots on a winter climb or ski tour. Heavy-duty plastic bags (like bread bags) work fine but aren't as durable as those sewn from coated nylon. VBLs are commercially available and easy to sew at home.

Drying Boots

Leather is skin, after all. **The same amount of heat that would burn your skin will just as quickly damage leather.** Keep boots away from intense heat unless you prefer warped, shrunken, and hardened leather uppers and midsoles. Heat also will damage glues that bond sole layers together, causing delamination. So don't cook your boots around the campfire! On a dry day in camp, remove laces and liners, then rack boots on branch stubs. Alternatively, dry them on a warm boulder in the sun. In winter, sleep with your boots inside your tent, or even in your sleeping bag, to prevent them from freezing overnight.

If you're not worried about freezing and can't imagine sharing a small chamber with your odorous dogs, set them upside down on a pack or stuffsack to keep the dew out.

At home, or during a motel break from the trail, remove insoles, stuff wet footwear with newspaper, and change the paper every few hours. Those skimpy little motel towels work wonderfully as boot dryers. Stuffing boots with newspaper during off-season storage is also a good way to prevent mildew from invading (or to deter creatures from filling your ski boots with acorns).

Chapter 7

Custom Fitting

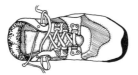

If the shoe fits . . .

−Anonymous

Little-celebrated miracle of moving parts, the foot endures perpetual abuse. Since each foot bears its own unique history, it is no small success to find a durable boot that fits both your needs *and* your crooked left metatarsals. A little time spent cus-tomizing each new boot to its intended foot will truly enhance comfort and performance.

Breaking In
You can best coax leather boots into the shape of

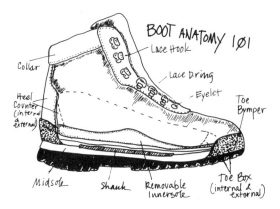

BOOT ANATOMY 101

Lace Hook
Collar
Lace D'ring
Eyelet
Heel Counter (internal & external)
Toe Bumper
Midsole
Shank
Removable Innersole
Toe Box (internal & external)

your foot when they're wet. Don't fill them with water—you'll invite mildew—but do take them for several rainy day strolls or meanders through morning dew. You should wear them around before attempting to weatherproof the leather for two reasons. One is to partially break in both uppers and midsole before softening the leather. The other is to clean off any lingering tanning resins, which prevent sealants from bonding to leather fibers. A stiff brush under a running tap will also help to remove tanning resins.

Boot-Fitting

Insoles

Perhaps the simplest way to adjust the fit of your boots is with insoles—trimmed to fit your needs exactly. Anatomically shaped liners add arch support and shock absorption, not to mention warmth. They're also available in varying thicknesses to adjust fit tighter or looser; thinner insoles give feet more room, while thicker ones snug-up a loose boot. You can craft your own insoles from a thin sheet of minicell foam by copying a pair of running shoe liners. Wool (felt) liners take up a lot of space initially, but pack down in time. They are breathable, absorbent, and very warm. (A spare pair of felt liners on a long paddling trip is my secret weapon—thanks to this trick, I am able to smile pleasantly even before my morning ban cha.)

If your boots feel *okaaay*, but still squeeze your foot here and there, trimming innersoles can yield surprising comfort. Cut away gradually where you require more room, and make sure to bevel the edge so you don't feel a ridge underfoot.

For boots that feel loose around the heel, try a pair of sorbothane heel plugs from the boot shop—or a matchbook—wedged under the innersole; snugging up this area helps prevent chafed heels (which, incidentally, are easily de-frictionized with a patch of duct tape).

More Sole Than You Can Control

External examination of a worn outersole reveals a lot about your gait. A little wear to the inside or outside of the heel is normal; extremely irregular wear will shorten sole life and may be corrected with orthopedic inserts, available through a podiatrist. Correctly fitted inserts can also improve stride efficiency.

Hotspots

Don't ignore hotspots! They usually don't go away, so stop where you are, take your boot off and attend to the offending harbinger of painful blisters. Cobblers have a secret tool called a "rubbing bar" that burnishes away irritating contact points. You can use the butt of your Swiss Army knife to solve this fit problem: Apply pressure and rub the spot smooth. You'll be surprised how well this works.

Lacing Tips and Tricks

- Nylon laces last forever, or at least until they become tent guys, sunglass retainers, or a cat's cradle game.
- Flat, braided nylon laces don't work well in lace locks (those flat, double-riveted hooks usually placed over instep), but are easy on the fingers. Some claim these stay tied better than round laces, but I disagree.
- Cotton or rawhide laces weaken when wet; once sodden, they're next to impossible to untie.
- For winter campers: Spritz a little silicone treatment on laces to prevent them from icing up.
- If you trim and heat-seal lace ends, make sure the lace will still run through your boot eyelets—you may need them for prussiks.
- Watch out for el cheapo hardware with sharp edges that will fray laces. Chintzy plastic eyelets on some fabric/leather lightweights are prime offenders, but so may be the metal lace eyes on a $300 pair of telemark boots! Use a small round file to eliminate sharp edges.
- Occasionally shift laces to and fro so they don't prematurely wear in one spot and break.

  Mountaineer's Lace.   Prevent laces from loosening with the **mountaineer's lace**. Simply change the direction as you wrap laces around hooks, so you're threading from the top down. The lace wraps over itself, providing extra friction so it's less likely to shift under pressure on the trail.

  Double-Hitching.   Maintain precise lace tension with a **double**

Mountaineer's Lace:
over and around
the hook
to maintain
lace tension.

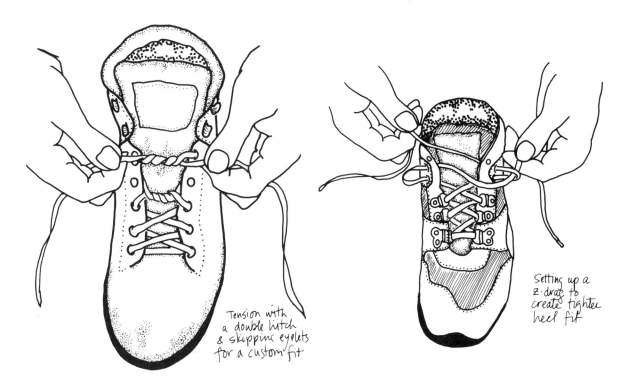

Tension with a double hitch & skipping eyelets for a custom fit

Setting up a Z-drag to create tighter heel fit

hitch. Wrap the laces around each other a few times and cinch, creating a stopper. This trick lets you create both a roomy toebox and a snug ankle, for instance. Use a double hitch before making a bow and the laces will stay tight even if the bow becomes untied.

Skipping Eyelets.   Have a niggling high instep? It's definitely legal to **skip eyelets**. Tension-off lower laces with a double hitch. Skip eyelets over the problem area, then crank another double hitch and finish lacing.

Z-Drag.   Direct and maintain tension with a mini **Z-drag**, which lets you pull your heel tighter into the boot's heel pocket.

Chapter 8

Boot Repair

The climbing shoes were made as follows: First we unravelled some sisal bags, obtained from the kitchen for a few packets of cigarettes. The threads were twisted together into a rope which was soaked in water, beaten and straightened between two poles of our barbed-wire fences. Finally they were sewn together in the shape of a sole. The uppers were cut out of a square yard of old tarpaulin.

—Felice Benuzzi, *No Picnic on Mount Kenya*

Typical Repairs

Torn Leather

Leather tears are traced directly to two likely causes: lack of maintenance and puppies. If you fail to weatherproof your boots, they'll either be too dried-out and brittle or too sodden and pliant to withstand abuse. A small tear is correctable with urethane adhesive, provided you've carefully prepped the area and cleaned any lubricants off the leather surface. Puppies are another story, and will

Regluing a Sole

gluing toe & heel bumpers or sole, then clamping & taping

- Regluing any major boot part is a surgical procedure—cleaning and prepping are key. Wash boot with soap and water. Once dry, lightly sand the gluing surfaces. Wipe down the clean, dry boot thoroughly with denatured alcohol before gluing. (*See Appendix A: Adhesives, page 225.*)
- Stuff the boot with paper to provide structure.
- Use contact cement (Barge brand is the most popular footwear adhesive). Spread a thin layer of adhesive on each prepared surface and let rest until almost dry.
- Align and mate parts carefully—you only get *one* chance with contact cement.
- Clamp the parts together with a C-clamp or wrap with strong tape, and let dry. Secure clamping is important to the success and life of your repair.
- Finally, seal the joint with seam sealer.

likely pick your new telemark boots for teething. If this happens, a consultation with a cobbler is in order.

Small Holes

Patching quarter-sized holes with urethane adhesive in a fabric boot is no problem. Just keep the boot level as it dries. (*See **Essential Techniques: Fabric Patching**, page 8.*)

Sole Reclamation

If your boots have a stitched (Norwegian) welt, rejoining upper to sole is better left to a cobbler. Most light- and midweight hiking boots sport a bonded sole with rubber toe bumper or rand to shield the joint, and these are easily repairable. Sole replacement, however, is the cobbler's bread and butter.

Blown Seams

In the field, a few turns of duct tape or a twist of baling wire will hold your blown-out boots together temporarily. If you have a little time, you might be able to restitch an opened seam with the awl in your sewing kit (the sailmaker's palm is ideal for this). Seamsealing will help lengthen the life expectancy of fraying stitches.

Ski Touring and Telemark Boots

Backcountry skiing involves a good deal more walking—a.k.a. slogging—than most "pinheads" would ever care to admit, and it's bloody hard work. Snow is wet and feet sweat, so regular boot maintenance is crucial. You can delay waterlogging somewhat by wearing gaiters and VBLs, but don't neglect leather treatment and seamsealing, particularly along the welt and around the toe area, where constant contact with bindings really abrades the boot construction. If your toebox area is chewed up and torn from unenlightened care, send the boots to a mountain boot specialist for rebuilding.

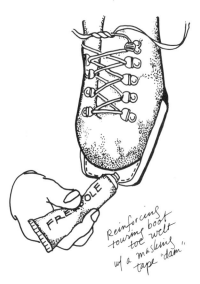

Reinforcing boot touring toe welt w/ a masking tape "dam"

Reinforcing Toe Welt

Protect the vulnerable toe welt of your touring boot with a coating of—you guessed it—Seamgrip or Freesole urethane adhesive. Clean and prep the upper and welt, then make a masking tape dam around the toebox edge. Apply the adhesive and set in a level position for the full cure time. Don't use for at least 48 hours.

Pinholes

Aside from water damage, the most common ski boot disorder is a cracked or broken sole under the toe, usually centered around the binding pinholes. This can be prevented with regular inspection, but if it happens in the field, three-pin bails alone will not hold your boot. In the field, jury-rig a cable binding with nylon cord, bungee, or wire. Once home, commit your boots to the clinic for a resole operation—when it's time for resoling, you can specify your desired midsole stiffness for a truly custom boot.

Good news for the spatially challenged: If the toe of your sole is riddled with divots from misstepping, you needn't race off to have a metal pinplate mounted. Those extra holes are cosmetic damage to the outsole—the "real" holes have metal eyes imbedded in the rubber to catch pins. Warns cobbler Komito, "Repair pinplates are put on with screws drilled through both sole and midsole, creating a weak spot that's bound to fracture. The cure is worse than the disease." You can avoid this problem entirely with a pair of cable bindings, or simply by being more mindful when stepping in.

Harvey Page has earned a mountainous reputation for leather "fitting" and rebuilding. Here he remounts tele boot buckles at brother Dave's cobbler shop.

Supergaiters

If gaiters extend the life of your ski boots, then supergaiters can render them nearly immortal. Well, not really, but the protective properties of supergaiters are worthwhile insurance for pricey tele boots. These insulated boot parkas have tight-fitting rubber rands that surround boots at the sole, so virtually no snow (i.e., water) can penetrate uppers. The only problem is keeping rands from slipping off the smooth, contoured leather. Solve this by applying a skim coat of ski binder wax to the leather or by spreading a thin layer of Freesole around the sides of the boot's toebox, providing a stickier contact for the rands.

WARNING: My friend John Harlin tossed his tele boots into a closet with tight-fitting supergaiters still attached. When he retrieved them the next winter, his boot soles were warped like bananas. Though we believed them to be wrecked, Dave Page the cobbler says they might be cured with a resole job that includes a new midsole.

Plastic Mountain Boots

Paul Cleveland, a peripatetic tramper, ski tourer, trail-maintenance guru, and wilderness EMT who literally *uses his gear up*, tried as hard as he could to think of an unusual repair situation. Paul finally recalled the hinge on his plastic double boot cuff that popped. While this minor failure didn't require field triage, a 33-cent stainless rivet from the hardware store proved a viable replacement.

Other than regular air-drying of the inner boots and obvious hardware failures like busted buckle systems or popped lace eyelets, there's little to attend to with plastic boots. Plastic doubles can be successfully resoled and re-randed by any mountain boot specialist. Also, if you've heard about custom-fitting or stretching the plastic shells by applying heat, don't. This should be handled by a mountain cobbler or ski shop, by a skilled, competent boot technician who knows the subtleties of heating and stretching plastics.

Rock Shoes

The Cinderella Syndrome

The more ambitious the route, the tighter the rock slipper, right? We've been forced to trade away more than one pair of shoes when this principle proved podiatrically unsound. The fact that rock shoes stretch constantly complicates this sizing dilemma.

One way to speed up the stretch process is to soften the uppers. Rather than soaking the leather in water, try wiping it down thoroughly with denatured alcohol just before initial wearing. The dampened uppers form right to your feet as the alcohol evaporates. An oil treatment will do a more radical job of softening, but may overstretch a leather upper.

We've heard of convincing slippers to fit by hammering the sole or driving cars over the last, but this will damage a board-lasted boot beyond repair by fracturing the midsole, heel, and toe counters. Consider this method a last resort.

Delamination

The sole of a climbing shoe is bonded to rand and last with heat-sensitive adhesive, and is designed to be easily removed for resoling. This means that any excessive heat source—like a campfire or (most likely) the trunk of your car on a hot summer day—will activate the glue and delaminate soles, rands, and other key parts. If you continue to climb on delaminated soles, you're likely to damage the rand, too. You can try to reglue and clamp the delam, but the bond is likely to be sketchy—you're better off with completely new half soles.

Holy Soles

When to resole? Most penny-pinching climbers wait too long before considering a resole job. New soles or half soles will adhere much better if you haven't completely worn through the original rubber in any one place, including edges at the toe. A good goal is to **try to preserve the rand at all costs**, since this part of your boot largely determines your edge control.

Climbers generally find half soles to be the most viable resole operation, since most wear occurs near the toes and ball of the foot, rarely at the heel (unless you're an off-width masochist). Slippers and slip-lasted shoes can handle just one or two resoles before losing their integrity, but other, more substantial boots may be successfully resoled several times. Home-resoling is both straightforward and economical. Your rock shoes set you back at least $100, so a $20 repair kit makes sense.

However, it may be well worth your while to spring for a professional resole, which runs about $40. The cobblers recommended in *Appendix F: Directory of Repair Services* (page 242) use machinery designed to recreate the original fit of your shoes, and their expert gluing and grinding methods minimize the risk of delamination (a likely result on a home job, especially your first one).

The Home Resole

Order a kit (*see Appendix G, page 246*), which contains directions, glue, enough rubber to make two pairs of half soles or one set of full soles, plus instructions and a tube of adhesive designed for bonding footwear. Sheet kits give you more options than pre-cut kits. **Resoling is really a two-person operation**, since there are moments when you need at least three hands.

If the rubber left on your old shoe is super-thin, you may consider applying a new sole directly to the old one. This popular solution adds stiffness and durability to slippers. Use the thin rubber kit for this, and sand or grind the original sole as thin as possible.

Cutting

Cutting the thick rubber is awkward at best; use a utility knife with a fresh blade or a very sharp, thin knife. The easiest way to slice the rubber is to have a friend spread the rubber apart as you cut.

Grinding

Resoling calls for a fair amount of grinding, which can be accomplished in a number of ways. The easiest way is with a belt grinder or sander. Lacking that, you can use a coarse, 3-inch grind wheel (about $3 at your local hardware store) on a power drill. If you're in the manual mode, spring for a Surform tool, which will work fine to both prep and shape the rubber.

A Surform tool works to prepare gluing surfaces and custom-shape new rubber soles.

Remove old sole over hot burner

Remove the old sole.

- Remove the old sole, or front half, as shown. Heat the rubber over a red-hot electric stove coil until it's hot to the touch (about 3 to 5 minutes). Do not let the rubber get so hot that it smokes.
- Use Vise-Grips or needlenose pliers to peel away the sole. If the rubber doesn't peel easily, continue to apply heat to the opened area and separate layers with a knife.
- Be careful not to tear away any of the rand or midsole, or you'll have to repair those gouges (by filling with Freesole or Aquaseal) before applying new rubber sole.

If you're adding half soles only:

- Don't heat the whole boot—just the part you want to replace.

- Slice off the peeled section; bevel edge of original rubber at the instep to create a larger gluing surface.

Cutting new soles
- Use the old sole as a pattern.
- Trace around the sole, allowing plenty of room between each boot pattern.
- Cut the patterns apart into separate, rough-shaped soles, leaving plenty of room (¼ to ½ inch) for the final trim.

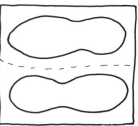

Cut patterns apart

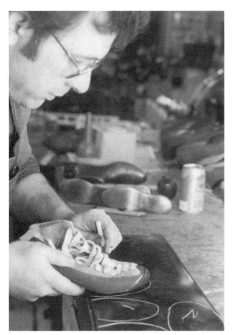

John Buckner traces around a rock shoe to pattern the new sole.

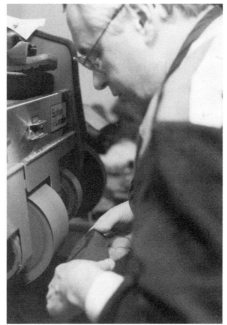

The professional edge: Dave Page grinds a new half sole to like-new performance.

Gluing
(*See* **Appendix A: Adhesives,** *page 225.*)
- If you've accidentally ripped out any sections of the midsole, fill with urethane adhesive and allow to cure completely before gluing sole.
- Make sure the rand edge is as square as possible. You may wish to build up the edge with urethane (making a masking-tape "form"), then trimming or sanding square once cured. This square edge is important for adhesion and later performance.
- Prep the surfaces to be glued by sanding, then brushing away any dusty residue.
- Clean the gluing surfaces with denatured alcohol. Do not touch

the cleaned surfaces with your fingers.
- Apply a very thin coat of contact cement (Barge brand is most recommended) to both surfaces. Wear a rubber glove to spread the cement into a thin, smooth layer.
- Allow cement to dry completely—at least 2 hours—before joining surfaces.

Sole Mates
- Stuff the boots with newspaper to add structure to the form.
- Heat both glued surfaces over a red-hot electric coil for no more than 30 seconds, making sure the rubber surfaces (or your hands) do not begin to smoke.
- Carefully align surfaces, starting at the beveled edge, then roll the sole toe-ward, firmly squeezing along the contour of the boot.
- Hammer along the edge of the bond to further convince mating.
- Allow glue to cure completely, preferably 48 hours.
- For a bomber resole on slippers (not board-lasted boots), *Climbing* magazine (No. 101) offers this slick trick: Carefully position the front wheel of your car onto the **front section only** of the shoe, and park the car overnight. Retrieve the flattened shoe and knead it to restore shape.

The Final Trim
- Trim away excess rubber with a utility knife.
- Use a vise or get a friend to help you separate the rubber for smooth slicing.
- Be conservative, since you can fine-tune the trim with a grinder.
- Grind the edge to your favorite angle.
- For small sections of delamination along the edges, sticky-rubber supplier, Five Ten Company recommends filling with Freesole or Aquaseal.

Ensure a solid bond by hammering new rubber sole, with a wooden mallet before trimming.

Rubber Boots

L. L. Bean built an institution on customer service, including a fine boot repair facility to which my grandfather sent his Bean boots for rebottoming every umpteenth year. My brother still wears those boots—the original tops must be 60 years old! Granted, both men qualify as fanatics when it comes to taking care of their stuff, always treating the leather uppers to generous waterproofing each spring.

Before treating the leather on your Beans or Sorels, apply a little urethane sealer around the stitching that joins leather upper to rubber bottom to help keep water out and protect the individual stitches.

Rubber waders or Wellies begin to suffer tiny cracks as the color starts to fade. Keep the material supple longer with regular applications of 303 Protectant. (Don't get any on the bottom or you'll wipe out.) Typically, the rubber will crack where the boot flexes as you walk. If leakage is a problem, consider gooping on a little Aquaseal. Take time to let liners dry out after wearing—remove any insoles and set in a cool place to allow canvas to dry without mildewing.

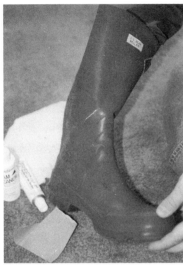

Rubber boots may fatigue and crack where boots flex.

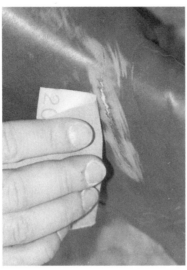

Prepare area by sanding, then cleaning with denatured alcohol.

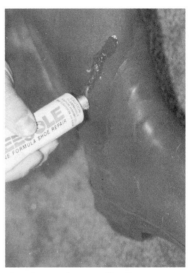

Apply urethane adhesive to caulk the leak.

Part III

Hardware

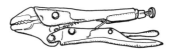

*Preparing for the worst is the only way
of giving the best a chance to happen.*

—Laurens Van Der Post, *A Far-Off Place*

The Rewards of an Inventive Nature

A visit with Win Ellis always leaves me with an original perspective on some everyday object or method. Ask Win, the quintessential inventor, about most any topic, and he'll respond slowly, "Well-l-l . . . I really don't know much about that, but I imagine . . . " and then continue with logical rhythm to explore the territory in question.

Win makes a living fabricating unique, techy yacht fittings and manufacturing and marketing a few of his own gadgets (like the Windspeed kayak spinnaker rig and rechargeable headlamp battery packs). He seems perplexed by the fact that most people seem content to leave the thinking to somebody else. "Those weekend warriors who buy all their gear at an outdoor store are letting someone else have all the fun designing and problem-solving."

Win continues to wax poetic with tales of his own resourcefulness: "Years ago in India, I had some time on my hands, but no money, and decided to make a backpack frame from bamboo and a little parachute cord. I braided the cord for straps, then padded them out with strips from an old Army blanket. That lashed frame was totally flexible and rugged—you could've strapped a car to the thing.

"Another time, walking through Nova Scotia in terrible weather, I made a fine lean-to shelter shingled with fish bags I'd found washed up on the beach. Any beach has all matter of goods for repairs or innovations: bleach bottles, floats, nets, potwarp, flip-flops . . . Say, an old flip-flop is the ideal fan to coax a smoldering fire into action."

Win speaks warmly of everybody's favorite repair essentials, including duct tape and dental floss: "Our first night out on Baffin Island, our tent vestibule blew off in the horrendous wind. We secured it with dental floss the next day, and it held up excellently."

Win's ingenuity with found objects serves to acquaint you with the skills required in this section. If something breaks on a trip, keep your eyes open and your brain in gear, and you'll be able to solve the problem at hand.

Chapter 9

Stoves & Cookware

Yet, instead of going out at once with the begging-bowl,
he stayed his stomach on slabs of cold rice
till the full dawn.

—Rudyard Kipling, *Kim*

The Crankiest Item in Your Pack

A camp stove is probably the most intricate, fiddly piece of equipment you're ever going to haul around in the wilderness. Yet, if you're like most rugged individualists, you've probably never even glanced at the operating instructions. It wasn't until starting this book that I finally perused the manual for any of our four camp stoves. Geez! If I'd only read the directions first, that little MSR episode in the Banff motel bathroom never would've happened . . .

"Reading the instructions is the single most important step for smooth operation of any stove," says Mike Ridout, MSR's tech lord and repair specialist. "If people read their instructions, I'd probably be out of a job." Ridout also emphasizes that there's no quicker way to ruin your stove than to loan it to a friend.

This section is less about repairing a specific model stove than about how to care for camp stoves in general and what sort of performance you might expect from the different types. With more than 50 packable stoves available, to dissect each unit here would be more painful than simply reading your particular stove's instructions.

Stove Types

Alcohol

Alcohol burners sport the fewest parts of any liquid-fuel stove and are therefore among the most reliable; as long as you have fuel, you're able to generate BTUs. Silent but slow, an alcohol stove requires more fuel to produce the same amount of heat as does a white-gas burner, so your tea break takes a little longer. A windscreen and well-fitted cook set are vital. Denatured alcohol is renewable, burns without pressurization, and offers low volatility, making it a favored cooking fuel for boat cabins and tiny tents.

Bottled Gas

Probably the most convenient and least-troublesome cooking option for average, above-freezing conditions, butane, isobutane, and butane/propane stoves are a little like giant Bic lighters, and unfortunately just as disposable. Fuel canisters are not yet refillable, and if the stove malfunctions you fix it by purchasing a new one (bring a spare unit on a long trip). Still, these stoves simmer like crazy and, because of their simplicity, are popular with high-altitude climbers. Bottled-gas stoves generally work great down to +40°F; below that, they become increasingly inefficient.

White Gas

Additive-free white gas (Coleman or MSR fuel) is the cleanest-burning and most popular fuel for all-season use in North America. These stoves work by pressurizing liquid fuel in a small tank by pumping or heating. The fuel is forced through a vaporizing jet to a flame spreader or burner to produce fast, hot, economical BTUs. This type of stove has a lot of crucially integrated parts—most field disasters and repairs relate to white gas or multifuel stoves.

Multifuel

These stoves are essentially variations on the white gas theme, with jets designed for burning other fuels, such as auto gasoline or kerosene. While care and maintenance are generally the same, you must clean the burner jets each time you light a multifuel stove, because the less-refined liquids used in these stoves tend to clog parts. Be sure to filter the fuel, too, and don't store any of these fuels in the stove. Solvents and detergents in automotive gas are especially likely to solidify and gunk up your rig.

Pressurized Liquid-Fuel Stoves, Simplified

Despite myriad spinoffs and innovations, liquid-fuel stoves still function along the same lines as the first-generation MSR X-GK or Svea 123 (many of which continue to fire, thanks to diligent, maintenance-oriented owners). Liquid-fuel stoves all share the same general parts.

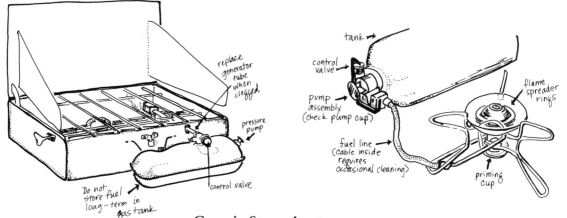

Generic Stove Anatomy

1. **The fuel tank** is pressurized in one of two ways: by compressing air in the tank with a hand pump, or by "self-pressurizing" when heated (fuel vapors expand inside a warmed tank). Tanks can be damaged by corrosion, storing fuel inside, and by a faulty seal (usually caused by stripped threads at the filler cap, pump attachment, or other orifice).

2. **A control valve** allows pressurized fuel to travel through a fuel line to the jet and burner. The control valve may be damaged by heavy-handed treatment (i.e., overtightening the knob), or by a cracked, worn O-ring seal.

3. In the **jet vaporizer or generator assembly**, pressurized fuel

passes through a smaller-than-pin-sized hole into the flame spreader. The brass jet is the greatest troublemaker of all stove parts, bar none. Lighting and extinguishing the stove cause carbon buildup that clogs the jet (as does dirt, oatmeal, and boiled-over Ramen noodles). A dirty jet means poor fuel flow and poor results. Many stoves now offer a self-cleaning jet—really just a built-in stainless steel needle that pierces the jet—activated by fully opening the control valve or by tipping the burner upside down. Older styles require hand-pricking.

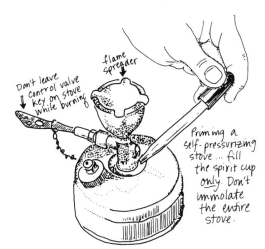

flame spreader

Don't leave control valve key on stove while burning

Priming a self-pressurizing stove ... fill the spirit cup only. Don't immolate the entire stove.

4. The **burner cup and flame spreader** disperses fuel so it burns cleanly and evenly. Although this is the least-troublesome part of your stove, the flame spreader may expand and distort over time; check that spreader position is recessed from the burner cup (it should be).

Priming Is Everything

No matter what brand of liquid-fuel stove you use, priming and preheating the unit are the keys to both short- and long-term performance.

With self-pressurizing stoves, dribble an eyedropper of fuel into the spirit cup ONLY—don't douse the tank, as many crag-crazed dudes are wont to do. Some people prefer the control and cleanliness of priming paste for this job. As the paste or priming fuel burns, the flame preheats the fuel jet and pressurizes the tank. The priming flame also preheats the fuel vaporizer tube so when you open the control valve you get a fine mist that burns blue rather than a smoky blast of yellow flame.

A stove with a remote, air-pressurized tank first requires pumping to compress the air in the tank, then priming and preheating the generator tube assembly, fuel vaporizer, and jets.

Allow the primer flame to burn down to candle-flame-size, then open the fuel control valve to start the stove. If the flame goes out, open the valve about one-quarter turn and re-light the stove. Now you're in the preheat phase. Allow the stove to burn at its lowest level (with a blue flame) for one or two minutes before increasing the flame for full-blast cooking.

General Stove Maintenance

Whether you use your stove frequently or occasionally, it's essential that you follow recommended maintenance procedures, particularly if your stove has a remote, pump-pressurized tank. Field "repairs"

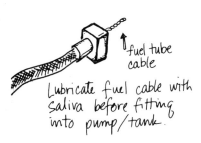

Lubricate fuel cable with saliva before fitting into pump/tank.

fuel tube cable

are more often just field "cleanings" that are much easier done at home on a sunny deck than in a howling wind with fumbling, cold fingers and a growling belly.

Stove maintenance tools and replacement parts are tiny, virtually weightless, and essential to sound operation. Carry your little bag of stove parts right in the sack with your stove, because chances are you'll need them. Tape the jet-pricker to your fuel bottle so it's always handy.

Maintenance Tips

- When assembling your stove, always lubricate the connecting parts with a little saliva or lip salve so you don't tear any tender O-rings.
- Gently, gently! Do not use excessive force to seal connections. You'll have a hard time separating the parts; you may even weaken them.
- O-rings act like the head gasket on your car. Replace them as often as once a year, since UV and penetrating solvents in fuels will deteriorate rubber compounds, increasing fire hazard during stove operation.
- Oil pressure-pump plungers as often as possible. Dry, mangled leather pump cups produce no air pressure and slide with no resistance when you stroke the pump. You can use any light-grade machine or cooking oil; in a pinch, use lip salve, rubbing it in until the leather becomes soft and pliable. In the field, you can fashion a new pump cup with a swatch from the top of a leather boot tongue. Soak in oil before using.
- Inspect vaporizing jets regularly. The jet-pricker or cleaning needle in your stove's repair kit is made of stainless steel, while the jet itself is soft brass. The harder metal of the needle can enlarge the jet hole and cause flareups and irregular fuel flow. You may need to replace the jet at any time—carry a spare in your repair kit. Sometimes carbon buildup is significant enough that your jet-pricker simply shoves a chunk of carbon back into the body of the jet, rather than breaking it up. Remove the jet and hold up to a light to inspect; clean from the inside or replace.
- Use a Scotchbrite pad to scour the flame reflector, fuel cable, or any other rusty or carbon-coated parts. Sometimes a generator tube will become sticky with fuel deposits. Clean these by soaking in white gas, then scrubbing with the abrasive pad.
- Compressed air (the canned kind, used for blowing dust out of a computer keyboard) is also effective for removing grit from inside a fuel tube or other hard-to-reach parts.

assure consistent fuel pressure; lube the plunger cup on pump assembly regularly. Never allow cup to dry out.

If you've cleaned the jet & still get sputtering flame... try heating the generator tube, then plunging into cold water... this breaks up carbon deposits

Troubleshooting: Likely Stove Problems

Insufficient priming. Burn performance is directly related to priming and preheating. An erratic or yellow flame is a telltale sign that your stove is too cold and cranky.

Fuel system leak. Air or fuel is escaping somewhere between the tank and jet.

For fuel leaks:
- Check all fuel tank orifices, including threads that may be stripped.
- Inspect connector seals and O-rings for damage, dryness, or decay.
- Examine pump valve and seal for damage.
- Look to see if the jet hole is enlarged.

For air leaks:
- Make sure pump is completely threaded into fuel bottle.
- Check the pump assembly for cracks, dry pump cup, fatigued seals, or damaged O-rings. Perform pump test (see page 106).

Jet malfunction. A jet may be clogged by carbon or other debris. An enlarged jet (from aggressive cleaning) can allow too much fuel to pass, resulting in flareups. You may be using an incorrect jet, designed for another type of fuel. A gasping jet may be telling you the tank is empty—check the fuel level or pump more air pressure.

Contaminated fuel. Fuel additives, condensation, and just plain sand in the tank will clog the fuel path and obstruct jets, resulting in an unreliable flame at best. Peer carefully into the empty fuel tank; if you see water droplets or sand particles, swish a little clean fuel around inside and discard (into your auto tank, not on the ground). Allow stove tank to dry completely with the cap off before storing.

Defensive Operating Tips

Protect your stove from impact and set up your camp kitchen away from the traffic zone. The first day into a two-week river trip is no time to stomp on the burner.

No Substitutions! Do not substitute another manufacturer's tank; use only parts designed specifically for use with your stove model.

Don't overfill the tank. Always fill to manufacturer-suggested levels; overfilling can result in pressurization problems and dangerous flareups during priming. A too-small air space means pressure fluctuates excessively over a short period, resulting in an

Cavity Cleaner

Chris Townsend, Scottish author and inveterate backpacker who once hiked the Continental Divide from Canada to Mexico, offers this account:

"During a December crossing of the Cairngorm mountains in Scotland, my soup boiled over and blocked the jet of my camp stove. After I discovered I'd forgotten to bring a jet pricker, I tried various alternatives but they were all too thick. Blowing down the fuel line didn't work. Not far away was a small bothy (a simple mountain shelter) into which I'd seen two walkers enter. I made my way there to ask if they had a jet pricker. They didn't, but suggested trying a toothbrush bristle. I did, it worked, and it saved my trip."

erratic, surging flame and requiring constant adjustment of the control valve.

Check for leaks with every refuel. With all valves shut off, turn both tank and burner upside down and watch for spreading gas at connecting points or dribbles from any orifice. If you spot a leak, do not use the stove. Repair or munch cold oats.

Prime time is precious. Be mindful as you prime and preheat your stove. This is when most flareups and accidents occur, and is crucial to the smooth operation of your burner. Follow instructions exactly.

Filter your fuel with a small felt-lined funnel (available where you purchase your Coleman or MSR fuel). This screens out water and debris that will bedevil you sooner or later.

Strive for a blue burn. If you can't achieve a blue flame after a minute of operation, shut down the control valve on your stove and re-prime it. Inefficient yellow or orange flames produce jet-clogging soot.

Pump Test

- Empty fuel bottle. Screw pump onto empty bottle. Open control valve and pump the plunger to empty any remaining fuel.
- Close control valve and pump plunger about 50 times to develop air pressure. You should feel resistance—if not, oil or replace the pump cup, then resume test.
- Remove plunger assembly at bushing.
- Submerge into tub of water and watch for a steady stream of bubbles to spot the leak. Minor initial bubbling at orifices is normal, but a steady stream indicates a poor seal.

Fuel Conservation

Try a Windscreen

Windscreens can help conserve up to 50 percent of your fuel. Use a wrap-around windscreen (available wherever you purchase a camp stove, or make one at home with heavy-gauge aluminum foil or flashing). Make sure the windscreen allows some ventilation, or your flame may sputter and die. Sometimes windscreens work too well, reflecting heat down to overheat tanks and fuel lines. Always monitor the temperature of your fuel tank—if it's hot to the touch, open the windscreen or turn off the stove for a few minutes and reorient your windscreen.

Blacken Your Pots

You might be employing fuel-saving cookware without realizing it. Simply using a lid decreases radiant heat loss, while a blackened pot accelerates heat absorption (*see* **Get the Most From Your Cookware,** *page 109*). Another fuel economizer is MSR's Heat Exchanger, a corrugated aluminum band that fits around your cookpot to channel hot air around the sides.

Simmering Hints

Simmering is notoriously difficult for a liquid-fuel stove with a control valve located tankside rather than at the burner. The steady, low flame required to simmer tends to flutter and sputter, clogging parts and generally frustrating the chef.

One method for simmering is to start with low fuel pressure (fewer strokes of the pump), or begin with a half-full fuel bottle. This means you'll compress a larger air space; as the fuel is depleted, the extra compressed air prevents the internal pressure from fluctuating (and the flame from sputtering), so you'll face less control-valve adjusting.

Use a skillet to insulate your cookpot

To extract a passable simmer from its blowtorch-like stoves, MSR recommends operating the burner at a high rate for about five minutes, then slowly adjusting the control valve to simmer.

We've found the easiest way to slow-cook a cheese fondue is to insulate the cooking pan with a metal spacer or a *plaque radiant* designed to diffuse heat, or by partially filling a larger pan or skillet with water to act as a chafing pan/double boiler.

Cold-Weather and High-Altitude Operation

At high altitude or in wickedly cold conditions, the temptation is strong to cook in your tent—something every stove manufacturer explicitly warns against. Peter Hickner of Feathered Friends tells about a nameless climber whose stove melted through his bag, sleeping pad, tent floor, and a good bit of glacier before wheezing to a permanent halt.

If conditions force you to cook inside a small space, do so in a fire pit dug just inside your tent vestibule, so you can kick the thing out the door before your entire tent poofs. If using white gas, be especially careful not to spill any supercooled liquid gas on bare skin when refueling: The resulting instant frostburn is incredibly painful, not to mention dangerous. Likewise, liquid fuel can blister or permanently contaminate your hi-tech tent and clothing fabrics, so refuel outside your tent. Always check for leaks by turning the fuel tank upside down before priming and lighting the stove.

Insulate your fuel bottle from snow with foam or a mitten.

Hand-warm butane canister to increase fuel pressure

To boost fuel pressure, dip butane canister in warm—never boiling—water.

Butane canisters need a little help from their friends for more efficient operation in cold weather or high altitudes.

Impurities—especially the paraffin in kerosene—can freeze and inhibit fuel flow to the burner.

Small-Space Safety

Alpinists often rely on nonpressurized alcohol stoves as the only safe alternative to butane canisters. Alcohol's low volatility and quick evaporation when spilled make this type of stove a certain, if slow, choice for cooking in a tent, snowcave, or boat cabin.

Faster boiling times make bottled-gas camp stoves more desirable than alcohol-burners, and the canisters actually become more efficient at higher altitudes (above about 15,000 feet), since lower pressure makes the gas vaporize at lower temperatures.

However, insulating the canister is the key to efficient cooking in cold temperature at lower altitude. Efficiency drops considerably as the fuel (and pressure) is depleted, so warming the bottle is necessary to keep the stove burning hot. Isobutane seems to offer more consistent fuel delivery than butane or butane/propane blends, but it pays to follow a few warming tips if you're using stove cartridges.

To insulate and increase the efficiency of your bottled gas:
- Use a foam beverage insulator for the fuel bottle (or make your own with a piece of an old foam pad and duct tape).
- Boost the flame by holding the gas cartridge in your hands to warm it.
- Sleep with the canisters in your bag, and carry them next to your back in the pack.
- Wrap a band of copper flashing around the canister, pointing the tail end to the stove flame. Transferred heat can be insulated with foam padding as suggested above.
- Hold the fuel can over heating water, even dipping it into the warming—but never boiling—liquid.
- Windscreens are crucial in the cold—a windbreak of snow or rocks will go a long way toward making your stove work more efficiently.
- Carry a firepan or nonflammable base to insulate the stove burner from the snow. Pan lids and old license plates are popular, and so is the scrap of aluminum flashing from your repair kit. Some stoves offer suspension kits so you can hang the rig from a ledge, or—*gasp*—inside the tent.
- When you're melting snow, mound it in the middle of the pan, don't pack it up the sides—you lose too much heat that way.

Packing Up
- **Blow out the flame** after you've closed off the gas, rather than allowing it to flicker and die. Once the flame is out, the

lingering raw gas fumes will cleanse the jet.

- **Release fuel pressure** in the tank before packing. Do this only when the stove has fully cooled.
- When dismantling your stove, **wipe off any fuel** dribbles, and carefully store your fuel bottles away from any food. An isolated, outer pack pocket is ideal.
- **Freshen your fuel.** Stored fuel suffers from condensation and leaves junky residue, and your stove suffers in turn. Pour off any unused fuel into your car's gas tank before storing your stove. Swish a few tablespoons of clean gas around inside the tank, then drain it off. Leave the cap off and allow any remaining drops of fuel completely evaporate. Screw the cap back on loosely.
- Store stove and tanks in a **cool, dry place**.

Get the Most from Your Cookware

- Rounded sides heat (and clean up) more efficiently than squared off corners.
- Blackened pans deliver heat more evenly and even save a little fuel. If your cookset is shiny new, you can cheat a little by purchasing some black, heat-resistant stove paint at the hardware store and coating the outside of your pots. Heat up several rounds of water in the newly painted pots before using them for cooking. You can also blacken pans by filling them with water and setting them on red-hot coals. The water prevents metal from overheating and losing temper.
- Never plunge a hot pan into cool water (likewise, avoid pouring cold water into a really hot pan) or you risk ruining the pan's temper.
- Always scour gunky stuff from pan bottoms immediately with a scratchy pad, sand, or fire ash. Even stains left from cooked-on food can cause irregular hot spots that cause later creations to stick and burn.

Cast Iron Cookware

Bargain barns and second-hand tool shops abound with iron treasure. Our corn-pone biscuit mold and mini Dutch oven were rescued from a forlorn state and now serve paddling appetites with dignity. A thin film of rust marks a pot worth saving; if the pan in question is pitted or flaky with rusty scales, don't bother.

Most rust can be worked off with steel wool or a wire "toothbrush," but the easiest way to prepare the pan for seasoning is with oven cleaner (*see **Appendix B: Low-Tox Cleaning Solutions,** page 229*). After removing as much rust as possible, evenly coat all surfaces of the pan with the cleaner. Wrap inside a plastic bag and allow to sit overnight. Wear rubber gloves to scrub away the grime in a sink or on newspaper. Clean thoroughly with the hot water method (*below*) before seasoning.

Seasoning

Despite their weight, cast iron skillets and Dutch ovens remain staples for backcountry chefs who like to cook over an open fire or for groups. Unfortunately, the secret to seasoning these beasts went with the sourdough trapper, and many wannabe traditionalists are stumped by sticking, rusty pans. To season new or salvaged cast iron cookware:

- Start with a clean, dry skillet, pot, lid, muffin pan, etc.
- Coat inner and outer surfaces lightly with mild cooking oil.
- Place pan in preheated 350° oven and heat until the oil just begins to smoke.
- Remove and allow to cool slowly.
- Rub entire pan with a soft, lint-free cloth.
- Repeat procedure three times to achieve a darkened, seasoned, dependable, non-stick pan.

Cleaning

It's true: You shouldn't use soap to clean your favorite cast iron. Heat an inch or more of water to boiling in the offending pan to draw out any lingering flavors. Scour with plain steel wool (not a pre-soaped pad) or synthetic scratchy pad. For nasty, gummed-on chili, scrub gently at the spot, using baking soda as a last resort. Rinse with clean water and dry immediately with a soft cloth. Check scrubbed spots that may have been stripped of seasoning and re-oil if necessary.

Chapter 10

Water Filters

The bottle had a fitting for a filter in the screw-cap.
We made a filter but it proved to be the only item of our
whole store which was definitely useless. It consisted of
two pieces of wire gauze found in the famous rubbish-
heap near the camp but boiled and otherwise disinfected,
containing layers of compressed powdered charcoal and
dressing muslin.

—Felice Benuzzi, *No Picnic on Mount Kenya*

A two-week paddling trip into beaver country quickly exposed the limitations of our group's water filters. The river ran rich from lodges and leaves, full of tannin and the murk of the northern forest. After a few days, the task of pumping 6 liters per pit stop became, well, a real pump—hardly a rest for cadence-weary canoeists. Peter, who had filtered his way through Pakistan without straining a vessel, was amazed when his trusty filter functioned only a few days before choking.

pump body

various filter elements

intake hose

prefilter

An equally frustrated Tom, our resident engineer, tinkered with his filter on a windy beach. Soon he bounced up the bank with a pail of water. "I've figured it out," he beamed, "you just remove all the elements and the pump works great."

Pump water filters, notoriously finicky widgets even under the best conditions, are a testament to the advantages of boiling. However, scant or nonexistent fuel—in the very places where you need water treatment most often—makes filters essential traveling gear.

Filters are a physical, rather than chemical, treatment. A filter that also "purifies" implies germicidal action, usually with iodine, in addition to physical filtering.

Unfortunately, filters can do their job a little too well, as in Tom's case, and clog. Ceramic filter elements offer the longest service life of filters on the market today, but other types combining activated charcoal, iodine resin, or microporous membranes have entered the market as affordable options. While effective, many members of this new generation of filters have more parts, require more care, and tend to break down frequently. Others are designed with less mechanical complexity and longer element life for easier maintenance.

No matter what they're made of, all pump filters will clog over time. The key to satisfactory performance is to try to reduce the amount of sediment pumped into the unit. Conscientious use, frequent cleaning, diligent storage habits, and periodic replacement of elements are all important.

Water Filter Operating Tips

- Allow water to settle in a bag or pail before filtering; draw breakfast water the night before if possible. Silt that settles out won't clog the filter.
- Use a prefilter. These are usually sponge-type strainers that intercept big particles that would quickly clog the main filter element. Easy to clean, a prefilter postpones inevitable dismantling and is well worth its modest additional cost.
- Pump the unit dry after each use; shake out the hoses.

- Carry the filter in a mesh storage bag that allows moisture to evaporate.
- In freezing temperatures, sleep with your filter (sealed in a plastic bag) to prevent moisture from icing inside the elements. Though freezing does not hurt your filter, ice crystals will slow down its operation considerably.
- Discard the first few cups of water coursed through your filter with every use. This flushes out any debris from the outlet, as well as stale flavors.

Filter Field Care

Regular attention in the field ensures that your filter operates smoother and longer before the inevitable clog. As with stoves, it is *essential* that you read your filter's operating instructions. If pumping becomes difficult, stop and clean filter elements. Wash your hands thoroughly with soap and filtered water before and after cleaning.

If you own a ceramic filter, you're in luck—cleaning is dead-simple: Remove the cylinder and wipe dry. Sometimes really dirty water will leave a film that's easily scrubbed off with a stiff brush.

To clean a depth filter with variable elements (the most common type currently available), don't try to forcibly remove any parts. Some filters require only that you swish the cartridge in clear water, then rinse the pump body. Gently scrape, brush, or flush any removable mesh screens. If a screen appears stained or turns color, replace it. Scrape carbon cartridges clean with a knife.

Most manufacturers suggest sanitizing a filter once you've handled the separate elements. Do this by dropping the filter into boiling water or by flushing with a bleach solution, as described here.

Carry a small bottle brush to keep your water filter clean in the field

Bleach Flush

Running a weak solution of bleach through your filter after a trip is a good practice. The diluted chlorine ensures that any hang-dog protozoa won't colonize inside your filter elements.
- Mix 1 qt. water with 2 tsp. household bleach.
- Remove prefilter and soak in the solution.
- Pump to cycle the bleach solution through the filter.
- Pump the filter 10 strokes to remove any lingering water.
- Dry with a soft cloth, then allow filter to air-dry overnight.
- Do not store in a sealed container.

Chapter 11

Knives & Multitools

Her most important tool is the ulo, *a curved knife with a
handle in the middle of the blade. From intuition, she
cuts her skins in the proper pieces and sews them
together, rarely measuring anything.*

—Peter Freuchen, *Book of the Eskimos*

Dad gave me my first Swiss Army Spartan. That
simple but versatile knife stayed with me for a dozen
years before slipping from an aerie into a jumble of
boulders. My friend Liz didn't skip a beat. "I'll
make you a present of mine," she volunteered,
"they're cheap in Germany" (where she lives)—
thereby sparing me a sentimental loss by an equally
sentimental gain. A rawhide umbilical cord now
secures my worn knife to rucksack or belt loop.

Part of the survivor's ten essentials, and certainly

a pivotal repair tool, your knife serves a hundred purposes and asks little in return. For some, honing their constant companion is an important ritual; others break down and attend to their knife only when it's so polluted with peanut butter and packed with pocket lint that it refuses to fully close, or to open at all.

Cleaning

During college, I often whiled away boring lecture hours with that godsend, the Swiss Army toothpick, meticulously removing crammed crud from the slots and recesses of my Spartan while daydreaming of wine-and-cheese repasts, high and far away. My blade-honing skills I'd picked up years earlier from Uncle Herb, the family chef and connoisseur.

Though cleaning a folding knife is certainly a fine pastime for long layovers, this task is made supremely simple by dropping a fully opened knife into a pot of boiling water for a few minutes. This also invites long-stuck knives to loosen up so you can get at a corroded blade or joint. Cleaning can be done in the field, of course, but if you expect your knife to fix, slice, pare, whittle, punch, or bore, you'll need to clean it at home.

Once you've removed the wretched detritus with an old toothbrush, work the blades or tools in and out. If you use your knife a lot, chances are the oils from your hands have kept appendages in good working order. Otherwise, apply a little light-grade machine or cooking oil to the hinges; work back and forth, then wipe off excess oil.

In the field, scour a stained, rusty, or gummed-up blade with wood ash from your campfire. (The wood ash is mildly abrasive; it also works great for scrubbing your cookset.)

Rust Never Sleeps
Dave oiled his leather belt sheath before heading off on a paddling adventure where, on the first day, he dumped. Even though the exte-

rior of the knife sheath was oiled for water repellency, the inside was not; his sheath remained damp for the duration of the trip, inviting rust to form on his prized multitool.

Treat the inside of a your knife sheath with an aqueous leather treatment, or heat a small amount of beeswax and pour it into a warmed sheath—work it in using a toothbrush. Excess wax certainly won't harm the knife but could make for slippery handling. For trips where you're certain to get wet, consider switching to a quick-drying nylon sheath.

Some knife manufacturers combine stainless steel blades with a weight-saving aluminum body. Left unused, the dissimilar metals will corrode by galvanic action, manifested by a furry, white film on metal surfaces, especially at hinge points. This type of knife requires regular lubrication to maintain easy operation.

Discoloration

Really hard steel blades will darken with a blue patina as they age. This natural rustproofing should be allowed to remain. High-acid fruits may leave stains on softer, carbon-steel blades—nothing to worry about.

Sticky Lockback

Wood-handled lockbacks (knives with blades that "lock" in the open position) are known to swell with humidity, making it just about impossible to extract the blade with your fingers. Other lockbacks may stiffen in a similar curmudgeonly fashion. Opinel Knives recommends using the "Savoyard Knack" to open the lockback: Grasp the hinge end, blade-side-down, and give the opposite end of the knife a sharp tap against a hard surface. The blade tip will pop out.

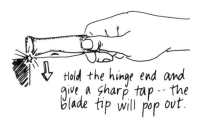

Hold the hinge end and give a sharp tap -- the blade tip will pop out.

Don't Pry

Your knife is not a crowbar, screwdriver, or hammer. Asking it to perform these functions will certainly endanger the blade. More than one innocent bystander has been nicked by the soaring, sheared-off tip of a prying blade.

Storage

Storing in a sheath is the most destructive act you can perpetrate against your trusty blade. Fabric or leather sheaths draw and hold moisture, which translates to rust. Store your knife unsheathed, or consider this option: Thoroughly clean and oil the knife, wipe dry, then sprinkle with wood ash and wrap in a soft cotton cloth.

Gaining an Edge

Whenever I'm cooking in someone else's kitchen, one thing is constant—the knives are always dull! A sharp knife is easier to handle and actually safer than a dulled, nicked blade. A dull blade means you have to use force instead of finesse to cut. There's nothing more frustrating and painful than slicing into your knuckle instead of a crusty boule.

Many people are stymied by the process of knife sharpening, probably because it's so simple. Although there are many ceramic sharpening gadgets available, nothing gives an edge like a stone. A sharpening steel may work well for skilled mystics, but anyone with a large-sized stone can sharpen any steel tool, including scissors, chisels, axes, or machetes. Sharpening a serrated blade requires a special file and patient practice.

Learning to hone blades on a stone is a matter of determining what sort of edge you need and applying even pressure at a controlled angle. A narrower angle means a more delicately finished blade.

Stones

A rectangular honing stone can be purchased at a hardware store or from most fishing outfitters. A small, thin, 3-inch stone isn't a bad choice for field use when skiing, ice climbing, or fishing. Large stones usually have a coarse side for working out burrs and roughening the blade, and a fine side to achieve a sleek, finished edge.

The Stone Is Too Dry, Dear Liza

If you never got it from the song, a honing stone should be lubricated with oil or water before you begin sharpening. This gives the stone a protective film from grit and metal shavings and reduces friction.

Sharpening Tips: How to Get 'Way Honed

- Keep fingers clear of honing surface!
- For a truly sharp knife, start with the coarse surface of the stone, always using an equal number of strokes on each side of the blade. Touch-ups require just a few strokes on the fine surface.
- Stainless steel blades may take twice as long to sharpen as carbon steel blades, but even then the process shouldn't take more than a few minutes.
- Steady, even pressure on the stone is key. Never push so hard that the blade takes a bend. Ease pressure with successive rounds and finish with a light touch.

SHARPENING ANGLES

blade
stone

10° for light-duty, fine work like fileting

20° good all-around angle for everyday use

30° blunt & strong for heavy work -- chopping

Easy method to sharpen at about a 20° angle: imagine half of 90, then half of 45.

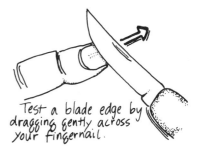

Test a blade edge by dragging gently across your fingernail.

The Strokes

Shaving Stroke. Elementary and effective, this is the stroke to teach a young person. Pretend you're slicing a thin layer from the stone.

Circular Stroke. This is best for large, long blades. Begin at the point and work toward the tang.

Figure-8 Stroke. Advanced only. This stroke requires focused attention to pressure and angle, but the alternating licks ensure even treatment to both sides of the blade.

- Count your strokes out loud, or establish a 5- or 10-stroke pattern.
- Wipe off the blade each time you start another round of strokes.
- Test keenness by dragging the blade lightly across the back of your thumbnail to produce a thin shaving of nail. Apply no pressure—just the weight of the knife is plenty. For the squeamish: The knife should slice smoothly and effortlessly through paper.

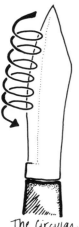

The Circular Stroke is the best way to hone a large knife blade.

Figure Eight Stroke

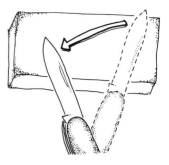

The Shaving Stroke
Draw the blade toward you

Chapter 12

Optics & Lights

"Everyone should have his own point of view."
"Isn't this everyone's Point of View?" asked Tock,
looking around curiously. "Of course not," replied Alec,
sitting himself down on nothing. "It's only mine,
and you certainly can't always look at things
from someone else's Point of View."

—Norton Juster, *The Phantom Tollbooth*

When you bring specialized instruments into the backcountry, you challenge fate. Wet weather, knocks, and rocks don't mix well with lights, binoculars, and cameras. Yet for most travelers the experience just wouldn't be the same without the advantages of their cherished widgets: light when it's dark, magnified vision, permanent memories on film.

When I asked regular backcountry binocular and camera users what their favorite repair item was, without exception the answer was a tiny screwdriver—a jeweler's or eyeglass screwdriver, or the little screwdriver that slips into the corkscrew on a Swiss Army knife. The next favorite tool: plenty of fresh batteries. After that, consensus held that there's not much a layperson can do to repair electronic or precision equipment. Long equipment life in the field depends on preventive maintenance and cultivated rituals for use.

Binoculars

General Inspection and Cleaning

Inspect lenses regularly—dirty optics directly affect binocular performance. Fingerprints, grit, and lint all contribute to fuzzy images and, if left unattended, to scratched coatings and lenses. Keep debris from collecting on lenses by storing your binoculars in their case with dust covers on.

The outer, glass-to-air lens surfaces of better binoculars have one or more antireflective coatings, which act like sunglasses to reduce glare. If left uncleaned, fingerprints and skin oils can permanently damage this coating. Clean lenses as recommended later in this chapter.

Quality binoculars have an aluminum body with some sort of rubber or plastic armor, or coating, which provides shock absorption as well as weather protection. Usually this armor extends beyond the

Binocular anatomy 101.

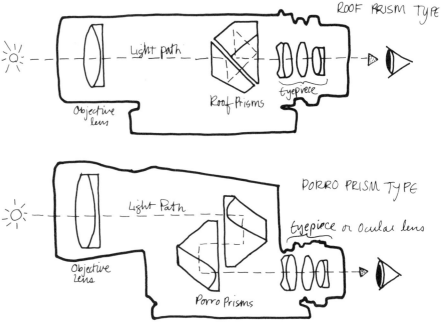

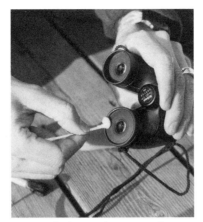

Fold eye cups back to access lenses.

A very light application of silicone will condition the cleaned fold on eye cups.

Brush/swab away any grit from rotating parts.

body to shield objective lenses and to form eye cups—channels where grit, salt, and moisture like to deposit themselves. Use your lens brush to remove any loose dust, then clean with a cotton swab moistened with a little clean, fresh water.

Eye cups fold over like turtlenecks for use with eyeglasses, and tend to crack with age. A little silicone lubricant or 303 Protectant applied with a cotton swab will keep them supple, but take care not to get any silicone on the lens. Wipe off any excess lubricant and allow to air-dry thoroughly before storing or using.

Center-focus knobs and barrel hinges that seem too stiff for easy operating can also be spritzed with a little lubricant—TriFlow, with the directional straw fit into the spray jet, is ideal for this. Apply a few drops and work the mechanism back and forth, then clean off any grit and excess lubricant with a toothpick or corner of a cloth. Lubricating the diopter ring is not recommended.

Waterlogged

What's the last sound your binoculars ever make on a paddling trip?

Ploop.

Most binocular troubles are water-related, caused either by the insidious enemy, condensation, or by the obvious threat of a full dunking.

If your lenses appear blurry but aren't fogged on the outside, hold the binoculars at arms' length and look through the objective lenses (never into direct sunlight). You can easily spot drops of moisture or crooked lenses.

The key to preventing condensation is to avoid dramatic temperature fluctuations, especially bringing cold optics into warm, damp rooms. If you enter a snug hut after a snowy ski tour, leave

Block light on diopter lens, focus with opposite lens

Next, block the other (focused) Rotate diopter to attain sharp focus.

Custom-focus your binoculars with the diopter setting.

the binoculars in their case to gradually acclimate to the temperature and humidity. Sealing optics inside a plastic bag will minimize moisture buildup before entering a warm space. While still outside, place binoculars or camera in a Ziploc bag, suck the air out and seal. Once inside, condensation forms on the *outside* of the plastic barrier.

Store binoculars in their case to protect from water and temperature extremes. For long-term storage, place binoculars in a plastic bag with a packet of desiccant or silica gel (a photo-shop item) to absorb any moisture.

Mindful storage can keep moisture from penetrating the binocular housing and staining the lenses or prisms from inside, but nothing prepares them for a catastrophic dunking. A sea kayak guide friend tells an epic tale of disassembly after his father's vintage WWII binocs had endured a capsize. After careful dissection and a freshwater bath, Chess managed to replace each lens, using a fork as a spanner, to the amazement of the native population.

Nitrogen-sealed waterproofed binoculars should not be futzed with—return them to the maker for service or replacement. However, basic models can be taken apart by humans, even though no manufacturer would recommend it. If you're in the field and your lenses are clouded and useless, you may be inspired to attempt the de- and re-construction process. **Remember the first law of tinkering: Save all the pieces, in order. Clean and dry each piece before replacing.**

Double Image—It Could Be You

If you drop your binoculars or they clonk around in your truck, chances are they'll become misaligned, or lose their *collimation*. Both right and left side should be in complete alignment or you'll experi-

Central Focus Adjustment

- With both eyes open, set the space of the barrels by moving them back and forth until you see one image circle.
- Focus on a subject about 50 feet away (don't focus through window glass, which creates distortion).
- Cover the objective lens on the side with diopter adjustment (usually the right side) with your hand. Turn the center focus wheel until you see a crisp, detailed image with your left eye.
- Lower the binoculars and rest your eyes for a moment.

- Without touching the focus wheel and while viewing the same object, cover the opposite lens, then rotate the diopter ring until you gain a sharp focus with your right eye.
- Look through both lenses simultaneously. If the two images do not produce a sharp focus, or one eye feels as if it's being "pulled," repeat the process.
- If you can't achieve a comfortable focus after several tries, your binoculars are probably out of alignment and should be serviced by the manufacturer.

ence double images, which in turn will cause eyestrain and headaches.

Many people can't tell if their binoculars are out of alignment because they really don't know how to regulate the diopter setting in the first place. (*See sidebar, page 122.*)

Cameras

It's amazing how an upright citizen can treat a camera in the most unspeakable manner, yet walk about with head up, oblivious to this cavalier, amoral behavior. Unfortunately, many of us forget that a camera is a precision instrument to be treated gently, respectfully. No matter how little attention you pay to the mechanics of your optics, at least follow a few preventive rules.

Protect from Impact

There's a reason why cameras come with straps. Shorten the strap to keep the camera from swinging into things. Use a 1-A or skylight lens filter—think of it as a $10 insurance policy for your $200 lens.

Use a padded camera bag or hard-sided case. This may seem obvious to some, but I can think of half a dozen friends who toss their cameras on the car seat or in a rucksack with the attitude that a case is too much trouble. There are hundreds of fine, streamlined and specialized camera cases available, at very competitive prices. Find one that suits your style and use it.

Rig your camera for comfort, safety, and quick-draw convenience during outings. Waistbelt rigging can be awkward when you set your pack down in the dust, rocks, or snow.

A skylight filter protects camera lens from moisture, dirt, and impact.

Protect from Heat

Excessively hot temperatures (as in your car parked in the sun on a summer day) can damage a camera's internal electronics as well as cook any loaded or unloaded film.

Protect from Moisture

Everyone consulted for this chapter—professional photographers, lab specialists, and manufacturers—cited condensation as the worst problem with cameras. When you bring your cold camera into a warm room, water vapor condenses on lens surfaces and wreaks havoc with lenses, electronics, and film. Unattended condensation may also cause fungus and rust. Fortunately, you can combat the menace of moisture in many ways.

Use the case. Carrying an unprotected camera inside your coat only contributes to fogged lenses as you crank out body heat and moisture. Foam padding in a hard or soft camera case insulates from both impact and temperature changes. Leave the camera in its case and allow to slowly reach ambient temperature. Treat the case with a water-repellent coating for even more weather protection.

Here's one field-professional's favorite way to **warm the camera** while minimizing the risk of condensation:
1. Remove batteries to keep them warm and functioning.
2. Place cold camera in a Ziploc bag, then suck the air out before sealing. Water condenses outside of the bag, not on the camera.

If you don't need to change the camera's temperature, don't. This

Lens Cleanse

Fingerprints will acid-etch the lens glass and coating if left unattended. Clean as soon as you spot them. Other nonadhesive substances that blur an image are dust, sand, and water vapor, all of which may contribute to corrosion and even fungus if ignored.

A lens cleaning kit (available from any photo supply house) should include a small blower brush, lens cleaner, and lens cleaning papers. You might also use a camel hair paintbrush reserved especially for the purpose. Find a clean, soft, lint-free cloth to use on your lenses. In the field, whatever fleece you happen to be wearing will suffice.

Optical glass is softer than ordinary glass and scratches more easily. For this reason, attempts to clean the lens in the field may damage the surface. Use a clear filter to cover your lens and you'll only need to clean the filter.

Never use alcohol to clean any lens—it may act as a solvent and destroy coatings. Also, do not apply lens cleaning fluid directly to the lens glass; place a little on a lens tissue, then use the moist tissue to clean the lens.

Richard Botley at my neighborhood photo lab insists you should NEVER clean a dry lens, or you risk permanently scratching and damaging it. Usually the fog from your breath will provide enough lubricating moisture to clear the glass. If the lens is really smudged, use lens tissue moistened with lens cleaner.

may mean leaving the camera (in its protective case) outside or in your tent vestibule. Remember to remove the batteries to keep them warm.

Avoid heavy breathing. A recent portage was particularly steamy, muddy, and otherwise memorable, but the photos came out entirely forgettable: My elevated body temperature had completely fogged the lens. Carelessly exhaled breath as well as holding the eyepiece up to your eye for unbroken periods are typical causes of condensation.

Keep a silica gel packet inside your camera bag or drybox. Remember to periodically dry the silica in a low-temperature oven or on a sun-heated boulder.

Protect from Dirt and Dust

Preserve your lens. Use a clear or skylight filter all the time, and use a lens cap. A pain, you say? Purchase (or make your own) lens cap leash to enforce the habit.

Dust the lens and body with a blower brush each time you load film—especially in field. Our comrade, photographer Peter Cole, ritually brushes each spool of film to keep any dust or snow from working into the camera body. After a trip, use the brush to remove dust, then wipe down the outside of the camera body with silicone cloth—especially if you've been around salt water, which is terrifically corrosive.

Open the rear cover and use a soft camera brush to get rid of any sand in the film chamber. Do NOT use a canned carbon dioxide-

Carry a blower brush in your camera bag, and use it to whisk lens, film, and any dusty surface each time you load film.

powered air jet (popular with computer users) to clean camera body or optics: You may cause damage by driving debris further into internal mechanisms. Neither should you touch the camera's reflex mirror, focusing screen, contacts, or shutter curtain with bare fingers—use air from a camera brush to clean away any debris.

Lens Cleaning
1. Dust off lens with brush.
2. Gently fog lens with your breath.
3. With lens tissue or soft cloth, wipe with gentle, circular motion from center to outer rim. Check cloth beforehand to make sure you haven't picked up any grit particles.
4. Remove any tough spots with lens tissue moistened with lens cleaner.
5. Repeat step 3.
6. To test lens for clarity, slowly breathe on the surface. If moisture evaporates quickly, you're all set. If one spot holds moisture longer than the rest of the surface, clean again.

Storage Tips

- Make sure your camera is clean and dry when you put it away. Follow cleaning tips outlined above.
- Make it a habit to set any switch options to OFF whenever your camera is not in use. This prevents unintentional current consumption or battery discharge, which can cause corrosion as well as run down batteries.
- If storing the camera for any length of time, remove batteries entirely.
- Store your camera in a cool, dry, well-ventilated place. If you're

Cold Weather Tips

Below-freezing temperatures take a particular toll on electronics. These tips will help you get the most out of your photo gear in winter conditions.
- Sleep with your batteries but leave the camera in the cold.
- Switch your autofocus camera to "manual" to save battery drain from the autofocus motors.
- Film becomes brittle in subfreezing temperatures. Load film and advance frames slowly to avoid tearing the film inside the camera. Film should also be brought to ambient temperature slowly, inside its canister, before loading (same rules apply if you store film in your freezer). Once you've shot the film, keep it free from condensation to preserve quality of the exposed images.
- Steve Howe, wildlife photographer and writer, suggests that if you do a lot of subzero shooting, consider sending your camera to the manufacturer to have its normal silicone lubricants replaced with dry graphite. This decreases friction at low temperatures, where wet lubricants become stiff and sluggish.

worried about humidity, place the clean camera in a heavy duty Ziploc bag with a packet of desiccant.

- If possible, periodically check stored camera for moisture, exchange silica gel, and check to see that everything still functions—just like you'd do with an old sports car stored in a barn.

Goggles and Glasses

If you wear and depend on glasses, your first line of protection should be to secure them with a strap or retaining cord. Bring a spare pair with you on trips.

The most common eyeglass failure is a broken or stripped hinge. Rather than repairing it with a Band-Aid, try a fishing swivel, pierced-earring wire, or section of monofilament line to secure bow to frame. These field fixes are so effective they may become semi-permanent.

When your nylon frames become stretched or twisted, not only are they uncomfortable but the stress may cause the lenses to pop out at the most inopportune moment. Restore the intended shape of your shades by dropping them into just-boiled (not boiling) water for several minutes. This should awaken your glasses' molded memory. Remove and clean. Your neighborhood optician can also custom-fit your glasses, often at no charge.

Cleaning
Old-fashioned soap-and-water remains the best eyeglass cleaner. Always buff with a soft cloth; a chamois or square of PakTowl is ideal.

Antifog Treatments: Do They Really Work?
The deal with any lens is that the surface next to your face is warmer than the opposite side—all the heat from a steep climb or hot chili escapes from your head, that great regulator. This temperature differential is what causes snow and water vapor to condense on the lens surfaces and blur your view of the tree you're about to hit.

Antifog treatments create a clear surface coating that makes water bead-up and roll off, rather than mist-over, the lens. The best treatment is probably McNett's Sea Drops, formulated for dive masks, though even this formula must be reapplied frequently.

Antifog applications do help dispel condensation, but are by no means a cure. What you really need is better ventilation. Double-lensed goggles or face shields solve this problem pretty well, but chronically fogged prescription-wearers should think about contact lenses. (Remember that lens solutions freeze in the cold.)

A Bit About Batteries

Most of us carry and depend on a flashlight, headlamp, or camera; some wouldn't venture far without an avalanche transceiver or weather radio. All these outdoor appliances share a common weakness: batteries. Learning to maximize the energy from each cell will spare you inconvenient failures.

One way to get the most current is simply to wipe off all contact points on both the battery and the gadget it powers. Also, use matching batteries where pairs are called for—that is, don't use a half-charged battery along with a fully charged one.

Battery Storage

As with any chemical product, batteries begin deteriorating from the moment of manufacture. A battery's service life depends on how much it is used and how well it is stored.

Get into the habit of removing batteries from your equipment before storing for any length of time—leaking electrolyte and other gases can corrode contacts, and this oxidization causes resistance between the batteries and electronics, resulting in erratic behavior, followed by failure. Most of us have uncovered a long-lost flashlight only to find a gummed-up, miniature toxic-waste disaster inside. Regularly clean battery terminals and camera contacts with an ordinary pencil eraser to alleviate any corrosive buildup.

Batteries should be stored in a cool, dry place (though freezing batteries does more harm than good). Even a properly stored battery discharges energy over time; you'll still get the same voltage out of the cell, but for a shorter time than from a battery of more-recent vintage. Try to "use up" rather than store a partially spent battery so you harness the most energy from it.

In cold weather, alkaline batteries lose up to half their power. Remove batteries from transceiver, camera, or what-have-you and carry/sleep with the batteries in a pocket close to your body.

Battery Disposal

Few communities collect batteries for safe disposal, so consumers should save spent cells at home rather than commit them to the waste stream. Store in a cool, dry spot in a well-marked container. Check with your local recycling center, dump, or town office about disposal options.

Try to limit, or at least reduce, your battery intake by conscientious use and storage, and seek alternatives whenever possible. For instance, plan a trip around a lunar calendar; try beeswax votive candles instead of a flashlight or lantern around camp. Although beeswax may seem expensive, it melts at a higher temperature than paraffin, and it lasts longer. Think of the sweet scent as a reward for not using a petroleum-based product. (The honey bee is the only creature utilized by man that naturally produces more than it needs, all the while propagating native plants. Support your local apiary!)

Rechargeables

As dead batteries accumulate in your home, you're likely to gain an interest in rechargeables. Once you've made the modest initial investment of charger and batteries, you'll enjoy savings. **The caveat:** Although rechargeable batteries work in most applications, their intensity and duration are less than alkalines (to say nothing of lithium cells)—so you need to pack spares. Additionally, nicads (nickel-cadmium rechargeable batteries) contain electrolytes every bit as caustic as those in other batteries—they're just kept out of the waste stream longer.

What about the white powder that forms on top of a nicad battery? Contrary to popular myth, this does not indicate that your battery should be discarded. Potassium hydroxide (the electrolyte) penetrates seals, reacts with carbon dioxide in the atmosphere, and forms potassium carbonate (the white crystals). The crystals are harmless and may be cleaned off with soap and water. After wiping dry, a little dot of silicone lubricant may retard the growth of more crystals.

Not surprisingly, it is the *internal* buildup of these same crystals during storage that may cause your cell to refuse a normal charge. This battery can be saved! The cure for this memory loss, advised by inventor Win Ellis, is to pass a high current quickly through the afflicted cell. Use your car battery to fuse internal crystal "whiskers" and restore the life of your rechargeable. This will also make you feel like a mad scientist.

Win's Nicad Lobotomy

- Wear safety glasses and gloves.
- Connect an insulated wire to the positive terminal of your auto battery.
- Hold rechargeable's negative end against the negative battery terminal.
- Quickly brush the wire across the rechargeable's positive end. You'll see a small spark. Repeat two or three times.

If the rechargeable does not respond to these ministrations, it is no longer usable. Store spent cells in a cool place until a disposal method becomes available.

Nicad lobotomy not tested on laboratory animals

Nicads are also prone to becoming oppositely charged over time. This reversed polarity may also be cured by the zapping technique described above. They can then be recharged in the normal manner.

Note: Check out the new generation of packable solar chargers, available at most well-stocked outfitters. These solid devices weigh just a few ounces and will charge your AA headlamp batteries while you paddle or backpack along your day's route.

Lithium Cells

If you're a cold-weather camper, your best bet is lithium batteries, which are super-reliable, and in frigid temperatures will outshine rechargeables by a factor of four. They are expensive, so it pays to cover battery contacts with duct tape when traveling or not using—nothing's more annoying than arriving in camp at dark with a $20 dead battery in a headlamp that turned itself on in your pack.

Tape over the contact points on lithium cells in your headlamp to prevent draining during travel.

Headlamps and Flashlights

Problems with these essentials are usually battery related. The key is to keep the lamp from turning on in a backpack—tape the switch in the OFF position if necessary.

Flashlights and headlamps are notorious for having terrible switches. If you have one of these beasts, do yourself a favor and replace the entire lamp rather than become frustrated by a poorly placed, poorly designed switch unit. Sometimes you can temporarily fix a balky switch by bending its contacts so they touch each other more securely.

The most trouble-free switch is the rotary type (where the entire lamp bezel twists on and off), though even these have been known to discharge themselves.

Many headlamps offer a nesting place for a spare bulb; make sure you have a spare and check to see that it works.

External battery packs are a good idea if you're heading into cold, wet conditions. You can wear the batteries next to your warm body so the light works when it should. However, the connector wires tend to pull out under tension. Prevent this by tying a knot in the wire between the connection and housing.

A flashlight is good duct tape storage: Wrap a few yards of tape around the barrel.

Glow-in-the-dark or reflective tape will make your light easier to locate in dark.

Chapter 13

Climbing Gear

Come, climber, with your scientific hat
And beady gambler's eye, ascend!
He pauses, poses for his cameraman:
"Well-known Climber About to Ascend."

—Robert Graves, *Dream of a Climber*

(See also: Footwear, *page 78;* Winter Gear, *page 142.)*

Climbing hardware featured in a book about repair? Since all climbers are taught to scrutinize their gear regularly and retire it before wear becomes a danger, "fixing" is rarely an option. Here's a case where *prevention* is key. So lower your eyebrows and read on to learn how proper care and maintenance will protect an investment that protects your life. **Note:** Periodic review of various climbing magazines will alert you to innovations and new technologies.

Carabiners

Carabiners are manufactured from aluminum alloy or steel to rigid specifications. While alloy carabiners offer the best strength-to-weight ratio, they are prone to gouges, dents, grooves, and, ultimately, minute cracking or stress fractures as they become work-hardened. Stainless or chrome-molybdenum carabiners are heavier, last longer, and are generally more rustproof than their alloy cousins. Anodized aluminum 'biners do offer more than cosmetic appeal. Anodizing prevents oxidation (the black film that rubs off on ropes and hands) and worse, corrosion, which manifests itself as a fuzzy white film, especially around salt water.

The Right Tool for the Job

Most climbers get the most out of their carabiners by using an assortment of styles suited to specific functions: steel or fat aluminum locking biners for anchors, belays, rappels, first clips/ground protection; standard Ds for clipping protection; bent-gates and ultralights for clipping bolts (use bent gates ONLY on the rope-clipping end of quickdraws); ovals for brake-rappels or hauling.

Oval carabiners continue to be popular for aid climbing and carabiner-brake rappels, but D-shaped carabiners offer a higher strength-to-weight ratio because their design distributes most of the load along the strong spine. Bent-gate Ds are just as strong, but are recommended only for linking runner to rope—never directly to protection. The bent gate facilitates the clip, but can also facilitate inadvertent unclipping.

Asymmetrical Ds or ultralights are manufactured with smaller diameter rod stock, which tends to be hard on your rope as it runs over this narrow radius. These carabiners don't last as long as more substantial models, are not as versatile, and are rarely worth the weight savings.

Hangdogs Beware

With the advent of indoor walls and sport climbing, many people have adopted new attitudes toward falling. Even though the "controlled" conditions of clipping bolts offer a certain security, most reported carabiner failures have occurred on sport climbs, and short falls can be harder on any climbing gear than long whippers. The thin steel hangers on most bolt anchors are extremely rough on carabiners. Better-quality hangers are thick, or have a rolled surface that protects carabiners from gouging, but sharp-edged hangers will stress and nick biners. So if you're a hangdog, use thick carabiners.

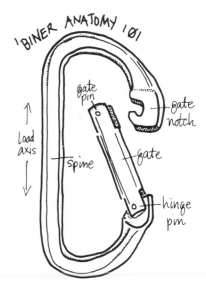

BINER ANATOMY 101

gate pin
gate notch
load axis
spine
gate
hinge pin

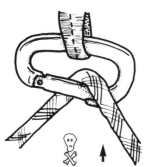

Stress cracks may occur over time

Open end

Hinge point

Carabiner Inspection

Inspection

A new carabiner should have a smooth finish and gate action, with no play in the axis and with a precise gate-latch or locking mechanism. Judge your carabiners by how much wear you see, not by age. Causes for immediate retirement include dropping from even a modest height (which may cause imperceptible but serious fractures in the metal), or whacking with a hammer. Don't buy used biners or employ a found one for anything but tying your dog out. If the gate or locking action feels loose (or, for that matter, very stiff), it's time for the pasture. Read the signs: Nicks, grooves, drops, gouges, or corrosion all spell "r-e-t-i-r-e."

Load axis
Carabiner strength is figured on its long axis. A cross-loaded biner has been substantially weakened and should be retired.

Care O'Biners

- If the gate latch feels sticky you can apply cross-pressure (with your hand) to the open gate to improve action.
- Lubricate gate axis with dry silicone or graphite lubricant—never oil, which will attract more dirt and can weaken nylon ropes and runners.
- Clean biners by boiling, sans soap, in a spaghetti pot, or by cycling through a dishwasher (again, no suds). Wipe dry, then spritz gate axis and latch with silicone.
- Grit can also be blasted out of a biner hinge with the powerful air hose at your neighborhood gas station, then lubed as above.
- True grit: Some sources suggest soaking in a noncorrosive solvent such as kerosene, then rinsing and wiping dry before lubricating.

Old carabiners never die—they become key rings, clothesline pulleys, dog retainers, bowline anchors for roof racking, and perform myriad household tasks. Take time to mark retired biners with paint or tape so there's no confusion about their history.

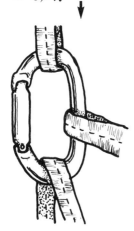

Cross-loading a carabiner may reduce its strength up to 80%

SLCDs, Friends, and Assorted Springy-Thingys

Spring-loaded camming devices (SLCDs) have either a rigid stem (Friends) or cable (Flexible Friends, Camalots, TCUs). All require the same inspection and care. Watch for metal fatigue (cracks); more likely, you'll spot wear on the cables, which may abrade, fray, and break strand by strand. Cables may take a twist or kink. You can

Spritz a little Teflon lubricant around moving parts of clean *cams.*

return your worn SLCDs to the manufacturer for service and for replacement of a tired cable stem. If you notice cam teeth are worn or splayed, or there's excessive play in the head, it's time to retire the unit as a Christmas ornament, or use for kayak haul-offs on a rocky shore. Also watch the nylon slings, which won't last as long as the hardware.

For best performance, treat your SLCD as you would a carabiner. Friends manufacturer Wild Country recommends a kerosene bath for the metal parts. Wipe down, then lubricate with TriFlow—not oil, which will attract more grime.

Other Hardware

Follow carabiner procedure for inspection. Retire anything with cracks, gouges, funky springs, loose rivets, or after dropping or whacking with a hammer. If, for instance, your ascender slips on a dry rope, that's a sign you'd be foolish to ignore.

Ropes

Since WWII, all climbing ropes have been woven from nylon, or Perlon, for its durability and elastic qualities. Today's climbing rope utilizes "kernmantle" construction—a multistrand nylon core, or kern, with a braided protective sheath, or mantle. The core provides strength and stretch to absorb the energy generated by a fall, so you don't stop with a jerk. The mantle holds everything together, protects the core from abrasion, and gives the rope its hand, or feel. A tightly woven mantle gives stiffer handling, but is less abrasion-prone than a softer one.

Kernmantle
Multi-strand
core,
protective
sheath

Each fall reduces a rope's ability to dissipate energy. Short falls near your belayer are actually much harder on a rope than longer falls, because there's less rope to stretch and absorb energy. Ropes, anchors, and belay hardware accumulate stress with each successive fall, so sport climbers should pay close attention during inspection. If you ever "catch hard" on the sharp end of the rope and don't feel any stretch, retire the rope immediately. We have climbed several times at a gym that uses disconcertingly worn ropes. While many people would never consider climbing at a crag with a squashed, furry rope, they seem to have no trouble dangling off a roof problem in the gym on a rope that resembles a molting caterpillar. Funny.

Dry Ropes

Dry ropes have been factory-treated with a water-repellent coating that extends the life of a rope in several ways. Coatings are usually Teflon or other fluoropolymer, but some companies employ paraffin coatings, which tend to attract grit and feel sticky. Dry ropes generally absorb less water, an important consideration for alpine or ice climbers, since a wet rope will double in weight, stretch endlessly (i.e., the rappel from hell), and possibly freeze solid.

A coated mantle's slick surface is significantly more resistant to abrasion and to UV damage, both archenemies of any rope. However, a very tightly woven mantle on an uncoated rope may be just as water-repellent as a loose, coated mantle. These subtle variations may be reflected by price. Don't be cheap; be safe.

Kinks

Your brand-new rope has a great hand but turns into pasta salad the minute you toss it for rappel? Kinky ropes are a frustrating malady, and only through trial-and-error with different brands and sizes will you seize upon the perfect rope for you. Smaller-diameter ropes kink more readily than fat ones, and certain practices and hardware may contribute to this pesky problem.

For example, a figure-8 device is more likely to introduce kinks than a Sticht belay plate. Lap-coiling is another perpetrator—try the butterfly coil. Unkink your rope by passing its entire length through your hands three or four times, until the rope feels smooth again. You can also hang your rope straight down the cliff while coiling to ease the twists. Stacking your rope loosely and randomly during and after climbing (in a rope bag) prevents kinks from setting in.

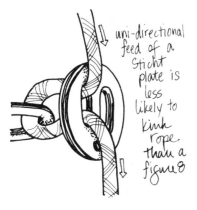

uni-directional feed of a Sticht plate is less likely to kink rope than a figure 8

Rules of the Rope

Ropes pick up a load of sand and grit with tiny, sharp edges that eventually work through the mantle and nibble at the core from inside. Keep your rope clean by stacking it out of dirt whenever possible, preferably on a rucksack or scrap of nylon, then storing in a rope bag. If your rope appears very dirty, give it a soak in the tub with non-detergent soap (see *Kinder, Gentler Hand-Washing*, page 35), then double-rinsing. Blue Water Ropes suggests adding a fab-

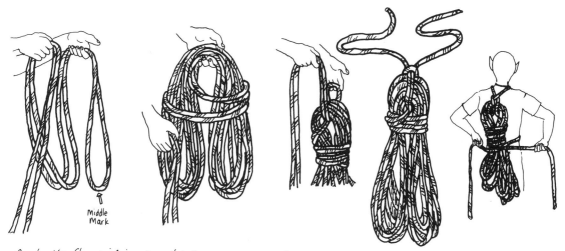

Middle Mark

a butterfly coil is less likely to cause kinking & will feed better; also, this type of coil may be carried like a backpack

ric softener like Downy into the first rinse to restore suppleness. DO NOT machine-wash or -dry; rather, loop the rope in a shady place to air-dry. Specialized rope cleaners are available from climbing shops or the Mountain Tools catalog.

How you transport and store a rope can also cause fatigue. Auto trunks are major culprits—heat, chemical fumes, and battery acid have destroyed many ropes. This goes for your Bosch or Hilti batteries, dudes, so pack ropes separately from the dread drill. UV damage is often cause enough for retirement; faded or stiff ropes reflect excessive exposure to sun or any heat source.

NOTE: At a mountain-rescue team meeting in North Conway, New Hampshire, members conducted an eye-opening experiment: During the meeting, they soaked a rope in DEET (N,N-diethyl-meta-toluamide), the active ingredient in many insect repellents. The group adjourned to a tug-o'-war, and broke the rope.

Stepping on a rope is bad juju, especially if you're wearing

When Should You Retire Your Rope?

The industry line:

- Immediately after a long fall.
- If there are soft or flat spots inside the sheath.
- If the rope has a frayed or worn sheath.
- If the rope becomes stiff.

- With holiday use only: retire after four years.
- With weekend use: retire after two seasons.
- With multi-fall use: retire after three months' constant use or one year of part-time use.

Finish rope ends or elastic cording with a quick dunk into some tool dip. Of course, tool dip is also useful for worn ice axe grips.

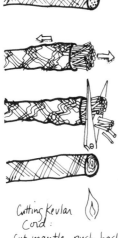

Cutting Kevlar Cord:
Cut mantle, push back trim core, pull mantle over then heat finish

crampons, since you can easily damage the inner core without obvious wear to the mantle. Feel for soft spots or lumps as you coil the rope. Avoid running ropes over a sharp edge, as when toproping. You can thread your toprope through a section of tubular webbing or over an old chunk of carpet to protect against cliff-edge abrasion. If you're hauling, consider wrapping duct tape around knots on the haul line to minimize abrasion. Use your rope only for climbing.

You alone should know the history of your rope; never loan it to a friend or buy a used rope for climbing.

Trimming

If you've damaged your rope near one end, salvage the remainder by hot-cutting the bad section. Take an old knife—even a butter knife will do—and heat to red-hot on your stove burner. Wearing mitts, slice through the rope. This works (and looks) infinitely better than melting apart with a torch or camp stove, all the while inhaling wicked black fumes. Finish the ends with a dunk into some rope sealer (see below) or tool dip (just the last half inch). Remember to re-mark the middle.

Marking

A taped middle mark will rarely last a week on a dry (treated) rope, and we've always heard that permanent inks are bad for the nylon. You can use adhesive tape (again and again), or you can purchase a Blue Water Ropes laundry marker designed especially for nylon. Mountain Tools also offers a whip end rope sealer (*see **Appendix G**, page 246, and **Alpine & Winter Gear Resources**, page 247*).

Slings and Kevlar Cord

When slings become fuzzy, abraded, stiff, or faded, replace them. Don't sew your own runners; home machines can't handle the tight-tolerance bartack stitching and heavy threads required. Send them to the manufacturer or to a credible custom sewer (ask if they'll bartack runners before you send your equipment).

Kevlar cording is made like a kernmantle rope, though the yellowish Kevlar core does not depend on the sheath for strength. Even so, if you see Kevlar peeking through the mantle, *r-e-t-i-r-e*. Because the Kevlar core and nylon sheath stretch differently (Kevlar doesn't stretch much), you'll have to employ a special method for trimming the ends of cut cording.

Harnesses

Inspection and treatment of harnesses follow the same general rules as for ropes. Dave and I argued for months over whether or not we needed to replace our harnesses. "Look at Ben," I insisted, "he's still alive and his Whillans is 15 years old!"

A few calls to gear manufacturers said differently. Turns out you should retire your harness about as often as you do a rope. ("No way," I protested, thinking of the dozen ropes my harness has outlived. "Way," say the experts.)

Wear or abrasion are obvious warning signs. As with ropes, your harness loses strength and resiliency each time it is stressed in a fall. Clean it as you would a rope. Pay special attention to bartacks and tie-in loops, checking for abrasion each time you use the harness. Also double-check any knots on racking loops—who wants to scatter pricey hardware all over the crags?

Ice Tools

Ice tools are fairly simple to inspect, since they're built stronger than you're ever likely to need. The head and spike are usually glued and riveted to the shaft and unlikely to loosen. Maintenance involves an occasional light coat of oil on steel parts to prevent rust, filing and tuning the teeth and adze, and periodically replacing the pick.

It's a good idea to carry a wrench of the correct size whenever you carry your ice gear; always be prepared to tighten bolts, but be careful not to overtighten and strip screws. No need to carry spare parts for a day's ice climb—bring a spare tool instead. Bring a small fish hook file or snapped-off section of a regular metal file to remove burrs and touch up edges in the field.

Sharpening

Always hand-file your axes and crampons; a machine grinder can overheat and ruin the temper of the metal, weakening it. Before attacking your axe with a file, determine what shape you're trying to achieve. General-purpose or mountaineering axes should have a negative clearance pick so the pick isn't too grabby during self-arrest. Techy ice climbers prefer a positive clearance for better hooking on thin placements.

Malcolm Daly, a Colorado ice climber and head of Trango USA (climbing gear imports) offers this method for sharpening the teeth of a technical ice tool:

- Use a 10-inch mill bastard file.
- File the end of the pick so it is parallel to the shaft of the tool.

For best results, sharpen ice tools in a vise.

Ice screw caveat: files are not effective, but grinders may overheat & weaken the metal teeth.

Negative pick for general purpose

Positive pick for thin ice

- Shape the end of the pick, beginning with the side bevels. The two sides should form an 80- to 90-degree angle. Any sharper and the pick will dull easily and cut (skin, packs, outerwear, ropes) more eagerly. The bottom bevel of the last tooth is critical to a pick's hooking ability. If the angle made by the flat bottom of the last tooth to the point where your weight hangs off the shaft is less than 90 degrees, the pick will slip as you attempt to hook. If the angle is greater than 90 degrees, the tool will hook well. Too steep and the point becomes fragile and tough to remove.
- Slightly bevel the top edge of the pick if necessary (most come from the manufacturer this way). The top bevel aids in removal.
- Bevel the underside of the secondary teeth so the pick won't stick frustratingly in deep placements.
NOTE: Malcolm warns that this technique results in a less-durable pick; if you bash a lot of rocks you'll file more often and wear out the pick sooner.

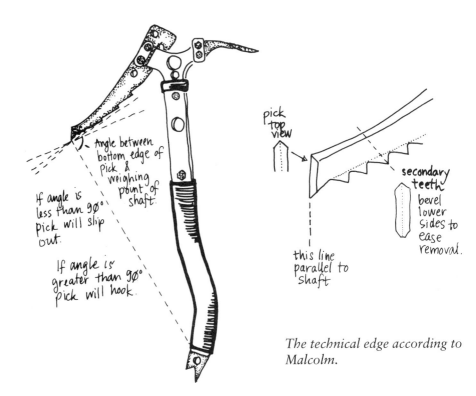

Angle between bottom edge of pick & weighing point of shaft.

If angle is less than 90° pick will slip out.

If angle is greater than 90° pick will hook.

pick top view

this line parallel to shaft

secondary teeth

bevel lower sides to ease removal.

The technical edge according to Malcolm.

Crampons

Whether you use rigid or hinged, straps or step-ins, most crampon inspection centers around the front points. Tiny stress cracks like to form just at the base of these two teeth. Other problem areas to watch: the base of upright side posts, hinge areas, and the crossbar between front points.

Strap-on crampons should be fitted to the boot snugly, so they will cling to the boot by themselves before the straps are secured. Check strap rivets and buckles, and carry a spare crampon strap. Straps are made of neoprene-coated nylon; melt back any frays with a lighter.

Step-in bindings vary by manufacturer, but all have a retainer strap for the heel clip. Make sure all parts are in working order, tighten all screws and bring baling wire for field repair. A little Loc-Tite on screws, at the beginning of the season isn't a bad idea.

Front points generally should extend at least ¾ inch, but not more than an inch, ahead of your boot toe. Always follow the original design of the point when sharpening. If the points are so dull that you can't tell, shame on you. Chisel-type points should be sharpened from the top down, while V-shaped points should be evenly refiled from each side. As with ice axes, hand-file only.

Crampons suffer from balling up in soft snow. Avoid this problem with a light coating of silicone on the metal as well as on any moving parts, hinges and strap buckles included. Another trick to prevent sticking snow is to stretch a piece of pantyhose right over the base of the crampon, punching teeth through the mesh.

In transit, crampons cause more damage to body parts, packs, tents, and miscellany than just about any other type of equipment. Store them in their own rugged stuff sack on the outside of your pack.

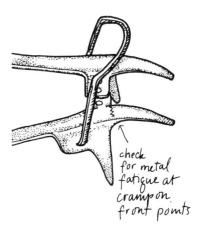

check for metal fatigue at crampon front points

Two types of crampon points—identify yours before sharpening: V-shape on left; chisel shape on right.

Chapter 14

Winter Gear

He carried his snowshoes and a blanket and the Blessed Sacrament on his back, and I carried the provisions— smoked eels and cold grease—enough for three days.

—Willa Cather, *Shadows on the Rock*

Touring Skis

Track or backcountry—the beauty of cross-country skis is that the essential forms are little changed from their Scandinavian ancestors (although performance certainly has, thanks to modern materials). No matter what type, age, or condition, your skis require the same general care. Make ski tuning and prepping part of those long winter nights and spring rituals. Your boards will reward you with many years of face plants and whoop d'whoops.

Ski Care

The best ways to ensure a long relationship with any skis, according to shop lord Tom Dolliver at Swallow's Nest in Seattle:

1. Regular hot-wax with base prep will both protect and enhance the performance of the skis. All skis have a porous base that can dry out.
2. Wipe off and dry your skis after each use, especially after they've been for a glide on your roof rack. Salt and road grime work their way onto the ski, rust the edges, corrode bindings, and dry out the bases.
3. Check binding screws before each use—the most common ski repair is a stripped screw.
4. When storing your skis for the season, clean off last year's wax and gunk, then rewax *without* scraping. This protects the edges and keeps moisture from penetrating bases. Don't store in a ski bag, which will hold moisture.

A Few Rules of Thumb

To get any leverage when tuning skis, you'll need to work out a vise system. If you're serious about ski care, a pair of sturdy ski vises is a worthwhile investment—they make the job efficient, safer and, a lot more enjoyable, so you're more likely to do it regularly.

Note: When waxing, scraping, or filing, always work tip to tail.

Single-Camber versus Double-Camber

Touring skis have double camber, which means they flex easily at the tip and tail, with a very stiff middle that only contacts the snow when all your weight is on that ski, i.e., when kicking or climbing. To check camber: Hold the skis base-to-base and press the waists together. If you can get the bases to meet in the middle with little effort, the camber is played—your skis are now *objets d'art*. If you have to squeeze hard, they're fine, so go skiing.

A single-camber ski flexes into a smooth, continuous arc with no defined wax pocket for carving smooth, powerful turns. You can easily press the skis together whether they're new or five seasons old.

Traditional Wood Skis, a.k.a. Hickory Sticks

With the advent of waxless skis, many frustrated folks tossed their "antique" but perfectly serviceable waxable wooden boards in the barn or tacked them to cabin walls. Today these skis are available at your neighborhood yard sale for less than $10; a surprising number of them remain in like-new condition, if dried out. A little preparation before storage would have preserved the skis' resiliency. Camberless wood skis are best used decoratively, but if you're lucky to find a pair with some life left, there's nothing more quiet and naturally springy than swishing through the trees on a pair of wood skis, complete with Tonkin poles. Retro. *Avant-garde*. Renewable!

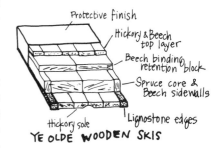

Protective finish
Hickory & Beech top layer
Beech binding retention block
Spruce core & Beech sidewalls
Hickory sole
Lignostone edges
YE OLDE WOODEN SKIS

Preserving Camber of a Wood Ski

If left unprotected during storage, exposed wood will absorb moisture—the camber killer.

1. Prepare skis for storage by cleaning and pine-tarring bases. Oil or varnish the tops.
2. Tie or band together at tips.
3. Place a wooden block at the waist. The block should be large enough so there's tension when you tie the tails together.
4. Rack skis on edge (typically in the barn rafters).

Wood skis require slightly more care than do their modern grandchildren, using old-time concoctions—principally pine tar—available at a hardware store, ski-touring center, or ski shop. Pine tar, or *grundvalla*, is wicked gunky stuff, but its resinous nature both protects the ski and holds wax well.

Preparing Wooden Ski Bases

1. Remove old wax and tar with scraper and/or hand torch with a flame-spreader attachment. After scraping, rub down the bases and edges with a rag soaked in turpentine or commercial wax solvent. (Best to do this job outside or in a ventilated shop.)
2. Hand-sand according to condition of the base. Don't use a power sander or you risk an undulating ride. Use 150-grit or finer sandpaper. Wipe clean.
3. Paint the base with pine tar. Burn tar in with the torch, taking care not to singe the ski. The tip of the flame should barely brush the ski, and the pine tar should bubble lightly but not smoke. Wipe behind the torch flame with a soft cloth to smooth the finish. (Remember, this is all flammable stuff.)
4. Oil or varnish the top surface of the ski as needed.

Spare Tips

If you ski any distance into the backcountry with wood skis, a spare tip is a good idea. Other field fixes include sapling-and-string splints, hose clamps, duct tape, and leather mittens.

Waxless Skis

Ski snobs may scoff at waxless skis, but for transitional snow (at or around freezing) and irregular terrain, these zithery-sounding boards make an hour lunch-break tour possible.

Waxless skis employ a pattern of scales or ridges underfoot to provide purchase for the kick. Hence, waxless—but only in the middle. The rest of the base needs waxing just like any other ski—hot-waxed with a gliding base wax at least once per season. Many waxless fans prefer to use a wipe-on liquid, like Maxi-Glide, which

Delams: The Seven-Year Itch

After some hard use—and poor care—any ski's core layers will begin to stray. Delamination marks the beginning of the end of your relationship with the skis, and you can spot initial phases (usually at tips or tails) with regular inspection. Fix minor delams early before they turn terminal.

If you're off in the boonies and the ski suffers a major, functional delamination, you can use splints, duct tape, or hose clamps to get you out of the woods.

Hose clamps and a metal scraper will go a long way to scrunch a ski back together.

Predrilled ski-scraper splints. While many folks recommend this as a great field repair, I've yet to see the scraper-splint in action or talked with someone who has. Start the screw holes in the ski with the awl on your knife. Sandwich splints top and bottom and hobble home. This works on fiberglass or wood skis; it's less successful on skis with full metal layers.

Another glue-and-clamp session. Once home, you might salvage the season by first cleaning the separating layers to remove dirt, adhesives, and damaged material. Use matchsticks to block open various layers. Slice away splinters, then brush on some denatured alcohol; allow it to evaporate completely. Inject two-part epoxy into the split with a disposable syringe. Remove the matchsticks, then C-clamp the area on both sides of the ski using two metal scrapers (top and bottom) to even-out pressure between the clamps. Start looking for a new pair of skis.

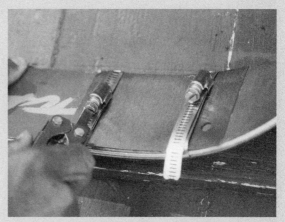

Ski scraper and hose clamp splint for serious delam in the field.

doesn't interfere with the scales and keeps nasty ball-ups at bay on warm spring afternoons.

Waxless skiers tend to be cavalier about their bases and are known to march across roads, streams, and barbed-wire fences without a second thought. That's fine, as long as you don't mind the interminably slow glide of fuzzy bases and a slippery, smashed grip area. Examine your scale pattern and trim any hangnails with a razor knife.

If the scales are really mushed, you can try to redefine the base by trimming the rounded scale edges square again. If smooth areas of the base are furry, hand-sand to prep for a therapeutic hot wax (*see Spring Cleaning, page 146*). My husband's waxless pattern was so mangled he had the bases stone-ground smooth at a ski-tuning shop, thus turning them into very effective waxable boards.

Sharpening metal-edged waxless skis is tricky because you cannot flat-file the grip pattern. Side-file the edges the best you can with the end of the file so you don't damage the base.

Waxable and Metal-Edged Backcountry Skis

Even the best sintered polyethylene (P-Tex) base will dry out over a summer with no storage preparation (cleaning and waxing without scraping). An unprotected base will lose its ability to hold wax, which can be insanely annoying on any tour. You can see if the base has deteriorated by looking for the presence of a film, or furriness under the light. This means your base has become extremely porous; any wax will fall right out of it and water will penetrate.

Restore your base by hand-sanding—not scraping—with a sanding block. Use 150- to 180-grit paper or an emery cloth. Better yet, take your skis to a competent alpine ski technician who can stone-grind them.

A few winters back, we headed into Baxter State Park, Maine, for some ice climbing. I was psyched to use my new red Valentine skis, hot-waxed the night before, and expected a glorious cruise to the hut. Less than a mile from the trailhead the slapstick waxing comedy began: zero grip going uphill, with hand-rubbed wax coats coming off every few hundred yards. I felt totally persecuted for 15 miles of rolling terrain, loaded with hardware, at – 10°F. Guess who reached the hut in the dark?

We didn't make the connection that my new skis had been drying in the shop for two seasons, victims of benign neglect. When you buy a new pair of skis, ask the shop to throw them on the grinder for a light touch-up.

Spring Cleaning

Lay your skis on the bench and survey the mileage. Clean off old wax, inspect and lube bindings, attend to bases and edges, then apply a thick layer of binder or base wax before storing.

Clean Off Old Wax

Scraping alone won't remove wax from pores in the base. Nasty wax solvents (paint thinner or commercial stuff) are the fastest way. A good alternative is CitraSolv (*see **Appendix B: Low-Tox Cleaning Solutions**, page 229*), which takes slightly longer to act. Let the citrus solvent sit 15 minutes on the base before rubbing off, then rub-down the base with citrus solvent on a clean rag.

Don't be tempted to use a torch to melt off old wax. This is just a good way of ruining bases unless you're highly skilled, which means you've ruined enough bases to know better.

Another method of removing old wax is to apply a generous layer of very soft wax (with a low melting point), then immediately scraping it off while the wax is still warm. Follow hot-wax instructions below; you may need to repeat the process.

The first run of the season is curtailed as Amy Fischer realizes she neglected to spring-clean her skis.

Removing Wax from Fabric

Forgotten tins of ski wax have a nasty tendency to glue parka pockets shut during summer storage. Establish a wax bag—a zippered, packcloth pocket is ideal—and save yourself some grief. For a stuck-shut pocket, first heat with a hair dryer or by dipping into just-boiled water. Peel apart the two layers of fabric. Next, freeze and crack off the wax. Then lay a scrap of clean cotton or a brown grocery bag directly over the spot. Iron the scrap, taking care not to overheat and melt the fabric underneath. This should draw out any shreds of base material, but will probably leave a stain. You can try a degreaser, but don't go overboard trying to erase a little mileage. Remember Lady Macbeth?

Soft waxes and klister are best removed using a commercial solvent wax remover, turpentine, kerosene or CitraSolv. When carrying klister-coated skis on your pack, make sure they're traveling base-side-out . . . trust me on this one.

Hot-Wax Treatment

Use a ski iron or yard-sale iron (you'll never get to use it for anything else again) at the "wool" setting. Dribble a pattern of wax along the base, but don't let the wax get so hot it smokes. Skim the iron over wax droplets to achieve a smooth film on the ski base. Don't hold the iron in one place too long or you risk delaminating the base in that area. Skis shouldn't become too hot to touch. Store skis without scraping.

Flesh Wounds

Preparing bases and hot waxing will take care of minor nicks and scrapes, but flesh wounds should be filled. A really deep gash exposing core material is best filled by a ski technician who has access to the actual base material and a plastic welder. For moderate lacerations and gouges, use a P-Tex candle, available at your favorite ski shop. After you've cut away any lingering hangnails, thoroughly clean the wound with alcohol.

Pre-warm damaged area with the heat from a blow dryer. Light the P-Tex stick and hold horizontally—molten plastic dropped on human skin produces a serious, painful burn. The trick is to keep the flame small, so you don't get blobs of black carbon into the repair. You can twist the stick on a metal scraper to keep it clean while burning. Rather than drip flaming blobs onto the ski, keep the stick almost on the surface and "flow" molten plastic into the gouge so the flaming tip helps preheat the repair area. Slightly overfill the repair area, then allow to harden until cooled to base temperature before scraping the base flat.

filling deep gouge with ptex candle

base is precleaned & warmed

Tuning and Filing

Check your bases for flatness. Backcountry ski bases are often higher than the edges, or the edges may "rail" higher than the base. A truly

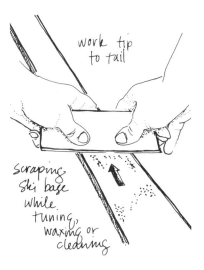

work tip
to tail

Scraping
ski base
while
tuning,
waxing or
cleaning

File scraper edges
square in a vise.

flat base means a more consistently responsive ski. Use a true bar (a machined cylinder—ask at an alpine ski shop) or scraper under a strong light to see where your skis are high or low—light will show under the gaps.

Scraping Bases

If your base is high, you can take it to a mechanic for an efficient, machine-ground treatment, or you can scrape it yourself. Use long, even, pulling strokes with a SHARP metal scraper tipped away from you, being careful not to bend the scraper into the base. Constantly check your work under the light to ensure you aren't overcorrecting.

A **sharp scraper** makes all the difference. Secure it in a vise and use your file to square-off the business edges. If you don't have a vise, lay the file flat, pointing away from you, and draw the scraper toward you.

If your edges are high, file them flat.

Burrs

Smooth over burrs with a sharpening stone (you can and should do this in the field) to maximize your fun quotient. Also, burrs terrorize skin, clothing, and your new gaiters. Once home, you can work out the ding when you file bases and edges.

Filing

Allow skis to reach room temperature before working on them. If you bring a cold ski into a warm shop, the condensation will make metal filings stick to the ski (and to you) and generally make a mess. Use a mill bastard file long enough (12 inches) to allow full grip with both hands. Files cut best at around a 45-degree angle to the ski—you can feel the action and adjust accordingly. Apply pressure where the file contacts the base, not out at the end. Use even strokes, tip to tail, constantly brushing metal flakes off both base and file.

Tuning skis is an art form that has generated protocols and controversies that transcend the scope of this book. If you want more performance from your skis, you'll need to develop your filing, waxing, and general tuning skills, including edge beveling. ***Appendix G: Resources*** (*page 246*) lists references that discuss tuning and waxing, as do countless other skiing guides.

These Modern Skis are Kinky and Twisted

Metal-edge backcountry skis are very difficult to break, but relatively easy to bend. You can spot a bent ski by pressing the bases together. As you press, a bent ski will pull away from its mate (usually at the tip). A bent ski still functions, but won't hold a turn like its designer intended. While possible to tweak a bend back into form, even experienced ski mechanics acknowledge this is a hit-or-miss operation.

When flat-filing, press down where file contacts base to make even, consistent contact.

Work carefully to maintain a 90-degree angle to the edge. Watch shiny area of new exposed metal to gauge cut.

Some suggest that bent skis might just be better for crud, since the tips won't dive!

Smashed Tails

A common malady, caused by stuffing your skis into a crusty snowbank at every rest. Prevent delamination—lean your skis gently against a tree or hut.

Bindings

No matter what type of binding you prefer, regular inspection and maintenance will save you the terrific hassle of fumbling with screws and glues in subzero temperatures.

Bindings undergo a phenomenal amount of stress and torque, which is transferred to the skis by a few little screws holding them onto the skis' top skin. Stripped binding screws are the most likely repair, but these can usually be avoided with regular inspection of your bindings.

Carry several extra screws in your kit, as well as glue and filler for field fixes. Virtually all binding screws are installed with Pozi-Drive screws, which take a specific bit available at hardware or ski shops (a Phillips head bit does *not* fit). If a screw tends to work loose but the threads still snug tight, try a little epoxy in the hole. If you're setting screws in a wood-core ski, use two-part epoxy; for foam/composite skis, use an adhesive like Elmer's Carpenter's Glue. Don't epoxy screws into foam/composite core skis: If you ever have to remove a screw, the core comes out, too—in big chunks—and you'll face major repairs.

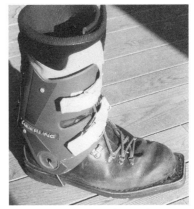

Soup-up tired tele boots by converting them to "Stein Comps." Scavenge upper boot and liner cuff from yard-sale alpine boots.

Bindings in the (Snow)Field

Galactic-certified powder hound David Goodman actually had a spare binding on hand last spring when his broke. Unfortunately, all the parts on the mountain did no good without a Pozi-Drive screwdriver (the Phillips head on a Swiss Army is too small). Even after that experience, Goodman will probably forget his Pozi-driver again—will he never learn?

To remove epoxy-set screws, heat your Pozi-Drive bit, set it into the screw head long enough to heat the threads, then back it out slowly. In the field, use a butane lighter to heat the bit. If the screws are stripped, pack a little steel wool or a matchstick into the hole. Goodman recommends using Superglue for setting screws in the field, which works better than epoxy in really cold conditions.

Binding Bindings

A squeaky binding can drive you and your tour mates to distraction. Regular lubrication with TriFlow or silicone on moving parts is a good idea. In the field, try a little lip goop or sunscreen.

If you suffer from snow sticking mercilessly to your bindings, smooth scratches and burrs with emery cloth or steel wool, then spritz liberally with silicone.

Basic Binding Styles

Three-pin

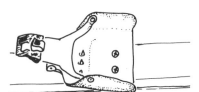

Typical backcountry three-pin binding

Traditional "rat trap" bindings are still favored for general touring. While older-style bindings had removable (read: *breakable*) toe bails and were notorious nuisances, today's three-pin styles have riveted bails that rarely detach themselves. Broken three-pin bindings can be creatively repaired in the field using baling wire or a spare old-style bail (robbed from yard-sale skis or from a dusty box at the ski shop). Since three-pin toepieces fit specifically right or left boots, on extended tours it's worth packing a spare pair.

Three-pin bindings are known to be hard on boots' pin holes, so take care when stepping in, and make sure the pins engage properly. Twisting from the toe also causes substantial wear to the boots' midsoles, rendering them over time as floppy as huarache sandals. Cable bindings are one way to reduce this wear: Cables offer more torsional rigidity, don't rely on pins, and can usually be completely repaired in the field.

Cable

Whether you have front-throw cables or popular heel-latch versions (there's little functional difference) get to know these bindings well and inspect them regularly. Watch for frayed, stretched or kinked cables, loose screws, cracked metal fittings, sprung springs. Our

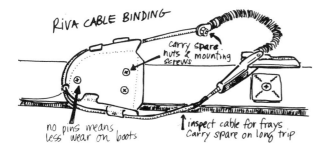

RIVA CABLE BINDING

carry spare nuts & mounting screws

no pins means less wear on boots

inspect cable for frays Carry spare on long trip

friend Ben managed to tour the better part of 40 miles with a broken cable binding, thanks to ingenuity, a bungee cord, and some nylon line. On a long trip, bring spare cables, plus the correct wrench and replacement nuts.

System Bindings

If you use a boot-binding system like New Nordic Norm Back Country (NNN-BC), be sure to pack a spare toepiece if you're going on a remote tour, since neither boot nor binding will be interchangeable with other types. There's not much you can wreck or fiddle with, since the torsion bar is molded directly into the boot and the binding's mechanics are housed in plastic. You can purchase flexor plugs of varying density to adjust the action. Otherwise, just pay attention to the mounting screws as with any other binding.

Ski Safety Straps

One of the least appealing aspects of retro-simple backcountry gear is the need for "safety" leashes at downhill areas. Always connect ski leashes to the boot, not your ankle. You can make a leash with a hook and some parachute cord girth-hitched around the binding. Clip this to a ring strung through boot laces at the toe. If you wear supergaiters, sew a loop to the toebox fabric. In the backcountry, stash these leashes in your wax kit so they won't snag on brush. Incidentally, a 50-pound-test fishing leader is a super-light leash alternative or spare.

Poles

All ski poles employ the same parts: grip, strap, shaft, basket, tip. Losing a basket or tearing the straps are common maladies; most serious is a bent, splintered, or broken shaft. Poles are natural spools for storing duct tape—wind a few dozen turns right under the grips for quick fixes.

Just one long descent without a basket will encourage anyone to carry a spare. (After once plunging, lunging, and wrenching desper-

Insulated mug lid
sacrificed for a
ski pole basket.

ately down a gully sans basket, I racked my brain for a substitute, and smugly sacrificed the lid of my favorite camp mug. Pure genius.)

While lightweight fiberglass poles are springy and resilient for woods touring, they are not torsionally strong, and often splinter along their length. If this happens, you can try to repair the split with fiberglass strapping tape (which isn't very weatherproof), or by splinting with a green branch, tape, or clamps.

El cheapo (nontempered) aluminum poles are fine for light touring, but tend to bend very easily and won't endure much abuse on the steeps. Be prepared to splint this type of pole. Alpine or collapsible probe poles are made with tempered aluminum and will break rather than bend, so they're much easier to repair.

Adjustable Poles

Adjustable poles have quickly become *de rigueur* in the backcountry, but their many parts invite quirky behavior. Identify the trouble-prone moving parts and pick up some spares—I went through three tips one ski holiday, though the manufacturer assures me that these are "old-style" tips.

It's common to bend or break the lower section, for various reasons. One is that you must never adjust any section beyond the "stop/maximum" line at a joint. Don't use the pole as a lever to pull

A Quiver of Pole Splints

Anything will do in a pinch, but common cures for pole fractures include:
- Aluminum tent stake, secured with duct tape or hose clamps.
- Aluminum flashing or soda can, wrapped and taped.
- Green tree branch plugged inside the shaft or used as splint.

- Ramer's Pole Patch (two steel sleeves that snap around a fracture).

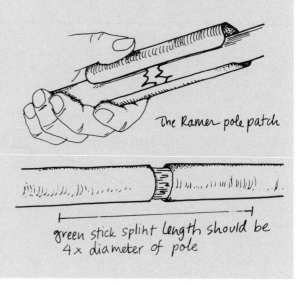

The Ramer pole patch

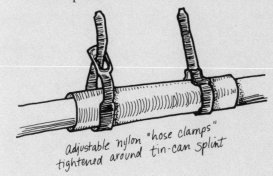

adjustable nylon "hose clamps" tightened around tin-can splint

green stick splint length should be 4× diameter of pole

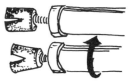

expander nuts

Extend lower section
to stop mark

Adjust length with
middle shaft section

stash of
duct tape

yourself up or do strange tasks. Telemarkers who take time to shorten their poles before descending will break fewer of them.

If yours is a three-section pole, pull the lower, more tapered section to its maximum length, and make fine adjustments with the middle section. Shortening the tapered end leaves too much play inside the barrel.

Collapsing Collapsibles

If your pole shrinks during a crucial plant, you probably unthreaded the expander when you adjusted the pole length. Take a few minutes to understand how the expander inside your adjustable pole works. Grasp the joint collar with one hand and loosen the barrel—one or two turns is sufficient. Pull the lower section past the stop mark to expose threads and expander plug. You can see there's a fine line between a secure fit and unpredictability.

If tightening the joint collar in cold weather seems unrealistically difficult, check to see that the plug is threaded properly and that there's no grit inside. Do NOT lubricate the pole; just clean it with a damp cloth if necessary. A wrap of duct tape at the bottom of each section will give you better grip to torque them tighter in the field. "Clacking" of older adjustable poles can be alleviated by clamping with a band cut from a bicycle inner tube.

THE AMAZING
SHRINKING SKI POLE
usually means the
expander nut has
become unscrewed.

Skins

Whether your climbing skins are made of mohair, nylon, or a blend, you should care for them all the same way.

Always fold skins adhesive-to-adhesive to keep glue from gumming up the business side—or other gear. Skins should be hung to dry after use, but never too close to a woodstove. In the field, drape them across poles or skis during a sunny lunch break. Many people stash skins in their gaiters during the day to keep them warm, dry, and sticky. For best adhesion, be sure to dry off your skis before applying the skins. Store your skins in a cool, dry place (especially during the summer). Even 80° heat can cook the glue and change its constituents, possibly damaging the skins.

Skin adhesive is toothy stuff, and with proper care will last several seasons. Occasionally someone will complain of skin glue coming off on skis. Usually this is because the ski base has dried out or

Fold skins to preserve adhesive and keep clean. Fold tail to middle, then fold tip to middle—adhesive to adhesive—then roll.

the base wax is very dirty—skin adhesives will cling readily to dirt or fuzzy bases. Your best bet for removing stuck adhesive is with a solvent, since heat or scraping will drive dirt deeper into the ski base.

Custom Fit

Many people are unaware that skins should be trimmed to fit. Cut the skins just before ski tails flare upward, since this is where they tend to work loose first. Use a round cut—sharp corners will catch and peel.

Another solution is to fit clips to skin tails; this also requires trimming skins. You can allow extra length at the tip for future adjustment.

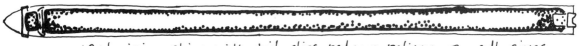

Customizing skins with tail clips reduces reliance on adhesives.

Tail clips eliminate the need to reglue tails as frequently, and provide a snug, custom fit. (*See **Appendix G: Resources**, page 246, for parts.*)

The Plush Side

There's a common assumption that a spritz of silicone on your skins will help increase their gliding potential. However, silicone coating causes the plush fibers to wick moisture to the adhesive side of a skin, and glue will not stick to silicone. Improve your glide instead with a bar of plain paraffin wax—just rub on skins as needed in the field.

Skins pick up dirt, wax, and pitch during an outing, which mats down the pile and inhibits performance. Once dry, you can beat or brush them to remove detritus, but at season's end you may want to clean them. Lay dry skins out on your deck or bench (or on the skis), spritz with citrus cleaner (with NO mineral spirits that might dissolve glues on opposite side) and let stand for 15 minutes or so. Use a stiff nylon brush to clean, then rinse with water. Allow to dry thoroughly. This session won't inhibit adhesion. If you have a tough spot of pitch, spot-clean with a little turpentine, but use sparingly.

Removing Adhesive

(*See **Appendix A: Adhesives**, page 225.*)

The easiest way to remove tenacious skin glue is with a heat-gun paint stripper. Lacking that, Paul Hebert of Ascension Enterprises recommends this technique: Lay a brown paper grocery bag on the area to be reglued, then iron through the bag using the "wool" setting. Peel the bag off the skin while still warm. Although this will remove old glue quite effectively, you may need to repeat the process.

Remove old adhesive by ironing over a brown paper bag.

Solvents are another option, but not recommended over the iron-and-paper bag-technique, since solvents will dry out and fatigue the skin materials. Hebert recommends Kwik Citra-Clean, a trade solvent used in ski shops, that contains citrus oils as well as mineral spirits. Ask your favorite ski mechanic to sell you some.

Hebert's cardinal rules for skin care:
1. Don't reglue more area than necessary—removing adhesive dries out your skins.
2. Always work in a well-ventilated area.
3. Minimize the amount of glue used. More is not better!

Regluing Skins

Ask three skiers what skin adhesive they prefer, and you'll get as many different answers. For home gluing, you're limited to solvent-based adhesives. While newer, water-based glues are certainly the trend and worth every effort to incorporate wherever possible, they just don't make it for skins—you're skiing on water, after all. Water-based glues also freeze into ineffectiveness faster than solvent-based types. Coll-Tex is a popular solvent brand, but if you're in cold coun-

Tried-and-True

Paul Hebert offers his tried-and-true skin-gluing method:

- Always work in a well-ventilated area, away from any heat source.
- Be stingy with the glue—too much and it's a real mess.
- Three thin coats 20 minutes apart gives best adhesion.
- Apply masking tape to the plush side; you're bound to get glue on them no matter what your finesse quotient.
- Use a staple gun to secure the skins taut on a deck or long workbench.
- Run a thin bead of glue down the center of the skin.

- Using an old credit card (or one with a high balance) as a squeegee, spread the glue from side to side. Lift the card at the end of each stroke, just inside the edge of the skin. Next, hold the card at an angle and skim straight down the center, trying not to let glue goop over edges. Add more glue as necessary, but remember—thin is good.
- Repeat process on second skin.
- Apply two more coats to each, 20 minutes apart, and allow to dry overnight (preferably longer) before folding or using.

try (below-zero temps), forget it, or plan to ski with your ski skins next to your own skin to keep them supple. Ascension Enterprises' Gold Label glue works well at lower temperatures.

If you wish to use non-solvent adhesive on your skins, Ramer Products will reglue your skins using a unique "hot-melt" laminating process with an inert adhesive that stays sticky down to – 50°. The caveat: If your skins have seen silicone, sorry, the lamination won't succeed. Ramer also offers a wide range of parts—tips and tail hooks, etc., as does Ascension Enterprises. (*See Appendix G: Resources, page 246.*)

Snowshoes

Wooden Snowshoes

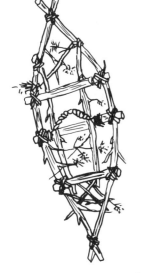

in a pinch you can use lashing skills to tie spruce boughs into functional snowshoes

Allegorical symbols of winter wanderers, wooden snowshoes evoke more romantic images than almost any other type of gear (which is why you see them so often above the fireplace or in urbane magazine ads).

Wooden snowshoes require modest but regular care to remain functional. If you're looking at a secondhand pair for real use and not for decoration, you can easily tell if they're dried out by poking the wood with a knife point—if the point enters easily, they're pretty far gone. Porous, splintery wood and brittle lacings won't last long underfoot. However, some splintering at the apex of the tip is not unusual.

If the wood's in good shape but the lacing is weary, consider renovating the shoes with a kit from Tubbs, one of the last holdouts of wooden snowshoe makers (*see* Appendix G: *Materials Resources, page 246*). Established in 1846, Tubbs offers repair kits and service for every imaginable style of shoe. The weaving of snowshoe laces is akin to advanced cats' cradle, and Tubbs supplies a terrific how-to booklet with its repair kits.

For those interested in the elegant art and intricacy of indigenous snowshoe building, seek out a copy of Henri Vaillancourt's fine treatise, *Making the Attikamek Snowshoe*.

An annual coat of varnish on the frame and rawhide webbing will maintain waterproofness and resiliency. If webbing is not protected, soggy rawhide thongs will stretch and weaken. Properly maintained, however, rawhide remains the most durable, longest-lasting lacing material, as well as the only renewable one. Neoprene laces (neoprene-coated synthetic fabric) require less care, but may fray and deteriorate over time. Pass a lighter back and forth along any fray to melt back stray fibers.

A break in the frame is a permanent structural failure, but you can splint the structure in the field with hose clamps, string and a stout stick. Laces may snap or cut along the frame, and splicing materials are limited only by your imagination: parachute cord, snips of woolen scarf, slices of belts, cattail reeds, and, of course, twisted duct tape.

If your laces are rawhide, once home you can soak the shoe in water to soften lacings enough to splice. The process is somewhat like darning mittens. Use soaked and softened rawhide of similar density. With a clove hitch around the frame, fasten one end of the rawhide to a structurally intact section of webbing. Follow the lacing pattern, working into the damaged area and beyond.

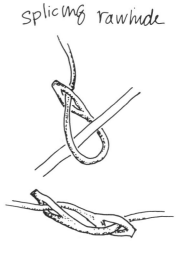

splicing rawhide

You can protect the vulnerable toe bend and laces with a wrapping of soft, soaked rawhide. Clove-hitch one end, then wrap snugly to the opposite side. Finish by tucking the lace under itself and pulling snug.

"Western" Aluminum Snowshoes

Modern snowshoes are virtually care-free. Crafted with tempered aluminum frames, integrated crampons, nylon bindings, and Hypalon or neoprene solid decking, these are quintessentially high-tech units. All employ modern materials to a design that's been around for two millennia.

Some versions attach decking with laces, using supple vinyl to lash a stiff synthetic deck to the frame; others simply stretch and rivet Hypalon decking around the tubes. Both styles are prone to abrasion on the outside edge of the frames; the riveted type will withstand more wear and tear before you're faced with repair. Periodically check rivets, however.

Laces commonly cut along this outer edge. You can protect laces

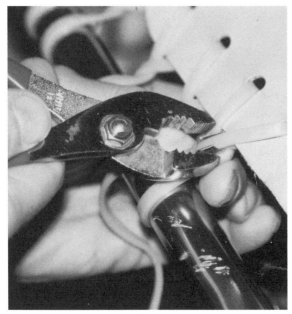

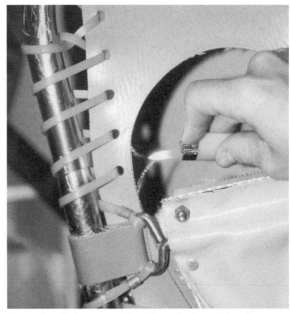

Secure vinyl laces with metal "cage clips."

Burn back frays on Hypalon decks with a butane lighter.

Traditional leather "H" binding

by wrapping duct tape snugly around a sensitive area of lashing (similar to toe winding on a wooden shoe), or with a patch of neoprene or webbing, stitched into place.

In the field, splice tattered laces with a length of nylon cord or twisted duct tape. These laces are tensioned and secured with metal clamps called "hog rings" or "cage clips," rather than knotted. You can purchase an inexpensive kit to replace hog rings—a special pincer is required—but the lacings are best obtained directly from the snowshoe manufacturer.

Hypalon decks are prone to puncturing from crampons, ski poles, and sharp sticks. These can be patched at home with Aquaseal. Watch for abrasion spots and melt back any fraying fibers with the flame of a lighter. Don't use a stove or torch—you may do more harm than good.

Snowshoe Bindings

Traditional

Wooden snowshoes often employ an H-shaped leather binding, complete with metal buckles. These must be well-oiled for smooth operating in the cold (wipe the buckles with silicone, too). Leather snowshoe bindings may not be as chemically stable as nylon, but the fit is excellent—like a moccasin. Another popular style is the speedy

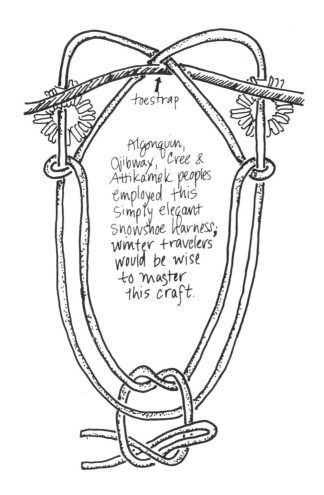

toestrap

Algonquin, Ojibway, Cree & Attikamek peoples employed this simply elegant snowshoe harness; winter travelers would be wise to master this craft.

"A" binding, which is simple and effective. You may want to silicone the laces to prevent icing up.

High-Tech Crampon Bindings

Aluminum snowshoes generally use nylon-web bindings with nylon hardware. Many parts of these bindings are likely to crack in the cold weather; bring spares or cannibalize parts off your pack.

Make sure crampons are secure and operating smoothly; lubricate the binding's pivot points underfoot with light oil or silicone. Snowshoe crampons are prone to balling up with snow. You can alleviate this problem with silicone or wax—silicone is equally effective in preventing ice-up on laces.

Snowshoe crampons made of hardened aluminum rarely bend; the teeth also remain sharper longer than non-hardened versions. If your lightweight crampons are bent, wait until the snowshoe is warm before hammering out any kinks, or you may shear the metal.

Bent snowshoe crampons are easily straightened with pliers.

You can often bring them back into shape simply by bending crampons in a vise or with pliers.

Collapsible Avalanche Shovels

Be careful not to pry when cutting snow

The most common shovel injury is a fractured blade caused by prying wet, compressed snow. The most effective shoveling method is to patiently cut snow into blocks.

Another area of weakness is the joint between blade and shaft. Check to see that it isn't wobbly. Loose rivets may be replaced with pop rivets.

Take your shovel apart occasionally and clean the shaft of grit. A little silicone spritzed on pop-pins will keep them from icing up. You should also rub silicone on the blade prevent snow from balling up.

Sleds and Pulks

If you're towing a wooden pulk or sled, treat it the same as you would wooden skis. Weatherproof each season with oil or varnish, watching for loose joinery or hardware. Treat the runners with pine tar and base wax.

Molded plastic or fiberglass sleds should be treated like their waterborne kayak cousins. Store out of sun, away from heat. Pay attention to the hardware, which is prone to jiggling itself loose. Loc-Tite on screw threads is a good idea. Inspect contacts where traces join the sled. Feel free to wax; a gouged bottom can be filled with P-Tex (for quality plastic models) or even epoxy and gelcoat on fiberglass versions. (*See **Paddling: Hull Materials**, page 173.*)

Molded plastic kids' sleds are popular for backcountry hikers because of their economy. Too often, though, they're tossed off the trail, discarded because of a crack in the bottom—they're cheaper to replace than repair, right? Well, you can have a sidewalk sale with these salvaged castoffs. In the field, use duct tape. At home, drill a small hole in each end of the crack to prevent it from spreading. Don't bother removing the duct tape. Next, pop-rivet a patch of similar material (semi-rigid plastic, if possible, or a scrap of vinyl house siding). Overlap the crack by at least an inch or so.

Part IV

Paddling

Murphy's Law:
If anything can go wrong, it will.

And a Few Corollaries:

- *Nothing is as easy as it looks.*
- *Everything takes longer than you think.*
- *If there is a possibility of several things going wrong, the one that will cause the most damage will be the one to go wrong.*
- *Whenever you set out to do something, something else must be done first.*
- *It is impossible to make anything foolproof because fools are so ingenious.*

—*from* Murphy's Law, and Other Reasons Why Things Go Wrong,
by Arthur Bloch

Consider the Alternatives

One glance at Audrey Sutherland tells you she's a woman with a mission. "Go light, go solo, go now" is her mantra; her vehicle, a small inflatable kayak. At 70-plus, Audrey has logged more than 15,000 miles in her "rubber ducky" during the last 30 years, touring coasts from Samoa to Scotland, Alaska, and Hawaii, where she makes her home.

Audrey's infectious energy sparks from crinkled blue eyes and radiates through her shock of sunbleached hair. While many people describe this world paddler as "tough," our family sees her as resourceful, practical, and beautifully balanced. Audrey's self-reliance is legendary, her fears unknown. What is most intriguing about Audrey is the way ordinary objects become essentials in her traveling kit. She may go out of her way to find a low-cost alternative to a high-tech piece of gear, but she'll gladly pay the price of a fine wine.

Here are a few care and repair tips and alternatives as prescribed by Audrey:

Favorite repair ingredient? "Dental floss—like the gut Eskimos used for sewing. Carry a needle with a large enough eye to thread it through. I've used it in place of wire, rope, duct tape, whipping line, eyeglass hinge screws."

Best maintenance tip? "A dental Water Pik with hot water at Force 10." Audrey uses it to get gunky peanut butter and old glue out of her Swiss Army knife and to blast lint out of shirt pocket corners. The pressure also succeeds at blowing carbon from camp stove jets or sand from the screw threads in hatch covers.

Unusual repair ingredient? "Condoms. Make a slingshot for survival; waterproof your watch or exposed film; carry water (reinforced by using inside a sock); make a spear gun for fishing; or use a fluorescent orange one for a crab trap float. Tie several together end-to-end as a long, super-strong rubber band."

Frugal tip: "Repair your water bag bladder by substituting a boxed wine bladder. Twice as strong, it uses the same cap/spout and can be used as a pillow, kayak seat, crab trap float, shower bag. Priced right, too."

Audrey Sutherland is quick to spot alternative uses for everyday objects.

Chapter 15

Boats

If you drive a small car and paddle a large double, it is probable that sooner or later you will impale a Winnebago at a traffic light. I have personally broken a kayak from whiplash when I drove over a curb, not realizing that an inch of rain had accumulated in the bilges overnight. But perhaps the most spectacular way to do in your kayak is to leave the bow line trailing so that the front wheel of your car drives over it. Even at modest speed, the effect of this is devastating.

—John Dowd, *Sea Kayaking*

Trying to demystify and qualify the gamut of materials used to build 20th-century canoes and kayaks could certainly justify a book or two in itself. For the average boater, however, a rudimentary understanding of hull materials provides the foundation for most any repair situation that might arise.

Regardless of design, purpose, or style, canoe and kayak construction falls into one of the following categories: ABS/Royalex, aluminum, fiberglass/Kevlar, polyethylene, wood-and-canvas, or skin-over-frame.

Whether you're a wild creek boater, quietwater tourist, or surf fanatic, you may well trash your hull before you ever reach water. We've seen a rotomolded whitewater boat launch from an auto roofrack at 70 MPH and suffer little more than road rash, but other, more tragic tales of terror abound:

One friend, speeding north through a subzero breeze for Christmas with a holiday-red poly kayak on the roof, was shocked when the boat shattered upon impact with the pavement . . .

After a surreal, nearly desperate crossing ahead of a looming thunderstorm, Mary and I reached the boat landing in a stinging downpour, leaped out, and literally threw our light glass double onto the waiting trailer—and punched a hole broadside . . .

An island friend—and a mountain of a man—helped us portage our loaded boats with his big truck. Geoff effortlessly hoisted one end while I wrestled with the fraying bow grab loop. His powerful heft was enough to break the loop; the sharp bowstem splintered on contact with the unforgiving island granite . . .

An uneventful Canadian odyssey culminated in a raucous packing-up session. I heard with horror the cracking canoe as an overzealous lout cranked the stern line just a little tighter . . .

These transport tales of terror aside, any paddler should know what sort of performance to expect from his or her boat material, how to deal with catastrophe in the field, and maybe how to prevent it in the first place. The following chart helps to illustrate the properties of various materials; you'll find more in-depth coverage in the corresponding discussions.

Once you've mastered the hull-material characteristics, other structural and rigging idiosyncrasies become specific to type of craft: leaking bulkheads, broken cockpit coaming, or worn rudder assembly on kayaks; cracked rails, torn seats, or blown D-rings on canoes. Replacing rigging and hardware teeters at the brink of outfitting—altogether a different bailiwick than maintenance and repair.

However, the wide world of outfitting still plays an important role in the safety and performance of your paddling paraphernalia (for instance, if D-rings are incorrectly applied they can cause serious hull damage). Trying to walk the line, I always ask myself this question: Could this job prevent a catastrophic failure in the future?

Hull Materials at a Glance

	ABS	*Polyethylene*	*Fiberglass*
Intrinsic properties: positive-vs-negative	+Tremendous impact resistance, sturdy, slips over rocks, resilient. −Floppy, hard to mold efficient shapes, heavy, low abrasion resistance, chemically sensitive.	+Great impact resistance, sturdy, inexpensive. −Floppy, heavy, can shatter in very cold, poor abrasion resistance, easily UV damaged, poor bonding surface.	+Inexpensive, stiff, efficient, abrasion resistant, moderate weight. −Limited impact resistance, stiffened areas difficult to fix.
Deform under its own weight	Yes	Yes	Minor
Special maintenance or storage requirements	Wood trim requires regular oiling, also preparation for cold storage. Rack on gunwales out of sun.	Must be racked on rails or decks, supported at bulkheads. Hanging also suitable. Keep out of sun.	Keep out of sun to prevent gelcoat from fading.
UV protection	303 Protectant	303 Protectant	303 Protectant to buffed hull. Wax has no UV inhibitors.
Abrasion resistance	Low	Low	Medium
Impact resistance	High	High	Low to Medium
Most common repair	Abrasions and dents filled, also cold cracks from improper storage, skid plates added.	Leaky fittings, leaking or shifting bulkheads. Abraded holes from pebbles between seats and hull.	Gelcoat chips, impact damage to stems, stress fractures (spiderweb cracks) in laminate.
Ease of repair	Easy	Very difficult	Moderate to difficult
Best bonding agent for repair & outfitting	Epoxy putty, epoxy resin for repairs and skid plates. VynaBond for vinyl, 3M Urethane structural adhesive, contact cement for outfitting.	Urethane adhesive caulk, urethane structural adhesive for both. Contact cement not recommended.	Polyester resin, epoxy putty for repair, urethane caulk or structural adhesive for outfitting. VynaBond or contact cement not recommended.

Kevlar	Aluminum	Wood & Canvas
+Super strong for weight, very light, rigid.	+Zero maintenance, stiff, immune to general abuse.	+Organic, renewable, warm, resilient, historic.
−Expensive, hard to make smooth repair, skin-coat prone to UV damage.	−Loud, cold, grabby, hard to restore smooth shape once bent.	−Expensive, moderately heavy, high-maintenance.
No	No	Yes
Store out of sun to prevent darkening of Kevlar, fading of gelcoat.	Racked on rails, un-level, to prevent water from pooling and producing cracks.	Requires regular varnish, fabric filling to prevent mildew. Rack on gunwales indoors.
303 Protectant to buffed hull. Wax has no UV inhibitors.	N/A	Varnish and canvas filler paint.
Medium	High	Low to Medium
Medium	High	Medium
Gelcoat chips, resin cracks that separate laminated layers, also stem damage.	Dents	Torn fabric, gouged rails and cracked ribs. Wood rot from outdoor storage and lack of maintenance.
Moderate to difficult	Moderate	Easy to difficult
Polyester or epoxy resin, epoxy putty for repair; urethane caulk or structural adhesive for outfitting. VynaBond or contact cement not recommended.	Metal-proved epoxy, urethane caulk or adhesive for repair.	Yellow wood glue, ambroid glue, epoxy, varnish, canvas filler paint, copper nails.

Chapter 16

Rules of the Resin

*This particular portage at Navaite Rapids not only cost
2½ days of severe and incessant labor, but also cost
something in damage to the canoes. The one in which
I had been journeying was split in a manner which
caused us serious uneasiness as to how long,
even after being patched, it would last.*

—Theodore Roosevelt, *Through the Brazilian Wilderness*

(*See also:* Appendix A: Adhesives, *page 225.*)

Bad Juju

Many experts interviewed regarding fiberglass or Kevlar repair discouraged home users from ever getting involved with the stuff. "By the time you've botched five or six jobs, invested a fair amount on toxic materials, and shortened your lifespan by breathing them all, you might be able to produce a viable glass patch," maintains one boatbuilder. Others simply point to the skull-and-crossbones warning labels. Enough said.

Unfortunately, many folks don't live anywhere

near an experienced glass technician or boatbuilder, and anyone heading out on an expedition should be prepared to patch a hole— you might be 100 miles from anywhere and the boat your only ticket back. Although the process is not all that difficult for an amateur, controlling the working environment is. The home user's best options for glass and Kevlar repairs are prepackaged kits from canoe or kayak manufacturers, because they come with exact mixing quantities and step-by-step instructions.

While they may seem expensive, the resins and fillers delivered from the manufacturer are developed specifically for use on your particular hull, and there's less room for error than if you cobbled together materials from a meager selection at your local auto-parts shop or hardware store. Finally, kits provide you with small, easy-to-use-up quantities of the often highly caustic stuff, so you don't have to deal with long-term storage and disposal hassles.

If you find the kits limiting and your glass-repair enthusiasm survives the learning curve, select a book on working with fiberglass and thermoset resins from the hundreds available. Better yet, take a course at your local community college or vo-tech school. Set up your shop accordingly and practice the art safely.

For most weekend warriors, boat repair involves filling gouges in gelcoat or substrate layers with suitable putty, and applying skid plates to the bow and stern of a whitewater canoe. Once you've mastered these procedures, you'll probably feel confident and competent enough to tackle a structural repair.

The First Resins

Pine tar and latex rubber are indigenous organic ancestors of the present-day distillates we recognize as polyester, vinylester, and other synthetic hybrid resins. Abby, my woodcarver friend, never fails to stop and gather spruce gum whenever she spots it along a trail (where trees are typically scarred). She uses it as fill in her sculptures, but we've heard many stories where gum smeared into a punctured fiberglass hull successfully sealed a leak for the duration (and longer) of a wilderness journey.

Early wood-and-canvas canoe owners employed a techy alternative to pine tar: white lead. While this canvas filler had less fumes than today's resins, the dust was just as nasty. Modern wood-and-canvas craft are built with either oil- or water-based fillers rather than a synthetic resin.

Thermoset Resins: How They Work and What to Expect

When liquid resin is mixed with a catalyst, the reaction produces heat. The polymerized material cures (and shrinks) as it cools to a permanent, hard finish. Curing begins in relatively short order (often in less than 15 minutes), leaving you with an urgently limited working time to effect your repair. Therefore it is essential that you be orderly and organized when working with these substances. **If the worst thing you can do is to be in a hurry, the second-worst thing you can do is to take your time.**

A good cure depends both on the resin/catalyst mix and the ambient temperature and humidity. The mix you can control somewhat, but not the weather. A typical resin-to-catalyst ratio might be less than two percent, but even this recommendation is based on an ideal temperature range between 50° and 70°F.

The best conditions for a consistent cure are low humidity and moderate temperatures, and it's smart to wait for cooperative weather. Dampness may inhibit the mix from curing at all, while a hot, dry day is likely to produce a brittle concoction that sets up long before you're finished with the patch—neither of which will help you fix your boat on a remote riverbank.

Patching with cloth and resin in the field is very tricky because the conditions are usually not conducive to a proper cure. Since a fiberglass or Kevlar patch is essentially a permanent repair, it's better to limp out with a makeshift duct tape or spruce gum patch and do a proper job at home. Glass patching on a wet, cold trip will likely produce a mess that will require a great effort to undo later.

Some situations do demand a structural patch, however, and if you ever find yourself having to make one on a sandbar somewhere, you'll be glad you practiced at home on an old hull, or even on an apple crate, to get the feel of handling the basic mechanics of fabric-and-resin patches. *(See **Standard Fiberglass Patches, Shopside** page 189.)*

Resin Types

Gelcoat

Gelcoat forms the in-mold, pigmented coating for fiberglass and some Kevlar boats. Essentially cosmetic, gelcoat is heavy and commonly cracks or chips upon impact. Gelcoat's polyester base limits its bonding ability to other poly or vinyl resins; gelcoat does not adhere to epoxy. Gelcoat does, however, protect the underlying cloth layers from premature UV damage.

Vinylester

Vinylester is the resin likely to be used in a Kevlar layup, primarily because of its higher elongation (flexibility) when compared with polyester. However, its expense and limited shelf life make vinylester a rare commodity at the consumer level.

Polyester

Polyester resin is more readily available and is found in most kits. A polyester repair is best for long-term fixes on laminate boats because it closely replicates the original hull. However, polyester does not bond especially well to wood, and will separate with repeated impact. Expect horrified gasps if you mention that you've decided to glass over your grandfather's wood-and-canvas canoe.

Epoxy

Epoxy is easy to mix and work with in small quantities, so it's particularly handy to use at home or in the field for filling small punctures or deep gashes. Epoxy works as a two-part system rather than as a resin-catalyst relationship. Epoxy mixes vary, but you can find a type that will bond to ABS, aluminum, wood or just about anything. You can paint over epoxy but be aware that polyester—including gelcoat—won't bond to it.

Epoxy is a popular solution for filling nasty dings in a sharp-entry bow or stern because it is very strong, has the least shrinkage of any resin, and can be combined with a variety of fillers. Its added strength makes surfaces tough to sand once cured; experienced users recommend smoothing the material with a Surform blade during the "green" phase, after the mix has set but before it's fully cured to a rock-hard finish.

Safe Sets

No matter what material you plan to use—gelcoat, polyester, vinylester, or epoxy—don't dismiss the importance of the following safety precautions. Most repair materials are just plain nasty, stinky, toxic goops. Use them sparingly and intelligently.

- Read all materials instructions and warnings carefully before attempting a repair. Any enlisted helpers should also read instructions and warnings.
- Carefully prepare by laying out all your materials and cutting patches before mixing resin. Recite to yourself or write a quick outline of the steps involved—a systematic approach is more likely to yield the desired results.
- Work in a clean, airy (but not windy) location, well away from

any flame source and out of direct sunlight. A garage or well-ventilated shop is ideal.

- If working inside a building, use an ordinary household fan to ventilate the fumes; place the fan at your feet facing out an open door to blow the heavy gases outside.
- Lock kids and pets in the attic until you've finished the job.
- Wear safety glasses, gloves, and coveralls to protect eyes and skin.
- Gloves work twofold: they keep the nasty stuff off your skin and they keep your own skin oils from contaminating the repair.
- Use a respirator to prevent inhalation of fumes. This and eye protection are most important.
- Mix resin and catalyst in a clean, disposable container. Any leftover mixed material cannot be saved. Allow to harden completely in a cool outdoor setting before disposal.
- Tilt the container away from you when pouring or stirring so you don't catch splashes.
- For a really thorough mix and even cure, count to 100 while stirring.
- Acetone is the typical prep and cleanup material—don't be lax when handling this volatile, extremely caustic substance. Acetone is quickly absorbed into skin and attacks the liver. Always use sparingly and wear gloves. Substitute denatured alcohol whenever possible.

Chapter 17

Hull Materials

An Indian at Greenville told me that the winter bark,
that is, bark taken off before the sap flows in May, was
harder and much better than summer bark.

—Henry David Thoreau, *The Maine Woods*

ABS or Royalex

Writing about maintenance and repair brings guilty moments—every glance at the fading hulls racked outside my office window is a reminder that our boats sure could use some TLC. So I felt a lot better after spotting Zip Kellogg's (a local canoe celebrity) 10-year-old Royalex Tripper in a parking lot. The thing had led a rough life: Dings, dents, and gouges nearly obscured its worn-through skid plates; the wood rails were splintery and gray; mildew blackened the cane seats. But the boat was still solid, ready to paddle, and obviously had some stories to tell.

Many paddlers (probably most) could never devote enough time on the water to accumulate that kind of wear. Even so, with some simple preventive maintenance through the years your Royalex canoe will likely outlive you.

This class of canoe may be labeled ABS (acrylonitrile butadiene styrene)—the plastic that forms the strong substrate layer in a Royalex laminate. ABS laminate is made from various plastic sheets sandwiched together, then heated under pressure to fuse the layers, crosslink the vinyl outer skin, and activate agents to produce a foam core that stiffens the hull, and provides shock absorption and inherent flotation.

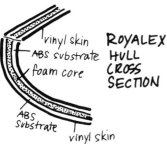

ROYALEX HULL CROSS SECTION

vinyl skin
ABS substrate
foam core
ABS substrate
vinyl skin

Royalex and its Evil Enemies

Three things have claimed more Royalex boats than all the world's rapids and rocks combined: sun, careless adhesive use, and improper winter storage.

Evil Royalex Enemy No. 1: The Sun

Although it's tempting to store something as care-free as a Royalex canoe outside, nothing could be worse over the long term. UV radiation will eventually fade and weaken the vinyl outer skin. Protected storage is crucial. Rack the canoe indoors, or at least under a shed roof. Regular applications of 303 Protectant will also help maintain the color and resilient qualities of your ABS hull. If you must store your boat outdoors, see that any scratches exposing ABS layers are filled or painted to protect against UV damage.

Even though the average canoe spends 90 percent of its life upside down on a rack, the interior of a well-used canoe should be treated, too. However, don't apply protectant to the interior just before a whitewater run, when you need purchase along the floor! A single application to the interior just before winter storage should be sufficient. Dorcas Miller solves the problem of a slippery canoe floor by strategically placing self-adhesive shower or stair treads. Glued-down foam pads are also popular.

D-ring

ABS Hull

adhesives can easily damage rather than enhance.

Evil Royalex Enemy No. 2: Careless Adhesive Use

Solvents such as acetone and those in contact cements can seriously damage Royalex laminates. If using acetone to etch a surface for adhesion, apply sparingly and don't rub too hard. Allow to completely evaporate before attempting bond. Use denatured alcohol whenever possible. Never touch a prepared surface with your hands—even momentary contact practically guarantees the bond to fail in that spot.

In the same vein, use special care when outfitting your ABS boat with vinyl D-rings or minicell foam. Contact cement or VynaBond users: Gluing surfaces should be almost dry to the touch—not tacky or shiny. If you join surfaces before solvents have completely evaporated, the solvents can migrate through the hull sandwich and create a soft spot likely to fail. Mad River Canoe recommends 3M-3552 urethane structural adhesive for outfitting purposes.

Evil Royalex Enemy No. 3: Below-Zero Temps

Royalex has a high shrink coefficient and will expand and contract significantly between a hot August day and a winter night when temperatures dip below zero. Many ABS canoes feature wood gunwales, which contract at a radically different rate; this difference can create pressures great enough to crack the laminate. These "cold cracks" may be up to 5 inches long, and must be repaired by removing rails entirely and patching the interior with Kevlar structural patches.

When preparing your ABS boat for hibernation, loosen the screws that secure the gunwales by backing them out several turns. Longer deck screws should be completely removed to open outwales and separate decks from the hull. Come spring, dab a bit of penetrating oil into each hole, then replace and tighten screws.

Scratches

When the outer vinyl skin is scratched deeply enough to expose the ABS layer, you should mask the substrate as soon as possible to prevent certain UV deterioration. Use a vinyl spray paint (available from the boat manufacturer or your corner hardware store) to touch-up surface scratches and abrasions. Remember to clean and prep the area first.

Dents

Whamming a rock demonstrates Royalex's charm: You slide off and keep going. Later inspection will reveal a dent, easily dealt with—just leave the dent exposed to the sun's warming rays and the depression will often spring back to its molded memory with no help at all. A hair dryer or heat gun will also do the trick. If using a heat gun or paint stripper, hold several inches away and use a circular motion to prevent overheating, which can cause delamination. Never let the vinyl skin get too hot to touch.

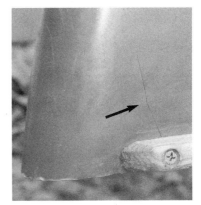

This hairline "cold crack" in a Royalex hull could easily have been prevented by loosening gunwale screws before winter storage.

Gouges

Full-steam, head-on contact with a boulder may bash a permanent divot in a bow or stern stem if your boat has no skid plates a.k.a. grunch pads—Kevlar reinforcements cemented on the hull to prevent this very occurrence. Epoxy putty can restore the shape, and grunch pads can prevent further damage.

Deep gouges should be filled with a waterproof resin. Ask at your local outfitter for a two-part urethane adhesive with structural integrity for Royalex hulls; the hardware-store alternative is waterproof epoxy putty like PC-7 or other quick-setting epoxy.

With most boats, the worst damage is often perpetrated during transport, as when a new tripping canoe arrived just in time for our big adventure—with two forklift scars gouged nearly through the bottom. Our initial disappointment abated when the manufacturer sent us a tube of Sea Goin' 5-minute epoxy. The stuff is clean and easy to use in the field because it will cure even when immersed. By all means carry this in your repair kit.

On an older Royalex canoe that's been stored outdoors, molding faults or heat-damaged areas may raise blisters along the hull, indicating delamination of the sandwich layers. This is something to be aware of, but not really to worry about. However, trauma from impact or freezing/thawing may cause a blister to break or crack, at which time you may decide to fill the resultant hole as recommended.

Creases

Creases that result from almost-but-not-quite folding your ABS boat around a midstream rock should be repaired with a Kevlar structural patch. A crease weakens the hull and may eventually become the hinge point for catastrophic failure.

Tears

Cold cracks or serious bites out of an ABS hull require structural evaluation and repair not really suited to the field. Mad River recommends its Kevlar patch kit with epoxy, applied to the interior as outlined here.

Skid Plates: A Pound of Prevention

Alan Kesselheim, a modern voyageur with many epic canoe adventures behind him, agrees that grunch pads are good additions to a boat, especially for long trips. However, added weight and change in hull performance complicate the decision of when to add them. "I now delay adding skid plates until there's a reason—deep gouges, abrasions, etc.," says Kesselheim. "Often it's years before I add them."

If you're ready for skid plates, take my advice: Buy a kit. The nice precut Kevlar patches and perfectly formulated resins infinitely out-

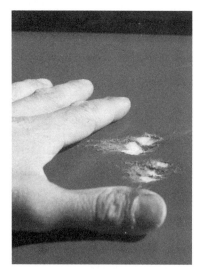

This abrasion damage to an ABS canoe occurred during shipping.

Patch and Go

The quintessential quickie patch: Cut away any damaged material so there's a bevel or V. Sand and clean to prep. Slightly overfill with quick-set epoxy—use a minicell squeegee to even out the fill. Next, lay a piece of waxed paper over the repair and squeegee over the paper to feather fill and give a smooth finish that requires little sanding. Once set—but before completely hard—peel paper, then sand down to hull shape; paint as desired.

Beveled edges provide best adhesion.

A small wedge of minicell foam serves as an excellent squeegee for smoothing out fill cement.

class any homegrown concoction. I tried fiberglass cloth and polyester resin grunch pads on a family "heirloom" and was distinctly underwhelmed with the results: The poly resin was way too brittle for the flexy hull, and my crude cloth patches didn't integrate as well as Kevlar would. Kits are modestly priced and yield neat, professional results. Order one from your canoe's manufacturer for the best match.

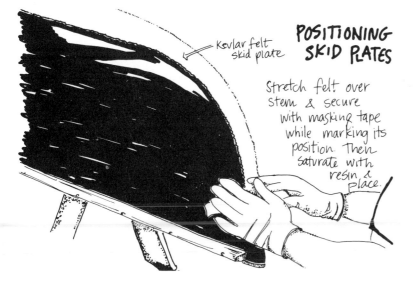

Kevlar felt skid plate

POSITIONING SKID PLATES

Stretch felt over stem & secure with masking tape while marking its position. Then saturate with resin & place.

ABS Structural Patch

- Read *Rules of the Resin* (*page 168*).
- Position boat so it will not rock and so the surface to be patched is horizontal and easily accessed.
- Remove gunwale if necessary.
- A hair dryer or other moderate heat source (even full, warm sun can suffice) will make the Royalex pliable enough to bend. Realign edges of torn Royalex material, joining the laceration as if preparing to suture.
- Use a sharp utility knife to slice away a beveled V from both sides of the tear (use a deeper V on the interior).
- Prep the exposed areas by sanding, then cleaning with denatured alcohol or a *small* amount of acetone. Be sure to prep a surface slightly bigger than the largest patch.
- Back the outside V with a slice of duct tape.
- Cut two or more layers of Kevlar to cover the tear. The first piece should just cover the tear; cut the second about 1 inch larger all the way around. Fraying an edge strand or two will make the cloth easier to feather.
- Mix the resin components thoroughly—count 100 strokes.
- Build the patch on a scrap of cardboard—it's easier to control the flexing fabric that way. Paint epoxy directly onto the cardboard. Lay the largest cloth into the wet epoxy, then spread more goop directly onto the cloth so it's thoroughly saturated. Lay second (smaller) patch on first, then spread on more goop. Repeat with smallest patch.
- Now fill the interior crack with adhesive.
- Pick up entire patch—still wet—and position over crack, with the largest cloth to the outside. Paint entire patch with thin layer of epoxy, building a topcoat with feathered edges for sanding.
- Apply waxed paper and smooth patch with corrugator, rolling pin, or foam squeegee.
- If you've removed the rails, clamp into place over patched, paper-covered area to make an impression in the adhesive—otherwise you'll have hard work sanding it down later. Remove the clamps after a few minutes.
- Allow to cure fully for 24 hours before filling the exterior V with putty.
- Remove waxed paper from interior patch, sand, then spray with vinyl paint.

A few general tips for applying skid plates:

- Read *Rules of the Resin* (*page 168*).
- Position the pad 6 inches from the peak of stem. Tape the top of the patch securely and slightly stretch along stem.
- Outline the precut pad with pencil.
- Prep just inside the outline—the adhesive will shrink the felt somewhat, and this allows for feathering.
- Pour mixed resin onto a cardboard slab, then lay the patch onto it. This allows the goop to penetrate up through the felt until it becomes transparent.
- Use a corrugator to laterally squeegee out excess resin and work into dry spots.
- After applying pad, squeegee out the resin from side to side, working from top to bottom. Run an acetone-soaked rag along edge of pad to clean hull.

Aluminum

Boat snobs may disdain aluminum canoes, but after compiling care requirements for other hull materials, "tin boats" look better all the time. Indeed, my father-in-law found a 16-foot Grumman washed up on a beach 30 years ago and the boat is still clipping along after more than a generation of outdoor storage with zero maintenance.

Wherever there's a classic canoe route, you can be pretty sure it has been successfully negotiated in strong, stiff, aluminum boats. Occasionally you'll also see where some gnarly twisting rapid has reduced one to silver shrapnel; any other craft would have been pummeled into matchsticks.

Storage

How you rack an aluminum canoe for the winter offers one of the few opportunities for preventive maintenance. Rack the boat slightly off-level, both lengthwise and laterally. This allows any water that might pool inside gunwales to drain. (If water collects, freezes, and expands, cracks could result.) As with other hull types, do not cover or let any fabrics or lines contact the boat, which can result in pitting of the hull.

Epoxy to the Rescue

Many aluminum hull repairs rely on epoxy fill putty (*see **Rules of the Resin**, page 168*). Make sure the epoxy you use is formulated to work on metal, like the popular PC-7 fill cement. Surface preparation is essential, and the repair area must be perfectly dry before applying adhesive.

Rivets

Most aluminum boats are held together by hundreds of riveted fasteners; though strong, they are somewhat prone to leaking after successive impacts. A ring of black oxidation around a rivet head means the fitting is loose.

Setting Rivets

Set or tighten rivets by holding an "anvil" (steel bar, axe head, what-have-you) against one side of the rivet while you whack the head—really hard—with a hammer.

A loose, leaky, or broken rivet can be patched in the field with a piece of duct tape, or filled with epoxy. If the rivet was holding a thwart or seat in place, you'll need to pop out what remains of the old fastener (use your camping axe as a hammer, and the awl on your knife as a center punch) and replace it with a bolt or baling wire from your fix-all kit.

At home under controlled conditions, rivets should be removed

The Fixall.

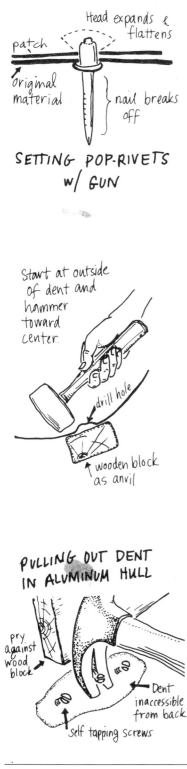

Head expands & flattens

patch

original material

nail breaks off

SETTING POP-RIVETS w/ GUN

Start at outside of dent and hammer toward center.

drill hole

wooden block as anvil

PULLING OUT DENT IN ALUMINUM HULL

pry against wood block

Dent inaccessible from back

self tapping screws

with care so the original hole is not enlarged—this makes installation of a new rivet easier. As when removing a broken snap, drill the depth of the rivet head, then pull off the head with pliers. Use a hammer and punch to pop the remaining half out the other side.

Be sure to use aluminum rivets on aluminum boats. Any other metal will cause galvanic corrosion, marked by powdery white fuzz. If circumstances do force you do place a steel, copper, or brass rivet into aluminum, use a rubber gasket to insulate the metals.

Typical hardware-store pop rivets work fine for repairs, though they often leak without further caulking. Just be sure to place the head end *outside* the canoe.

Scratches

Aluminum's tendency to grab and stick to rocks causes burrs and pocks along the hull surface. These minor scratches and dings are best viewed as mileage markers, but you might wish to grind down any sharp-edged gouges with emery cloth or a power sander.

Dents

Small dings that do not affect hull performance are also better left alone, since constant hammering or working the metal stretches and somewhat weakens it. However, a fist-sized dent below the waterline should be "convinced" back into shape with a wood or rubber mallet. In the field, a stone in the toe of your Bean boot should do the trick. Another, infinitely tested riverside option is to beach the canoe in sand or grass and jump on the bump.

Hammering Out a Dent

Use a wood block as an anvil. Hammer the dent from its perimeter and work toward the center. Extremely stretched metal is likely to rupture—drill or punch a hole at the apex of the dent before pounding to circumvent a likely tear. Patch the hole with duct tape, spruce gum, or epoxy fill cement.

Coaxing Out an Inaccessible Dent

A divot in the curved bow or stern may be gently pulled out by drilling one or more small holes directly into the dent. Drive a self-tapping screw a few turns into each hole, then pry each screw outward with a claw hammer braced by a wooden block. Sand and fill screw holes with epoxy.

Creases, Cracks, and Tears

A large dent with a crease in the metal should be treated as a crack, since the crease will eventually become a hinge point for the hull. Cracks must ultimately be repaired with a structural patch, usually a tape or fiberglass patch in the field or a pop-riveted patch at home in the shop. You might also consider taking a severe repair job to a welding shop that works on aluminum.

Field Patching

Depending on terrain and circumstances, most folks will fill cracks in an aluminum hull to stop a leak rather than perform a full-fledged structural patch in poor conditions. Spruce gum, chewing gum, duct tape, and epoxy putty are all viable plug options.

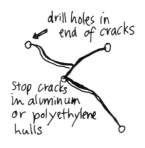

drill holes in end of cracks

Stop cracks in aluminum or polyethylene hulls

Temporary Glass Patch

Though many bush pilots carry a full aluminum patch kit and rivet gun for aircraft repairs, paddlers are not likely to haul all that gear into the outback. In the field, your best chance at restoring integrity to a cracked aluminum hull is with a fiberglass-and-epoxy patch.

Hammer the damaged area into shape as much as possible, working torn metal with a stone (the stone also works to roughen and prep the surface). Back the crack with tape (on the outer hull surface) and follow instructions for fiberglass patching (*page 189*), but substitute aluminum-approved epoxy for the polyester resin.

Remember, this is a field patch, to be removed for the long-term repair once home. Therefore, don't bond the patch closer than an inch to a structural element such as a gunwale or keel; you'll need that extra inch for fixing a permanent patch later. A glass patch can certainly hold a metal boat together for a season or so, but different flex and expansion patterns between the two materials will eventually cause the patch to loosen.

Riveted Patch

A riveted patch—covering the entire mess with a proper metal patch—is the only truly permanent solution to a torn hull.

- Try to use the same thickness and alloy as your boat—contact the manufacturer for specifics.
- Hammer the damaged area back into contour, drilling holes in crack ends as shown.
- If the tear is jagged, trim with a file or saw to make a clean edge.
- Center the patch and hammer it to replicate the curvature of the hull.
- Mark patch position on hull.
- Drill rivet-sized holes in each corner of the patch. Position on hull and mark placement of holes.
- Drill corresponding holes into hull, then bolt the patch into position.
- Mark placement of interior rivets about 1 inch apart, and drill holes through patch and hull.
- Remove patch and use a stone and file to clean off burrs and

cut line

For large tears in aluminum, cut away damaged area.

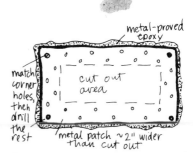

match corner holes, then drill the rest

cut out area

metal-proved epoxy

metal patch ~2" wider than cut out

soften edges. Lightly sand patch face with emery cloth.
- Apply urethane caulk to the face of the patch—unless you don't mind if it leaks!
- Fasten patch to hull with corner bolts.
- Rivet through all holes, remove corner bolts, and rivet corners.

Skin-Over-Frame a.k.a. Folding Boats

Typically, a big part of boat maintenance involves circumventing UV damage. Since most boats spend most of their lives exposed to the elements, does it not follow that a craft stored indoors would last longer? Ideally, yes. Yet many a folding craft has returned from an epic voyage unscathed, only to expire slowly in its pack.

Skin Disease

Other than catastrophic events like being hit by a ship, truck, whale, or tsunami, most damage to folding boats is to the skin rather than to the frame. Sunlight fatigues the deck, while abrasions, lacerations, and punctures from sand and rocks nibble both inside and outside of the hull. Add a dose of mildew from improper storage, and your fabric skin may no longer be seaworthy.

Cleaning

Most modern skin-over-frame hulls are made of super-durable Hypalon laminate—a combination of urethane-coated nylons reinforced with areas of rubber or urethane.

Whether or not you break down your folding boat after each use, it is very important to rinse sand and salt from the inside with fresh water as often as possible. Otherwise, grit deposits in the joints of the frame—and worse, between the frame and skin—will cause certain abrasion damage from the inside out. A garden hose is ideal for blasting out the cooties, but during trips, dousing with the bailer or sponge is usually sufficient. Examine the skin for cuts and worn spots as you rinse.

Cleaning the fabric is best done when the skin is stretched. Non-detergent soap and a soft brush will remove most grime from the hull. Vinegar or super-diluted CitraSolv (gently scrubbed and quickly rinsed) should take care of tenacious cling-ons. Commercial degreasers may be too harsh and damage the fabric—and what's a little stain but a good story? Rinse again and allow to dry completely before making any repairs or disassembling the boat.

Before applying any fabric treatments, determine if any areas might require a urethane adhesive patch (*see **Patching**, page 183*).

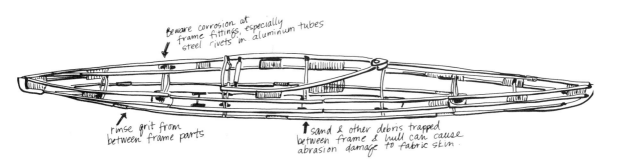

Beware corrosion at frame fittings, especially steel rivets in aluminum tubes

rinse grit from between frame parts

sand & other debris trapped between frame & hull can cause abrasion damage to fabric skin.

303 Protectant applied in moderation to the entire hull exterior will help shield against UV deterioration.

Patching

In the field, use good old duct tape. Urethane adhesive patches are the general *modus operandi* for filling gouges in Hypalon or for small, thumb-sized patches in nylon decking. Larger fabric patches may be applied with urethane adhesive. Hypalon patch kits usually bond to the hull with contact cement—ask a whitewater outfitter for a raft patch. The only truly permanent deck repair is a sewn patch, which requires a section of decking material from your manufacturer, both straight and curved sewing awls, heavy-duty nylon thread, and good seam sealer to caulk the stitch holes.

Storage

Mark Eckhart at the North American Klepper Service Center sees long-term storage as the most important area of maintenance, and offers these suggestions for preserving a fabric hull:

- Never pack away your boat wet.
- The skin should be cleaned and thoroughly dried, and should be kept in a cool, dry location out of direct sunlight.
- A light sprinkle of talcum powder inside and outside the hull is a good idea.
- Optimally, the skin should have as few folds as possible— storing folded in half under a bed, on a carpet, is recommended. The folds should be changed every six months, no matter where you stash it. Avoid folding along narrow sections of rubber (like a keel strip) or you risk stressing the adhesive bond.

Frame Care

Wood Frame

Wooden skeletons should be carefully rinsed of sand and checked for worn finish, which is where water penetrates and rot can begin if left unattended. Clean and coat wood frame sections with spar varnish, Varathane, or Thompson's Water Seal as needed, taking care to apply only very thin, successive coats. Thick coats will not dry properly and will cause the framing to stick together most unbecomingly.

In the field, be prepared for breakage: Keep a serrated saw blade and an assortment of brass wood screws and rivets, plus wire and cord in your kit. Small packets of epoxy may also be useful for bonding wooden sections. Duct tape is likely sufficient for most field repairs.

Aluminum Frame
Aluminum-tube frames require less attention, but are vulnerable to sand binding up section joints. As with tent poles, stiff joints can develop teensy hairline cracks. Regular cleaning with soap and water will eliminate the need to lubricate sections. For an unusually tight joint, first check to see that it is not kinked or cracked and that it is still round. Try dry graphite lubricant or a tiny dab of TriFlow as a last resort. (Try to keep silicone off the fabric, in case you need to patch it with adhesive at some later date.)

Doug Simpson at Feathercraft recommends bringing hose clamps and a "pocket chain saw" (an abrasive cable with rings) on long trips: "As long as the skin is intact, you can improvise . . . One day in a big surf, a friend bailed out of his boat, which filled with water—the bars were bent a full 90 degrees! By cutting bent sections, bracing and cannibalizing tubes, and splinting with duct tape, he managed to paddle home a weird-looking boat!" (*See* **Winter Gear: A Quiver of Splints,** *page 152.*)

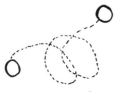

"pocket chain saw"

Fiberglass and Kevlar

Most paddlers rely exclusively on duct tape to repair
fiberglass canoes in the field. With enough duct tape and
ingenuity you can usually repair anything . . . Furnace tape
on a canoe is a paddler's gray badge of courage.
        —Cliff Jacobson, *Canoeing Wild Rivers*

Fiberglass and its spacier cousin Kevlar are manmade fibers that, when filled with a hardening resin, can be molded into sleek, efficient, rugged shapes. Both fabrics serve the same function in a laminated boat and are cared for in essentially the same manner. The fabrics look similar but are fundamentally different.

Fiberglass

Fiberglass building blocks include alumina, magnesium, and silica, which are melted together with other inorganic ingredients, spun into yarn, and woven into cloth. Resins and other "sizing" treatments are applied during the weaving process to prevent fiber breakage; adhesion between resin and filaments is critical to the strength of the resultant fabric.

There are many types and weights of fiberglass cloth, with varying compositions, including E-glass and S-glass, both of which are commonly built into small boats. Heavier-weight fiberglass used for reinforcement comes in coarsely woven sheets called roving or mat, a felt-like material that is to fiberglass what pressboard is to plywood. Cloth weights range from 4 to 20 ounces per square yard (strength correlates accordingly). Typical repair weight is 7.5-ounce cloth.

Canoe and kayak manufacturers—and consumers—continually strive for the best compromise of resins, cloth weights, and number of layers to achieve a light, durable, affordable mix. Once you're ready to make a repair, carefully examine the damaged area to identify both the weave and weight of the fiberglass layers you'll need, or contact the manufacturer.

Kevlar

Kevlar has been around since the early 1970s, when DuPont won the first heat of the race to develop a "superfiber." This manmade Aramid fiber's highly oriented molecules (they line up in formation) provide great tensile strength, thermal stability, and low density. In fact, Kevlar fabric is so rugged that the real limiting factor in a Kevlar hull is the resin used to bind each layer—upon impact, the resin will crack before fibers tear. Similarly, Kevlar's resilient fibers can spring back after extreme stretching, while resin cannot. Vinylester is a popular match for Kevlar layups because of its high elongation properties (flexibility).

The distinctive golden color of Kevlar darkens as it ages. Any light source will cause some discoloration, and in a superlight layup with a clear skin coat, the "suntan" is most obvious. Of course, excessive exposure to UV is a limiting factor, but the darkening is generally nothing to worry about. Some manufacturers sacrifice a little weight for a very thin, nearly clear, gelcoat layer that provides sun protection and more even coloration.

Kevlar fabric can be difficult to work with. Tough to cut, the stuff is even tougher to sand—it frizzes and fuzzes like cotton candy. For this reason, most people patch Kevlar hulls with fiberglass. If you're planning to lay a Kevlar structural patch on your Kevlar hull, first cut away the damaged area as best you can. Next, apply a thin coat of activated resin over the working area and allow to harden overnight. When you're ready to patch, sand the resin-primed areas (no fuzz) and prep accordingly.

Chewed-Up Stem

As with most materials (and personalities), the strengths of a fiberglass or Kevlar layup also represent its greatest weaknesses. For

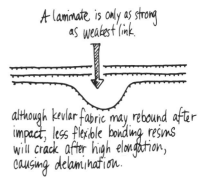

A laminate is only as strong as weakest link.

although kevlar fabric may rebound after impact, less flexible bonding resins will crack after high elongation, causing delamination.

instance, the deep, squared-off bow stem of our 18-foot cruiser makes a nice slice through the water but is too sharp for its own good when we scrunch into things. The stem looks quite a bit worse for wear, its chips and dings corrected and recorrected with epoxy and gelcoat of many colors.

For nose jobs, epoxy is probably your best bet, since you need to restore the structure with a strong fill. Epoxy sticks just fine to cured hulls of any layup, and you can paint the hardened material. However, polyester-based resins and gelcoat do *not* adhere well to epoxy. Use a marine-grade epoxy like the WEST SYSTEM kit (which includes fillers of different densities); Marine-Tex epoxy putty is another favorite. I have tried adding gelcoat pigment to an epoxy mix with fair-to-good results, but the color is nowhere near exact.

If you wish to make a gelcoat patch on a glass boat with severe divot damage to the stem, you can chop up fiberglass and use it as thickener in a polyester resin fill. Apply as a putty and allow to cure fully before sanding and adding gelcoat.

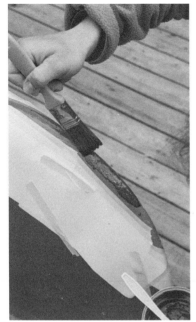

Take the time to mask hull around repair area.

Stem Reinforcement

*(See also: **ABS or Royalex Hulls: Skid Plates,** page 176.)*

Fiberglass and Kevlar designs are generally well-suited for low-impact, performance paddlers, but are not the best choices for cavalier whitewater warriors. For this reason, skid plates are not very popular with Kevlar or fiberglass hulls; another layer adds weight but not substantially greater impact resistance. But if you're a hammerhead who likes to motor, the added bow and stern protection (the stern gets equal abuse) is probably a good idea.

You can purchase pre-formed graphite plates for some designs from your boat's manufacturer. A stiff, super-thin graphite layer does not appreciably change your boat's needle-nose shape and adds a fair

Wet-sand cured gelcoat by hand using fine-grit paper wrapped around a foam block.

degree of protection. A cheaper but less-rugged alternative is to paint the stems with a few thin coats of clear epoxy.

Abrasion

Most fabric layups are molded with a thin gelcoat outer finish. Normal wear includes scratches in the gelcoat that appear white. With repeated abrasion, i.e., beach landings, even the tough gelcoat can be worn through, exposing the Kevlar or fiberglass weave. Hopefully you'll spot the abrasion before it gets to the fibers; if not, the simplest solution is to apply a thin layer of clear epoxy or polyester resin to the prepped surface. A gelcoat patch may also be appropriate (*see* **Gelcoat Patching,** *page 192*).

Abrasion Prevention

Brad Finn of Indian Island Kayak Company in Maine applies colored duct tape to the bow and stern of his glass sea kayaks for lightweight but effective abrasion protection from Maine's rocky beaches. For a more permanent abrasion guard, Brad has often painted worn areas on his hulls with Marine-Tex; he swears by this technique, but warns that the application should be very thin and the surface well-prepped.

Punctures, Creases, Nasty Bites

Whenever your fiberglass or Kevlar layup is bashed hard enough to crack through the gelcoat and into the resin—marked by fine cracks on the inside of the laminate and a soft spot that flexes under hand pressure—you must repair the area with a structural patch. More obvious wounds warrant the same treatment.

The real beauty of glass becomes apparent upon repair. A patch can completely restore the strength and rigidity of the original hull material, and the process is fairly straightforward. Still, it's not a bad idea to practice laying up a glass patch on cardboard scrap before you attack your boat. It's possible to make a patch too strong (using too many layers of cloth or excessive resin), which can cause eventual fractures at patch joints. Carefully assess the damage and try to match the number of fabric layers in surrounding areas when planning a repair.

Patching in the Field

The basic patching technique is the same for most fiberglass or Kevlar patches. On shorter trips, duct tape and epoxy putty patches are favored as quick fixes (duct tape has sealed a thumb-sized, below-waterline crunch in my kayak for two seasons), but for long expeditions, when the structural integrity of your craft is crucial, you must be prepared to make a resin/cloth repair. This means carrying (in addition to duct tape): a few feet of repair cloth, rough sandpaper, adequate resin and catalyst, mixing container, alcohol swabs, and applicator brush.

In the boonies, conditions are rarely conducive to a good cure. Expect your patch to look funkily rudimentary unless you have a lot of time to prep the surface and food to eat while you wait for perfect ambient temperature. To compensate for damp, coolish conditions you may have to add more catalyst (perhaps twice as much as recommended) and work fast. If using epoxy, remember that once cured, it is difficult to sand and/or remove.

While your emergency patch should be perfectly functional, you will probably want remove the patch once home and start over. Polyester is easy to sand, and removing the quick patch is quite straightforward: just sand resin away at the joints (wear a mask!) and pop the patch out. The patch is likely to be very brittle because of its catalyst overdose.

"Fast Patch" Prepackaged Glass Patches

Perhaps you've heard of Syntho-Glass, a prepackaged fiberglass patch that is water-activated and also cures under water. While this sounds like a paddler's dream come true, the product is not really designed for flat-patching applications (as on the hull of a canoe or kayak); rather, Syntho-Glass was developed to be wadded and stuffed into hardware fittings on large vessels. Syntho-Glass does stick to itself, and thus may be used to wrap a broken paddle shaft or stuffed into small cracks in a coaming, but its usefulness to paddlers is rather limited.

However, new on the market is the E-Z UV Cure Patch, which may indeed turn out to be a paddler's dream come true. The patch consists of an 8-inch by 8-inch fiberglass mat and cloth sandwich impregnated with a unique UV-activated resin. To use, you simply tear open the pouch, place on a fiberglass, Kevlar, aluminum, or Royalex hull, and wait for the sun to cure the patch—in as little as 30 minutes. Luke Hallman at Headwaters, the only source for this tripper's dream (*see **Appendix G**, page 246*), says the patch will even bond to wet surfaces. Resin left inside the foil pouch hardens, too, so packing out is no trouble at all. Wow!

Cold Cure

To aid curing in cool weather, you might try external heat. First tape plastic wrap smoothly over the repair to protect it and retain heat, then apply warm (not hot) pebbles in a plastic bag; or use a small, clear plastic 'tent' taped over a repair to provide a greenhouse effect to trap sunlight or heat from a campfire. I have used a Ziploc bag in this way for paddle blade and joint repairs in cool sunlight quite a few times.

—Randel Washburne,
The Coastal Kayaker's Manual

Cloth-and-Resin Patch

When repairing a canoe, the main structural patch goes on the hull *interior*; a cosmetic patch seals the exterior. This allows you to restore the hull's integrity with minimal alteration to its shape or drag.

Standard Fiberglass Patch, Shopside

(*See **Rules of the Resin**, page 168.*)

- Wear protective mask and gloves.
- Use paint stripper to remove interior paint from repair area, following manufacturer's instructions. After removing most of the paint, another coat of stripper may be applied and hand-sanded with coarse (60-grit) paper to remove residual paint from within the weave of the cloth.
- Remove all damaged material from hull laminate. Wrecked glass appears white, fuzzy, frayed. Use a razor knife or power grinder. Bevel or feather the edges as much as possible.
- Prep repair area by sanding for the largest patch.
- Apply backing to the hull exterior to retain a smooth profile. Use duct tape, cardboard, or wood over a layer of waxed paper so temporary backing won't stick to the repair area.
- Cut patches. How many layers depends on size of the damage and whether or not it's below the waterline (larger areas and those under water require more layers). If you're working in a curved spot, bias- or diagonally cut fabric will lay easier. Or try narrow strips, as if making a *papier mâché piñata*. For really tight curves (inside the stem or cockpit coaming), cut up chunks of cloth or use non-woven mat, which is easier to shape (but not as strong as) strips of cloth.
- The first layer equals damaged area plus 1 inch. Each successive layer should extend 1 inch farther all the way around than the previous one.
- Fray several strands of weave from each patch perimeter. This makes feathering, or blending, easier.
- Just prior to mixing resin, prep the sanded area with denatured alcohol, taking care not to touch the surface with your fingers.
- Mix resin according to manufacturer's instructions.
- Paint hull area to be patched with a thin coat of resin.
- Place smallest patch. (Schools of thought vary: You can either presaturate the patch on a cardboard work surface, or place the patch and saturate it in position.)
- Both fiberglass and Kevlar become transparent when saturated. If a whitish dry spot appears it's usually due to an air bubble between the cloth and previous layer. Use a corrugator or squeegee to work out the bubble and properly saturate cloth.
- Continue to add saturated layers of cloth, working from the

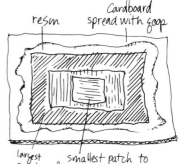

Build a glass patch on cardboard—easier to control flexing fabric & saturate fibers.

resin

Cardboard spread with goop

largest patch first

smallest patch to fill hole in hull

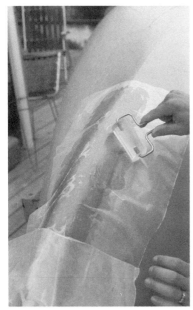

Use a roller or corrugator for consistent bond and feathered edges.

center of material and forcing air to the outer edge. Roll out excess resin this way as well.

- Wipe any drips or runs off the hull with a rag soaked in denatured alcohol.
- Place a sheet of waxed paper over entire patch area. Use the corrugator or squeegee to create a smooth, feathered surface.
- Clean brushes and corrugator immediately.
- Set remaining activated resin outdoors to cure before disposal.
- Once cured, sand any rough edges or high spots, then apply gelcoat (cosmetic) patch to the exterior for abrasion- and moisture-resistance. (*See **Gelcoat Patching,** page 192.*)

Exterior Fiberglass Patch
Unfortunately for sea kayakers, Murphy's Law kicks in: the most likely area of damage at the very bow or stern is going to be in a totally inaccessible spot. Not to worry—you just repair the hull exterior. If you're even more unlucky, the damage will occur just within reach of the cockpit, requiring that you perform the surgery with your head and torso inside a fume-filled hull. In that case, build the entire patch on a slab of cardboard first (*see **ABS Structural Patch,** page 178*), in order to limit your time trapped in a toxic airlock. Wear a respirator mask.

Follow glass patching instructions (*above*), but with these variations:
- Cut away damaged area of fiberglass.
- Make a serious effort to sand edges inside the hole—awkward but important. Feather exterior edges and sand as well.
- Clean with alcohol.
- Cut a scrap of cardboard about 2 inches larger than the damaged area.
- Thread the center of the cardboard with thin wire around a backing stick as shown, then back through.
- Cut a patch the size of the cardboard; cut a second patch about ½ inch smaller. Fray edge strands on both.
- Mix resin. Lay first (larger) patch on cardboard and saturate with resin. Add second layer and saturate.
- Paint inside hull edges with resin.
- Gently work cardboard into the hole, bending but not folding, and bridging stick across the center.
- Once cardboard is inside, tug the wires to create tension. This forms the backing for an exterior patch, and the stick allows you to pull the form taut.

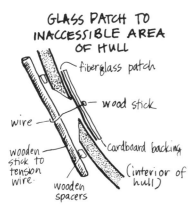

GLASS PATCH TO INACCESSIBLE AREA OF HULL

fiberglass patch
wood stick
wire
wooden stick to tension wire.
wooden spacers
cardboard backing
(interior of hull)

- Wrap wire against a second, exterior stick or lath, then block as shown to maintain tension during cure.
- Paint resin around exterior edges for additional sealing.
- After the patch has dried, snip the wires flush, and perform a cosmetic gelcoat patch.

Key to a Successful Fiberglass Patch
Spend a lot of time preparing the hull, preparing yourself, and preparing your work area. This methodical approach will naturally limit the amount of time spent in contact with toxic resins, and will ensure a cleaner, superior repair.

Gelcoat

(See also: *Fiberglass and Kevlar,* page 184; *Rules of the Resin,* page 168.)
Fiberglass and other laminated boats generally sport a gelcoated—not painted—exterior surface. Gelcoat forms the first layer in a mold, and its polyester resin base bonds with the resin in the layup for a finish more durable than enamel. Besides polyester and cosmetic pigments, other added promoters and inhibitors determine the flow characteristics, flexibility and UV-resistance of the gelcoat.

More is not better with gelcoat. It is heavy, and a too-thick layer will crack with normal flexing of the hull. Cracks usually result from impact, abrasion, or overtightened hardware, however, and show up white. Most boaters accept these as mileage scars and ignore them.

Gelcoat is somewhat porous: Water and any coatings (like wax or surfacing agents used in manufacture) can permeate and cause deterioration over time. On an older hull, latent imperfections (air bubbles) in the layup may manifest themselves as pock marks on the surface.

Despite its UV inhibitors, gelcoat fades quickly; constant exposure will lighten a hull by several shades and leaves a chalky finish. For this reason, many people prefer a *white* hull, which will not show age or wear and tear as markedly.

Minor gelcoat faults can be treated with elbow grease, rubbing compound, or sandpaper. Rubbing compound from a canoe manufacturer, auto parts store, or marine shop will go a long way to restore the overall color. Shallow cuts in the gelcoat are probably best left alone, since damage from overzealous cleaning can be worse than the original wound. Wet-sanding will expose underlying color and smooth hull surface. If you own several glass boats, consider investing in a power buffer, available for under $60.

Scratch and Fade Removal

Tips for those who can't countenance a faded, scratched bottom:

- Wet-sand by hand, beginning with 320-grit wet/dry sandpaper wrapped around a foam sanding block. Use a lot of water. This both lubricates the surface and makes your sandpaper last longer.
- Sand with successively finer grit to remove the scratch. Spend longer with each grade of paper; i. e., if you spend 5 minutes sanding with 320-grit, spend 8 minutes with 400-grit, 15 minutes with 600-grit. This obsessive sanding ensures you'll remove heavier scratches caused by the previous sanding, but is practiced only by those with many long winter nights to fill.
- After sanding, polish with rubbing compound, using a sheepskin, chamois cloth, or PakTowl. If you're as lazy as me you'll opt for the sheepskin sanding disk that fits on your power drill. Power buffers should only be used at low speed settings—you don't want to heat the gelcoat unnecessarily.
- Many people like to wax their fiberglass boats for maximum performance, but wax offers no UV protection; 303 Protectant works to sunscreen a gelcoat hull.

Gelcoat Patching

After making a structural repair to your favorite cruiser, a moisture-proof seal should be applied to the cracked outer hull. Remember that gelcoat's polyester base will not bond well to cured epoxy; if you want to restore the gelcoat finish to a large patched area, use polyester resin for your repair. Again, the easiest way to achieve a structure close to the original hull is to use a kit from the manufacturer. This also gives you the best odds of approximating the original finish and color. Even then, matching gelcoat exactly is virtually impossible. The older, original coating will have faded, and no two mixes are ever the same. Don't turn into an axe murderer trying to achieve an identical color match!

Gelcoat is available two ways: the **putty** form is easy to work with and suited for filling chips, but cures brittle. **Liquid gelcoat** is more versatile, goes on thin and is easier to feather into the original gelcoat for a less visible patch.

Gelcoat shrinks as it cures, so when using putty, overfill. When filling a scratch with liquid gelcoat, several thin layers may be needed, spaced at least an hour apart, to overfill the gouge. Liquid gelcoat may be thickened after catalyzation. Use talcum powder or even powdered wood putty (from the hardware store) to make a paste or putty. Be forewarned: once you thicken liquid gelcoat, it will shrink more as it cures.

CAUTION: Gelcoat's catalyst is MEKP (methyl-ethyl-ketone peroxide). Don't even *think* about making a gelcoat repair without

The gelcoat on this kayak bow stem has chipped off to expose underlying fiberglass cloth. Epoxy putty offers the most durable repair here.

gloves or eye protection. Always mix the smallest amount possible—just a teaspoon is all that's required for an average chip or gouge. (*See* **Rules of the Resin,** *page 168.*)

Surface Preparation

- For best color match, the hull should first be buffed or sanded as recommended above; this exposes original, unfaded gelcoat.
- Cut, sand, or grind away the damaged, flaking material, grinding deeper than the actual area and beveling edges slightly for best adhesion.
- If you're making a cosmetic patch over a cured structural patch where you have backed the laminated patch on the exterior of the hull, be sure your patch has been made with poly resin, not epoxy. Epoxy resin must be painted with enamel, epoxy, or urethane paint; gelcoat will not adhere to an epoxy patch.
- Clean the patch area with denatured alcohol; wear gloves to prevent contamination of the repair.

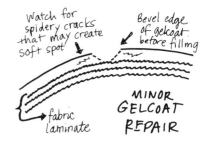

Home Color Match

If mixing your own gelcoat, it's worth the extra time to test for a good color match.

- Purchase appropriate tubes of coloring agents—having the three primary colors may be enough.
- Mix the color into clear gelcoat on a scrap of plastic (a clear coffee can lid) until you think you have a match.
- Draw off a teaspoon of gelcoat and add a minuscule drop of catalyst (which will affect the color).
- Spoon the test on a scrap of waxed paper and allow to dry. Compare to your original and make any necessary adjustments.

Filling Chips and Gouges

Chips that expose the underlying fabric should be filled to prevent water from penetrating the laminate. Gelcoat putty offers the simplest fix. Fill the void with material obtained from the hull manufacturer (for best material and color match), or with putty from an auto parts store. Cover with waxed paper, squeegee to feather the edges, and allow to cure about eight hours. Wet-sand, then use rubbing compound to finish.

You may also fill chips with liquid gelcoat applied in layers, as discussed above.

Old Screw and Hardware Holes

Holes should be filled with putty, but not gelcoat putty. For small holes that you wish to fill and cover with a cosmetic gelcoat patch, use a polyester-based fairing putty (like Bondo) to fill the gap. Bondo is not recommended for repairing large areas because of its great stiffness, although its structural properties make it suitable for filling small holes.

- Prep the area as instructed. Carefully remove any traces of sealant that may have been used to caulk the fitting.
- Isolate the repair from the rest of the hull with masking tape.
- Back the interior of the hole with masking tape.
- Use a razor knife to make one or two tiny slits in the tape. This prevents air bubbles from forming inside (which will weaken the repair).
- Slightly overfill the hole (to allow for shrinkage). Let dry.
- Once dry, sand flush to hull, taking care not to oversand the original gelcoat. Carefully create a shallow dish in the repair to allow for a liquid gelcoat patch.

Serious Gelcoat Cracks

Make sure there is no damage to the laminate (*see **Standard Fiberglass Patch, Shopside**, page 189*). Remove surrounding gelcoat all the way to laminate layer, creating a V-shaped channel with the laminate at bottom. Use the edge of a file if you don't have a grinder. Be sure to follow the crack to its terminus, or your repair is likely to fail.

Super-Thin Liquid Method

You can never be too rich or too thin. The closer the laminate fabric to the outer hull, the better. At a canoe symposium I watched Sandy Martin of Lincoln Canoes create a perfect, invisible gelcoat patch—quite a feat for a patch at least 6 inches square.

After prepping and masking the exterior area opposite a cured structural patch, Sandy got out his secret weapon: an $8 Preval sprayer from the auto parts store. He catalyzed the liquid gelcoat, then thinned the mix to a paint-like consistency with acetone to allow it to pass through the sprayer valve.

handheld sprayer for sealants, gelcoat

Sandy used short, controlled side-to-side strokes, gradually building the gelcoat surface. Short spritzes decrease the likelihood of drips—if you suffer drips, wipe off the sprayer head and shorten the length of each spray, as when painting. Once cured, wet-sand and finish with rubbing compound.

Polyethylene Hulls

Polyethylene is the plastic material used in single-wall, rotomolded kayak hulls and multi-layer rotomolded canoes. Most people buy a polyethylene boat for two reasons: low price and low maintenance. However, just because your boat can withstand being hammered on a rocky coast does *not* mean it is care-free.

If you own a polyethylene boat, how you store, transport, and protect the craft from unnecessary UV exposure can mean the difference between a 6-year hull and a 10-year hull. A basic understanding of polyethylene's properties will help you accept your plastic boat's idiosyncrasies and care requirements.

Polyethylene Primer

Your polyethylene kayak or canoe differs from Tupperware in several respects. First, it is manufactured from a high-density polyethylene designed for abrasion- and impact-resistance. The basic building block (polyethylene monomer chains) may have either a linear or cross-linked molecular structure—different schools argue for one or the other.

Cross-linked polyethylene, while more structurally durable and impact-resistant, cannot be recycled or remolded, which makes patching virtually impossible. **Linear polyethylene** can be remolded, and therefore can be patched. Various additives to either mix provide other desirable qualities: lubricants for better molding, plasticizers for increased flexibility, stabilizers for UV-protection.

It should be said that plastics technology is improving all the time, and even five years marks huge advances in the trade. So a kayak from '92 is a whole lot different from a vintage '88, and a '95 model is another animal still.

A typical **single-layer polyethylene** kayak hull is molded in a rotating form: Plastic resin or powder is poured inside the mold, which slides into a giant oven and spins like a high-speed rotisserie. The plastic melts and coats the inside of the form.

A **multi-layer polyethylene** canoe hull follows a similar procedure, except that three layers are "dumped" and melted into the form—an outer skin, a foam core for stiffening and flotation, and an inner skin.

Once all these ingredients are cooked and spun around in a vacuum, the resultant hull is allowed to cool before it's removed from the mold, outfitted, marketed, and sold as a care-free kayak. However—and this is important—like an infant, timing is everything. Some hulls are popped from their mold-womb too soon, or spanked too hard, and this inner-child stuff is recorded in the polyethylene memory bank. If your kayak seems tweaked to the left, blame it on a right-brain memory (and get yourself a rudder).

Flippancy aside, the memory of your plastic hull is an important key to performance. Heat and improper storage can seriously distort a hull, but often that initial memory can be regained with time by hanging the boat from a grab loop and letting gravity have its way.

Storage and Transport

Because plastic boats are not nearly as stiff as fiberglass, they are fabricated with thicker, heavier walls that can deform by their own weight. Consider your boat's original design when you rack or carry. Try to keep the weight off its rounded bottom as much as possible. Store upside-down on a rack with supports located under bulkheads (which provide structural integrity). If stored outside, watch any snow and ice buildup. Keeping the boat out of the hot sun is very important, lest your new boat develop a Dali-esque droop.

Likewise when cartopping: Carry the kayak on the rails (on edge), or locate rack bars and contoured cradles directly beneath bulkheads whenever possible. When one of our vehicles prohibited proper rack crossbar spacing, we made a wood "bulkhead" for transport use to protect the hull from rippling. If you don't have kayak saddles on your roof rack, carry the boat deck-side-down to eliminate the possibility of denting the bottom.

Hull rippling, or "oil-canning," makes for inefficient paddling and unnecessarily stresses the hull; if ignored, it can result in permanent deformity. If your hull is waving at you, take this as a sign. Correct by placing the boat bottom-up to face the sun for even, gentle reheating. Then press out the dents and cool the hull that way to reawaken the memory of a smooth-skinned inner child.

Hogged
Paddling around Downeast yacht harbors quickly teaches the meaning of the term "hogged," as applied to the hull of a well-used wooden craft whose keel lost her line a grandfather ago. A hogged polyethylene kayak can usually be traced directly to unmindful roof-rack practices. Hogged boats should be hung to correct the bend as shown.

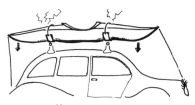

an all-too-common sight: over-zealous tying down bottom "oil-cans" as a result on poly hulls

Sun Protection

Store your polyethylene beast deck-down, out of the sun. UV is its worst enemy, so take precautions. As your boat ages (after six years a poly hull has reached maturity), it becomes ever more susceptible to impact damage, just like your grandma's hip. Regular rubdowns with 303 Protectant are vital to sustain its flexibility and resiliency.

Bends and Buckles

Any acquired wrinkles (like from broaching on a boulder in a tricky reversing falls) may be corrected with an afternoon's sunbath. If you're living in a foggy, cool region, you may have to resort to a hair dryer or heat lamp placed several feet away so the skin doesn't blister. Allow plenty of time for your plastic hull to relax from its traumatic experience.

Scars and Stripes

Smooth out your furry, battle-scarred plastic hull with a Surform planing tool, which allows you to remove peeling ridges without compromising the hull surface. A sharp metal ski scraper works great, too. Save the curls and peels for melting into patch areas later. Review any deep gouges for structural damage and possible need for patching.

Cracks and Worse

When you notice fine cracks in the hull—usually around areas where flex is greatest (beneath the seat or along unsupported sections of the hull)—it's time to retire your boat to planter duty. The plastic has deteriorated to the point that the craft is no longer safe.

It's important to realize the effects cold weather will have on an aged plastic hull—frozen, brittle boats have been known to crack and even shatter upon sharp impact (falling off a roof rack, or during a long drag across frozen territory). Older poly hulls probably should not be invited on arduous journeys.

Patching Wounded Polyethylene

Actual punctures rarely occur without high drama—a high-velocity meeting with rocks during a surf landing or unintended roofrack ejection. A puncture may appear as a deep, leaky dent or as an obvious hole. As you examine the dent, crack, or puncture, look for fragmented hairline cracks that radiate from the point of impact, as on a broken windshield. These indicate that the plastic hull has become brittle from exposure and is a candidate for early retirement.

New boats (a season or two old) suffering cracks should be referred to the manufacturer for possible warranty coverage. The manufacturer will ask you for the boat's serial number, which reveals the type and vintage of the original hull resin. The manufacturer may choose to replace the boat or supply you with a section of your exact hull material with instructions for patching.

Polyethylene Adhesives

Manufacturers struggle with this problem a lot: Find an adhesive that bonds to polyethylene yet remains elastic enough to withstand constant flexing. Caulking bulkheads is challenge enough, but sealing a leak or drilled fastener hole? For some time the most popular bet was clear silicone caulk, which produced a temporarily viable bond. Now manufacturers and outfitters commonly offer Sikaflex or Lexel polyurethane caulks for sealing jobs. Another popular adhesive recommended by those in the trade is 3M-5200 urethane.

NOTE: While there are some successes with welded patches and fillers, bonding requires heating the hull, which changes the structure of the plastic, thereby weakening it. Your repair will stop leaks, but does not restore the boat to its original integrity. You also run the risk of overheating your hull and *really* ruining the boat.

Hot Flashes

If manufacturers can't get a good bond, how can you? Sources say you can make P-Tex (ski base repair material) or resin filler stick by first flashing the surface of the hull with a torch or heat gun. This draws out and evaporates residual oils and plasticizers that inhibit adhesion. Stroke the blue tip of a torch flame across the area to be repaired as if using a paint brush. Don't melt (bubble) or blacken the surface.

If you're going to try to fill the hull with plastic, whether P-Tex, matched plastic from the boat's manufacturer, or low-density plastic (used in plastic welding), first flash the hull, then roughen the surface with a Surform plane, rasp, or piece of Dragonskin abrasive sanding sheet. Clean with alcohol, then attempt to fill.

As with ski bases, the damaged area should be prewarmed to accept molten plastic fill. Do this with a hair dryer or heat gun held several inches from the hull. The idea of preheating the hull over a fire or campstove *seems* viable, but these dirty heat sources would probably inhibit a bond.

Old Town Canoe Company offers a two-part polyurethane resin/adhesive for repairing its line of multilayer polyethylene Discovery canoes. According to tech rep Scott Phillips, this material works for filling gouges and sealing cracks once the hull has been flashed.

Pop-Rivet Patch

Occasionally, a pop-rivet patch, though somewhat ungainly, makes an effective, permanent repair. A crack in the hull should be bored or

Field Fixes for Leaky Polyethylene

Manufacturers often recommend this field fix, which combines an adhesive "primer" with the fabric structure of duct tape.
- Warm the hull if possible.
- Prep the damaged area by sanding, then purify with alcohol.
- Apply a very thin coat of marine contact cement (Sea Bond or HydroGrip) to an area slightly larger than the duct tape patch will be.
- Allow glue to dry almost completely (it should be only slightly tacky), about 5 minutes. While glue dries, cut duct tape to size, rounding the corners.

- Apply duct tape patch. If possible, warm the patch area slightly to fix bond. Burnish.

Mojo Rogers at Dagger suggests that a thin slice of absorbent minicell foam secured with duct tape is a sufficient patch for most field situations. (Even a simple duct tape job requires thorough preparation as suggested above.)

FIELD PATCH FOR CRACKED POLYETHYLENE HULL

adhesive & duct tape combination

drilled at each end to limit the fracture. Then prepare the area for a patch. (*See also* **Riveted Patch,** *page 181.*)

- Use a band of vinyl siding, a slice of your child's sled, or (best) a section of hull material obtained from the manufacturer.
- Cut the patch larger than the hole, and try to trim the edges with a knife, file, or rasp to feather the profile so the patch won't catch on rocks.
- Drill holes in crack termini as suggested above.
- Flash the hull and allow the repair area to cool.
- Apply contact cement to both boat and patch before positioning.
- Position patch on hull, then drill rivet holes.
- Rivet the patch, using washers to prevent rivets from pulling through.

Welded Patches

Plastic welding is not a recommended home repair, unless you own a plastic welder and have had plenty of chances to practice this arcane art on a trashed hull. For an interesting discussion of the craft, consult the winter 1992 *Sea Kayaker* feature by Rick Williams, a Seattle engineer who's repaired boats in this way for several years. A scattering of backyard welders around the country will also weld your kayak—with no guarantees. You'll need to do a little investigative work—start with your favorite outfitter.

Wood-and-Canvas

Artful, renewable wood-and-canvas hulls, like rawhide-laced wooden snowshoes, are often overlooked as viable craft today. Yet these boats can be resurrected, restored, rejuvenated, and revitalized to original form more completely than any other type of canoe. Your grandfather's perfectly good duck boat was probably racked in favor of a maintenance-free aluminum skiff and quickly forgotten.

Fortunately, the art of building and restoring these canoes has not died, and may even be entering a renaissance as enlightened folks seek non-petroleum-based alternatives. Today's wood-and-canvas construction is lighter than you remember, and every bit as practical as a glass hull—if you have a barn and like to putter around in it. Wood-and-canvas hulls really must be stored out of the sun and weather. *If* you can't store your historic craft indoors, at least rig a waterproof tarp to shed rain and snowload (make sure the tarp doesn't touch the hull itself).

If you plan to work on a wood-and-canvas boat of any vintage, order a copy of *The Wood & Canvas Canoe*, by Jerry Stelmok and Rollin Thurlow. This book is the best available guide to anything you'll ever need or wish to learn about wood-and-canvas hulls, including where to get materials. The book, plans, kits, supplies and advice are all available from the Northwoods Canoe Company. (*See Appendix G, page 246.*)

Many people think they must paint their canvas hull each year, but this adds unnecessary weight to the boat. Multiple paint layers are more likely to crack and chip upon impact, too. Simply touching-up dings and scratches is a better practice; Stelmok and Thurlow recommend filling deep gouges with two-part plastic auto body compound (Bondo), applied with a putty knife.

For field repairs, a scrap of canvas with ambroid glue—a liquid waterproof cement—constitutes the traditional kit. Ambroid glue is fast-drying and requires no mixing, so is ideal for field use. This is also available from Northwoods Canoe.

(*See also **Canoe Inspection**, page 201, for tips on how to keep gunwales and other wood trim in shape.*)

Chapter 18

Canoe Inspection

Our Indian said that he *used* black *spruce roots to sew canoes with, obtaining it from high lands or mountains. The St. Francis Indian thought that* white *spruce roots might be the best.*

—Henry David Thoreau, *The Maine Woods*

(*See also:* Hull Materials, *page 173.*)

Once you've taken the time to study the options, and then addressed the nature of your canoe's hull material to determine the appropriate care, your energy and attention must next be applied to the furniture—rails, seats, and thwarts—and finally the rigging and hardware. The myriad materials involved in creating your canoe's furniture require myriad specific repair approaches, whether it's sanding an aluminum gunwale or replacing a cane seat.

Gunwales

Aluminum and Vinyl Rails

Occasional sanding of any burrs in the bare metal is about all you can find to mess with on an aluminum-railed canoe. Vinyl gunwales are really vinyl-coated aluminum. Apply 303 Protectant to the vinyl when you treat the hull.

Other than that, these types of gunwales are essentially maintenance-free. If you wrap the canoe and bend the rails, however, you must replace the entire section, because they cannot be spliced. You can temporarily work the kinked section back into form, but the bend marks a structural weak place and invites material failure.

Wood Rails

Wood is usually preferred over vinyl for several reasons: Ash or spruce gunwales are aesthetic, highly resilient, surprisingly impact-resistant, and easy to repair—you can glue cracks or splice-in small sections if necessary. However, regular maintenance is important to prevent the wood from rotting, splintering, and cracking—or even from causing cracks in the hull due to shrinking of dried-out wood. A wrinkle in any laminate beneath gunwales indicates that the wood has shrunk, pressuring and deforming the layup. Oiling should restore the wood's expansion ability and correct the problem.

Gray Wood

Ash trim in particular goes gray naturally as it ages and weathers, but this does not necessarily mean the wood has deteriorated. You can test your wood rails for integrity with the point of a knife: If the point enters the grain only with effort, the wood is sound; if you can bury the point easily, then you may need to consider new rails or at least a substantial overhaul.

Splicing Wood Rails

Gunwale sections can be spliced successfully to restore your gunwales to their full strength. Obtain a compatible section of ash from our canoe manufacturer (who will also provide four pages of single-spaced instructions for the procedure). Suffice to say that if you are not a woodworker, this is a more involved process than it appears on the surface—you basically must take the entire canoe apart. While you can certainly splice-in a section of hardwood from your local lumberyard, a rail from the factory will be milled precisely to match your original. Consult your local outfitter, a wood-and-canvas guide, or your favorite canoe manufacturer for advice.

Oiling Procedure for Wood Rails

Regular applications of penetrating oil (at least once a year) will eliminate the likelihood of rotting, drying, or cracking upon impact, as well as cold cracks developing in the hull. Watco Oil, once highly recommended, has been discontinued. Deks Olje brand is the recommended replacement: It contains fungicides and soaks deep into the wood, offering a flexible, abrasion-resistant finish. Varnish is not compatible with the constant give and bend of canoe rails and soon cracks off.

- Treat small, splintering cracks or gouges to a fill session with a water-based yellow wood glue or epoxy. Clamp until cured.
- Mask-off the hull with masking tape to protect from sandpaper scratching and oil buildup. **Note:** Don't leave masking tape on the hull for more than a week or so; otherwise it will be a bear to remove the residue.
- On Royalex canoes with top-mounted decks, remove decks to gain access to the entire length of gunwales.
- Prep rails by sanding with medium sandpaper (150- to 220-grit, depending upon condition of wood). Don't use too fine a grit or you'll polish the grain hard rather than opening it to accept oil. Steel wool is not recommended because the iron residue tends to block oil, resulting in a gummy, non-penetrating finish.
- Turn the canoe upside down and sand the underside of the rails just as thoroughly as the tops (this is usually the most weathered area due to storing upside-down on racks).
- If you wish to apply stain to darken or restore the finish, apply it before applying the oil and allow to dry. Stain does *not* protect the wood as oil does, so continue with the treatment.
- Use a brush or rag to apply a generous coat of oil; make sure to get oil into screw holes, which are likely entries for rot and mildew.
- Allow the oil to sit for 10 minutes or so, then wipe off any excess not absorbed by the wood.
- Repeat this process several times, with 12 to 24 hours between each coat. With each application, less oil will be absorbed until very little penetrates at all. This means your wood is saturated and protected.
- When you've fully saturated the rails, allow to dry completely, then wet-sand with 400-grit sandpaper, using oil as the lubricating agent. Change the paper frequently and keep both rail and sandpaper wetted with oil. This gives a smooth, satiny topcoat.
- Follow procedure for any other non-varnished wood surface on your canoe.

(*For tips on maintaining varnished seats and thwarts, see also **Resurrecting a Tired Wooden Paddle**, page 217.*)

Furniture: Seats and Thwarts

In the event of a wilderness mishap, you may need to replace or back-up a broken, bent, or cracked thwart. This is an easy but essential repair since thwarts maintain much of a canoe's structural integrity. Use a section of green sapling approximately the same diameter as the original thwart.

Seats

Hanging seats bear your weight, plus terrific torquing and twisting as you pry or draw. Regular inspection of the hardware is important. Tighten bolts as needed, but also watch for cracked wooden supports. Seats are usually coated with spar varnish and need annual touchups to prevent mildew.

Sliders

Adjustable sliding bow seats flex more than regular hanging versions and should also be inspected regularly. Clean away any sand, salt, or grit, but don't lubricate the sliding rails or you'll slip back and forth constantly. If the slider moves too easily, consider drilling holes at regular intervals along the track for a stopper pin. Don't drill the hole larger than one-quarter the diameter of the track.

The Pain of Cane

Elegant cane seats can quickly degenerate into pain seats if you neglect their seasonal varnish requirements. The cane becomes brittle with exposure and either pulls from its seating or fractures with the slightest pressure from a bony derriere. Unseated cane can be worked back into the groove that holds it onto the frame and encouraged to stay there with epoxy. Don't bother trying to reweave a broken section—replace the webbing once you've punched through part of the cane.

In the field, stretch a scrap of pack cloth from your repair kit over the frame and secure with needle and thread. Woven cording will give stout support for a foam pad seat, too.

Fortunately, most modern cane seats are constructed of prewoven panels; replacement seat panels are readily available at most outfitters or from manufacturers.

I do not recommend attempting to reweave a classic cane seat, though there are many books available to illustrate the arduous task. Here is one instance where the repair does not really save costs, especially since the materials are renewable and degradable. Because caning is a traditional, skilled profession, one might heartily support its practitioners. Wood-and-canvas guru Rollin Thurlow recommends contacting the Perkins Company for thorough caning instructions, supplies, and advice (*see **Appendix G: Materials Resources**, page 246*).

For those who store their canoes outside, unscrew the cane seat panels and bring them indoors for the winter. One nice alternative to cane seats is a woven webbing seat—you can make your own on a deposed cane frame, or purchase the seat panel as you would a cane version. A webbed seat is comfortable, flexible, and more durable than cane, and looks handsome.

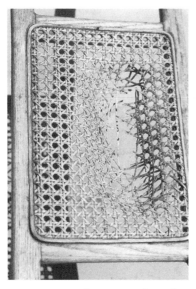

Forget it. It's best to replace the webbing once it reaches this point.

Nylon web seat is a good alternative to cane for those who store canoes outside.

Not *a roof rack!*

If you like *your canoe, space crossbars as far apart as possible to support the canoe's length.*

Rigging

Since canoe painters (bow and stern lines) are generally used as tie-downs on auto roof racks, you should inspect them regularly for friction burns and cuts from metal eyes, bumpers, and exhaust pipes. Likewise, check grab loop knots for frays.

Flotation lashing should be made with cord no stronger than 3,000-pound breaking strength—otherwise your canoe may get permanently hung up midstream by the lacing.

Other Outfitting: Lash Points, D-Rings, Saddles

As mentioned earlier, the line between outfitting and maintenance gets blurry, but remember, the wrong outfitting adhesive may lead to serious repairs. (Imagine if your thigh strap pulled out during a crucial draw . . .) Check all D-rings and other glued accessories, and be aware of the hazards of contact cement on ABS hulls (*see Evil Royalex Enemy No. 2: Careless Adhesive Use, page 174*). For rigging ABS boats, most outfitters are beginning to recommend two-part urethane adhesive, which traps less solvent in the bond.

For terrific service, knowledgeable advice, and all the outfitting accessories you could possibly imagine for any small boat, consult a whitewater shop (*see Appendix G: Resources, page 246*).

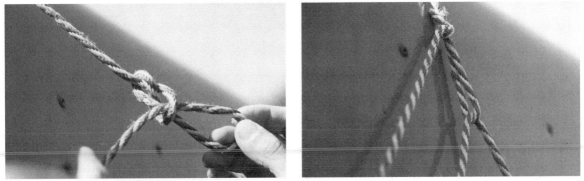

Use a trucker's hitch for solid tiedowns. (See Appendix E: Useful Knots, page 239.)

Chapter 19

Kayak Inspection

If you want a boat for the living room,
keep it in the living room.

—John Abbenhouse, Northwest Kayaks

(See also: Hull Materials, *page 173;* Rules of the Resin,
page 168; Appendix A: Adhesives, *page 225.)*

John puts it exactly right. Kayaks are designed to negotiate rugged seascapes, absorb constant wave action, and withstand pounding surf landings and drags along rocky shores. That's a lot to ask of a slim little craft, and to expect your boat to come through these trials unscathed is unrealistic, if not downright unreasonable.

Kayaks are built with a lot more parts than canoes, so naturally require more maintenance and repair awareness. On long trips with big crossings, the key to healthy performance is to check all elements for secure fit, trying to circumvent or plug any leaks before they cut into your fun factor.

In his book, *Sea Kayaking*, Derek Hutchinson tells of discovering, well out to sea, that his back hatch was filled with water. During the sandy beach launch, his boat had scraped along a broken bottle and acquired several small punctures. In this situation, he and his partners were able to perform a rescue on his boat because he had his minimum repair kit (duct tape) handy in the cockpit.

Bulkheads

Bulkheads serve two purposes: Structurally, they stiffen a hull and act as deck supports; as interior walls they seal off a section of the boat to create flotation chambers and watertight storage compartments. The best bulkheads are molded or glassed into place, but the standard for many years has been a block of minicell foam wedged and caulked into place. Periodically check the foam for mildew and give it a spritz with vinegar to kill any cooties.

Rudder Assembly

Losing control of your rudder in a following sea is more adventure than most paddlers bargain for. That's just what happened to me on a long crossing when a cable popped and the chop prohibited any attempt to fix the dang thing while afloat. Thankfully the day was fair, but the tension and effort to hold my course took their toll. After landing, I was useless for the rest of the day.

Now I am completely paranoid and futz with the rudder assem-

Cable   Swage

Carefully monitor the condition of rudder cables for smooth, safe operation.

bly before each outing. A foot-controlled rudder system, though simple, is like any machine—*expect* its moving parts to break and you'll get along fine.

Check all mounting hardware, especially if the rudder is hanging

Recaulking Foam Bulkheads

Foam bulkheads need periodic caulking to remain watertight (and to stay put in their designated place). Working inside a kayak is awkward and claustrophobic—allow plenty of time so you can take plenty of breathers, and wear gloves and a mask. Use urethane adhesive, not silicone. **Warning to family members:** People who are working wriggled up inside a kayak are apt to be cranky and demanding.

- Remove old caulk from each side of bulkhead with a sharp scraper or knife.
- Mark placement of bulkhead very clearly.
- Push bulkhead back about ½ inch (not too much, and be deliberate, especially if there are rudder cables running through the foam).
- Clean grime and slime away from around the bulkhead. You'll probably need a scratchy pad and some vinegar. Don't use CitraSolv, which contains oils that may inhibit the adhesive. Make sure you can still see the bulkhead marker.

- Use 150-grit sandpaper to prepare gluing surface. Clean with denatured alcohol; wear gloves so you don't contaminate the bonding area. Also clean the edge of the foam block with alcohol. Allow surfaces to dry completely.
- Push bulkhead back to original position.
- Begin caulking an inner bead, forcing the nozzle *underneath* the edge of the block—don't just push the gun, because you may break the nozzle. Apply outer bead immediately to the joint.
- Dip a gloved finger into a cup of cold water and tool along the bead of caulk to give a smooth, even texture. (The water keeps caulk from sticking to the glove.)
- Allow adhesive to cure completely according to the manufacturer's instructions. If you flex the hull before the glue has dried you risk ruining the bond, and you'll have to stick your head inside the hull again.

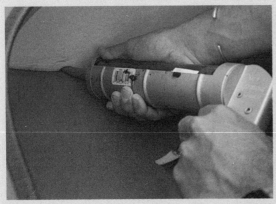

Carefully insert caulk nozzle between foam and hull to direct a bead of sealant well underneath bulkhead.

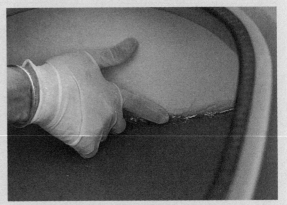

"Tool" caulk with a gloved finger dipped in cold water.

off the stern by a pin. On a long trip, bring extra bolts, spare rudder cables and plenty of cable swages, plus Vise-Grips for prying the old stuff apart and squeezing the new stuff back together. You'll also need something to cut the cable with, or make sure they're the right length before setting out.

Although you probably cannot visually examine an internal rudder cable, the most likely points of damage are where it connects with the rudder or passes with a bend through the hull. Watch for frays or corrosion in the cable and lubricate lightly with TriFlow.

Some rudders rely on nylon cord for retractors or to control the action—easy to fix, but also quick to wear out in sun and salt. Clean these lines as you would rigging: check knots, then trim and melt the frays. I was surprised to see that one otherwise solid system relied on a cheesy little plastic loop to secure the retractor, and I immediately replaced it with a stainless fixture.

Hatches

Spritz a little silicone lubricant wherever rudder cables bend or pass through fittings.

Hatches vary by design, but their job is the same: to provide access to a sealed chamber for stowing gear, and to keep water out of the chamber if the boat swamps. Most hatches have rims, or coamings, to be treated as you would a cockpit coaming. The covers may be made of neoprene, molded glass or plastic, or some combination of materials, secured either by straps or a self-locking closure. A few hatches are screw-on types, and the threads must be kept clean.

Always remove hatch covers before storage, especially neoprene covers, which rot quickly in the sun (*see **Sprayskirts**, page 212, for care*).

Some of the best, most watertight hatches ever made are rubber with a self-locking band, as on Valley Canoes. The trouble with these is that they work almost too well. If left on for extended periods dur-

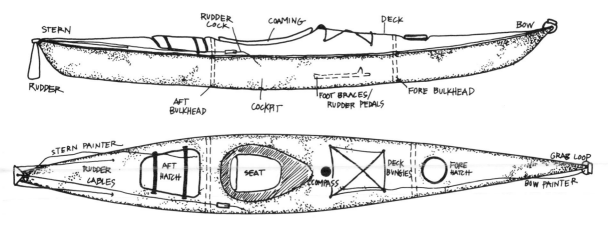

ing storage, condensation inside the chamber can cause a vacuum or vapor lock, making the covers almost impossible to remove. This situation can also occur on a summer day when warm air is trapped inside the warm hatch. Once the boat is immersed in cold water, the warm air contracts, creating vacuum-like stress on the deck, which may actually crack. One remedy for this problem is to drill a tiny hole through the bulkhead to allow air exchange. (Where it's appropriate to drill this hole is up for debate: If at the base, water will travel from your cockpit; if at the top, it's the first place to leak in a capsize. The middle seems a good compromise.)

Cockpit Coaming

On polyethylene kayaks, coaming is typically rimmed with automobile trim—vinyl-clad aluminum braid—that buffers the sharp-edged plastic. If this trim does not fit snugly, use pliers and crimp it every few inches to bend the wire core into shape.

Sometimes poly coamings don't provide much gripping surface for sprayskirts. If your skirt persists in popping off, use a rasp or piece of Dragonskin to rough up the underside of the rim slightly.

Molded fiberglass coamings are known to fail. Every time you enter and exit the cockpit you place great stress on the rim—even more if an attached seat is not sufficiently blocked (*see Hanging Seats, below*). If the rim fails while you're on the water, you lose structural integrity as well as a watertight seal. Check coaming before launching.

Normally you can fix a broken rim with duct tape to get you home and weather the season, but on a long journey you must be prepared to make a more substantial fiberglass repair. An emergency rim re-seating is probably best accomplished with quick-setting epoxy putty—bear in mind that this is a permanent fix. A poly resin repair is best made by adding filler (mat or other milled fibers) to the catalyzed mix to make peanut butter–consistency putty.

Hanging Seats

An unsupported seat is the source of much fiberglass boat angst. Examine yours carefully to see that its mounting hardware and surrounding layup are not becoming unnecessarily fatigued from the constant flexing of the boat. Even under normal use, seat mounting screws work loose and wear an elliptical hole that must be repaired. Grit trapped beneath the seat will gradually sand and grind its way through the hull.

Avoid these problems by ensuring that your hanging seat is supported with a block of minicell foam, caulked into place as recommended for bulkheads. This foam acts as a shock absorber each time you step into the boat, and it keeps debris from lodging in a vulnerable area.

Regularly tighten bolts, and on long trips bring a few bolts of the next-larger size to fill enlarged holes. Once home, drill a new hole and plug the old one with putty or a patch as needed.

Footbraces

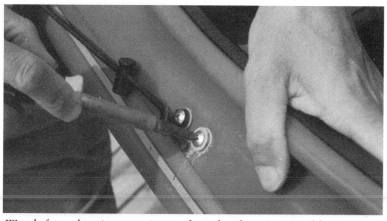

Too-tight mounting hardware may cause cracks in hull.

Too-loose screws will vibrate & create an enlarged, elliptical hole.

Due to the curved nature of a kayak hull, footbraces may abrade through the layup if not protected by a track. The track is mounted with screws at or near the waterline, and they will eventually corrode, even if they're stainless. Prevent galvanic corrosion and leaks by spacing with rubber gaskets rather than aluminum, and watch the fittings—if a corroded metal part breaks off it will be a bear to dismantle. Because the footbrace mounting hole is something you may at some point wish to fill and reposition, don't apply any lubricant containing silicone to the hardware, which will inhibit later adhesion of the fill. Plastic or rubber spacers will deteriorate and shrink, so gently tighten these fittings and replace washers as necessary.

Regularly remove footbraces and clean sand and salt out of the mounting tracks. If you have plastic footbraces and tracks, make sure they're clean and give them a coat of 303 Protectant as flexibility insurance. For aluminum, watch for reactive corrosion. If you spot any white, powdery buildup, sand with emery cloth (not steel wool), then clean with soap and water. Rub down the metal with a little TriFlow lubricant and allow to dry. This will improve the action and help prevent corrosion.

Watch for galvanic corrosion on boat hardware, caused by contact between dissimilar metals (usually steel and aluminum).

Sprayskirts

A sprayskirt's job is to provide a watertight seal around the cockpit rim. The elastic should fit snugly around the coaming.

There are two basic types of sprayskirts: coated nylon fabric and neoprene. No matter what type you opt for, the sprayskirt gets blasted by sun and salt, and must be treated like the delicate and critical garment it is. Regular rinsing with fresh water is essential.

Suspenders on a nylon skirt are not a fashion statement—they serve to tension the fabric so water won't puddle up and leak through the seams. Seamsealing may be necessary. Treat the coated nylon as you would a tent or shell garment to maintain water-repellency. (*See Fabrics & Insulations: Seamsealing, page 37, and Coating or Recoating Synthetic Weaves, page 37.*)

Neoprene skirts are by far the most effective water barrier. Unfortunately, neoprene is also one of the materials most quickly damaged by UV, so try to minimize the amount of exposure time. (Don't use your skirt as a travel or storage cover—invest in a nylon fabric cockpit cover).

A neoprene skirt will first fade and break down wherever it's stretched over the cockpit rim. The neoprene itself doesn't give any structural strength—the nylon fabric facing does. One really good way to add durability to your sprayskirt before the fabric tears (and it will), is to use McNett's Iron Mend, an iron-on nylon patch designed specifically for neoprene repairs. (*See Wetsuits and Neoprene Care, page 38.*)

Neoprene patching is a little tricky, because even the most flexible urethane adhesive becomes rigid over time and won't stretch with the fabric. If you are patching a large surface area (more than a few inches), then stretch the skirt over the cockpit before attempting to repair with an adhesive patch.

The top of your sprayskirt gets blasted by UV.

Fabric weakens where bent over

Hardware

If you're trying to track down a persistent, minor leak, check all deck hardware meticulously. With constant hull flexing, bolts regularly work loose or enlarge their holes. Tighten any bolted fittings until snug, but don't overtighten and pinch the hull material. Use plastic or rubber washers with stainless bolts—not aluminum.

If a bolt hole is leaking (likely), create a seal around the bolt with a rubber gasket or dollop of urethane adhesive caulk. Do NOT use silicone caulk, which will migrate into the laminate, rendering future adhesive repairs unreliable.

Watch around fittings to see that they're not too tight and causing hairline cracks to radiate out from the hole. If a too-loose bolt has caused the hole to become elliptical, reseat the bolt an inch away if possible, then fill or patch the old hole.

Although cheaper, lighter, and less-reflective than stainless, nylon or plastic deck fasteners are UV-sensitive and will not last as long. Expect these fittings to break, especially if they become faded or mottled in appearance, which means they've turned brittle. Preventive maintenance: 303 Protectant and covered storage.

Seams

If you've exhausted all possibilities for pinpointing a leak in your fiberglass boat, consider the seam joining hull to deck. Typically, seams are bound with a ribbon of glass cloth and are stronger than any point of the hull. Often the exterior seam will be covered with vinyl tape rather than gelcoat, and any damage or irregularities may be difficult to spot. You may have a better chance of spotting a soft spot from inside the hull with a flashlight. Otherwise, inch along the seam with your fingers, feeling for any give or ridges that may have delaminated.

A typical spot for a seam to separate is at the vulnerable bowstem of a low-volume kayak. After a few rocky landings, chips in the gelcoat open this area to water. Repair with epoxy putty or a fiberglass patch from the inside if you can (*see Standard Fiberglass Patch, Shopside, page 189*).

Deck Rigging

Deck lines soak up salt and sun just like all your other gear. When you rinse your boat, make sure you brush and rinse the deck lines, too. Every now and then, scooch the lines so sharp bends are not always wearing in the same spot.

If you find elastic rigging has stretched out, the rubber core is probably fatigued and the internal strands have become brittle. You

Trimming Bungee

Ed Stebbins at Northwest Kayaks offers his method for trimming deck bungees:
- Mark the cut with a wrap of masking tape.
- Cleanly cut the cord in the middle of the tape with very sharp diagonal cutters.
- Peel off tape.
- Pull sheath to extend around end of core.
- Use a torch or small flame to seal the sheath.
- Dip the last inch of the cord in vinyl tool dip (from the hardware store).

can buy a little more time by tightening at the knot, but expect to replace the cord soon after. The nylon sheath may be frayed at the ends or where it bends through eyelets; simply melt back any threads with a lighter. Don't attempt to burn the rubber core!

Painters

Bow and stern lines, or painters, should also be reviewed for strength, since you may rely on these for haul-offs on rocky coasts, and for cartop tiedowns.

Grab Loops

My friend Mary's bow grab loop is so flimsy looking that I just about lose sleep over it. Maybe a worn grab loop doesn't seem like some-

To Find an Elusive Leak

1. Dry off the entire boat, especially caulked bulkheads.
2. Suspend kayak with loops from rafters, trees, etc., so that you can easily adjust level from either bow or stern.
3. Pour a gallon of water into the cockpit.
4. Raise one end of the hull just slightly—an inch is plenty.
5. Observe bulkhead from opposite side as well as the exterior hull.
6. Watching carefully, turn hull from rail to rail, varying the level of the kayak to move the water around.
7. Repeat procedure with water in other compartments.
8. Mark any leaks and repair as needed.

Brad Finn, kayak guide and sauna tender, maintains his boats by hanging them in adjustable slings.

thing to worry about, but if the thing snaps when you're hefting a loaded boat over ledges, you'll be faced with a full-fledged hull repair. Also check the holes or hardware drilled for the loop for signs of fatigue or cracking. Sharp edges that might abrade the loop can be sanded or filed smooth.

Storage Tips

- If you use a rack, support kayak directly beneath the bulkheads.
- Hanging from grab loops is okay, but tends to increase hull rocker over time.
- Hot tip for storing plastic kayaks: Stand them on end, bow on ground. This is how manufacturers warehouse new boats, and so should you—if you have the headroom.
- On the side: Rack boat on edge, where sharper hull curves support the weight of a plastic hull with negligible deformation.
- Store with hatch covers off. This prevents your kayak from becoming a giant petri dish for mildew inside the hull.

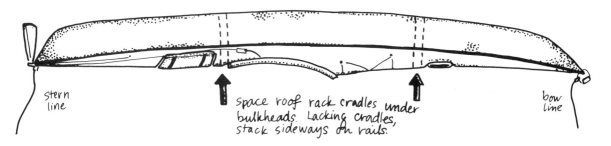

stern line

space roof rack cradles under bulkheads. Lacking cradles, stack sideways on rails.

bow line

Chapter 20

Paddles & PFDs

Frichette shook his head and spread his thick fingers apart on his knees. "There is no future for me if I cannot paddle a canoe up the big rivers any more."

—Willa Cather, *Shadows on the Rock*

Wood Paddles

Nothing beats the natural spring of a fine wood paddle, which will remain resilient for years with just seasonal varnish touchups. Varnish does two things: It protects the wood from drying from the inside out and from rotting from the outside in. But even the superhard finish of a fine marine varnish cannot withstand constant abrasion from rocky shorelines and zillions of strokes; worn spots on blade and shaft expose wood to the increasing effects of sun, salt, and water.

Unchecked moisture penetrates the grain and will soften or delaminate blades and cause further blistering of varnish (making a bigger repair job later). Regular, thin coatings of marine varnish or polyurethane are essential and easily applied. Pre- and post-season coats keep the gray at bay.

Copper tips on our dinghy oars made me realize the benefit of a protective blade sheath. Those tips are heavy, though! Use epoxy resin to clearcoat the edges of your paddle blade and waylay the inevitable furring or splitting of the end grain.

Resurrecting a Tired Wooden Paddle

- Allow the paddle to dry completely in sun.
- Sand dulled, gray, and furry endgrain to a fine, tapered finish. Start with medium (150-grit) and finish with fine (320-grit) sandpaper.
- Also sand any areas where varnish has blistered, peeled or abraded, or any stained spots. If the paddle is nearly varnish-less, remove all finish and replace with marine-grade oil (*see* **Oiling Procedure for Wood Rails**, *page 203*).
- Check T-grips for security. If at all loose, chip away glue or heat with a hair dryer to soften. Remove the grip, sand well. If you have no plans to shorten the paddle, you may as well epoxy the grip; if you want the option, use yellow wood glue, and varnish the joint well.
- Coat blade tip with protective epoxy shield.
- Correct any gouges or splits with epoxy as well.
- Allow epoxy to fully cure overnight.
- Apply several thin coats of varnish (or oil) to sanded area, finally working the topcoat over the entire paddle.
- Varnish is not normally applied to a canoe paddle grip because it can cause friction blisters; the oil from your hands lubricates bare wood to develop a fine sheen. Sand any splinters with fine sandpaper. If you wish, apply a little tung or linseed oil to the unfinished wood.

Split Blade

During a low-flowage session of "fightwater" with my husband, my favorite laminated bent-shaft paddle developed a 2-inch crack. This was easily repaired with epoxy and some careful clamping.

Paddling upriver with the repaired paddle, the blade cracked again. Duct tape made a fine field repair, and is still holding a hundred miles later.

Broken Shaft

Nine times out of 10 you'll crack the blade before damaging a shaft. Field repair of a broken paddle shaft is usually accomplished with a

Sand the end grain to a fine, tapered finish.

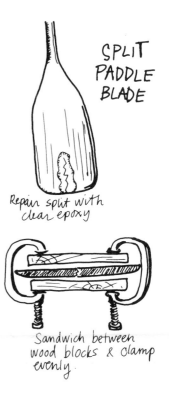

SPLIT PADDLE BLADE

Repair split with clear epoxy

Sandwich between wood blocks & clamp evenly.

section of bow line and sapling splint. If you're touring, chances are you'll have a kit with hose clamps or duct tape for a techier, sleeker splint. (*See* **Winter Gear: Poles,** *page 151.*)

Composite Paddles

Exotic composites of carbon fiber, epoxy, and various structural forms have brought us 12-ounce paddles so tough you could almost chop kindling with them. Even so, the best way to protect your composite paddle from damage is never to loan it; you alone should experience the satisfaction and chagrin of chipping, cracking, or otherwise wrecking your pricey technopaddle.

Catastrophic paddle breakage usually happens during transport—by stepping on the blade in camp, or in an unexplained, unapologized-for airline trauma. Take your paddles as carry-on luggage if possible, and use a paddle bag, even for portaging. Always secure paddles to the boat when beached, or stash them safely upright among tree limbs, out of the way of wind and tromping feet.

Paddle parks can be rigged with a utility holder from the hardware store, or with deck bungees.

While carbon-and-fiberglass blades are incredibly strong, use your noggin and don't pry with excessive torque. Digging a few clams in loose sand is one thing; levering stones is quite another.

The most likely wear your composite paddle will exhibit is along

Digging clams is OK, but don't try levering a boulder.

Plug Them Holes

blade edges and tips—points of contact with rocks, ledges, or sand. Carefully inspect the blade for furry or frayed exposed fibers. A stray fray can catch on rocks and cause a splinter that tears along the blade's length. Prevent chips and shears by coating the last half-inch of blade with a thin layer of epoxy. This will add negligible weight to your paddle and is worthwhile if you're hard on gear.

You can correct any cracks, gouges or chips in your paddle blade by treating it as you would any fiberglass boat (*see Standard Fiberglass Patch, Shopside, page 189, and Gelcoat Patching, page 192*). Maintenance is also similar, including buffing and waxing or coating with 303 Protectant as recommended for hull care.

Take-Aparts

Two-piece kayak paddles are favored for their versatility—you can adjust the feather, adapt into two canoe paddles, or break down the shaft for more manageable transport and storage. The joint is usually as simple as a molded ferrule with a spring-loaded button that snaps into correlating holes on the other section. Wood paddles rely on brass or stainless collar to fit the two pieces together.

Whatever the material, salt and fine sand build up around the joint, at times effectively gluing the sections together if left unat-

Once you've cleaned up the joint, check it for roundness; splits or fissures may be causing fit difficulty.

tended. Regularly rinse the joint with fresh water, then wipe down the fittings and hardware with silicone lubricant. If your paddle seems hopelessly stuck, try saliva at the joint. You might also let it soak in fresh water (tethered) overnight, or spritz TriFlow into joint and snap-lock. Once separated, inspect for roundness; splits or fissures may be causing fit difficulty.

PFDs

(*See also:* Fabrics & Insulations, *page 26;* Zippers, *page 13.*)

The Test

Holding up the tattered, bleached web of fabric that somehow holds an old flotation device together, I am resolutely skeptical. Yet I manage to zip the vest shut and jump into the lake with a yowl. Surprisingly, a moment later I am bobbing with nose and mouth above the water. Old Orange makes another season.

All your PFDs (personal flotation devices) should be subjected to this annual dunk test, since the sun cooks the life right out of both shell fabrics and flotation fillings. And even if you float, the fabric may be so rotted from sunny fun in the salt sea that it's ready to give up the ship.

Always rinse your PFD with fresh water after every outing. Salt water is the obvious enemy, but so are body salts from perspiration, plus other unknown contaminants found in our less-than-pristine lakes and streams. An excellent way to delay UV damage is to coat your PFD fabric with 303 Protectant at least twice a season; store it out of the sun when not in use.

Treat life vest zippers as recommended in the zippers section (*page 13*), keeping in mind that the device only works as well as its fastener.

Chapter 21

Dry Storage & Flotation

I must tie up the letters in oilcloth. That is something to do first—else they will get all sweated . . . He bound them into a neat packet, swedging down the stiff, sticky oilcloth at the corners, for his roving life had made him as methodical as an old hunter in the matter of the road.

—Rudyard Kipling, *Kim*

Flotation and dry bags are made with one of two synthetic materials: vinyl or coated nylon (usually urethane-coated). Since each type of bag is designed to be airtight and waterproof, maintenance means preserving the fabric and repair means sealing leaks.

Coated-nylon bags hold many advantages over vinyl bags. Although pricier at the outset, woven nylon fabric has more structural integrity and is less likely to puncture than vinyl. Coated fabrics don't need to be as thick as vinyl to achieve the same durability; the lighter nylon therefore folds more tightly and seals out water better than vinyl. When it comes to seams, adhesion and burst strength of urethane-coated fabrics are much greater than vinyl. Finally, nylon offers a lower friction coefficient; that means it's easier to stuff into a kayak hatch (think what it's like wearing shorts and unpeeling yourself from a vinyl car seat on a hot day).

Patching

When patching either type of bag, patch both inside and outside to ensure a watertight seal. A urethane patch alone will not be as effective as a glued fabric patch.

Whatever patch you apply, make sure the adhesive is allowed to fully cure before using the bag. Of course, duct tape is the field solution (apply tape to both sides of the puncture or tear).

Most manufacturers offer a guarantee against seam leakage. Once a welded seam springs a leak, you'll have a hard time correcting the problem. It's worth pursuing the warranty.

Dry Bag Tips

- Most damage to dry bags comes from the inside out, when a hard or pointed object inside the bag (like a tuna can, boot heel, or cracker box) concentrates abrasion in one area.
- Never store sunscreen or insect repellent containing DEET inside a dry bag (or any synthetic bag). DEET will literally melt the material.
- When opening a dry bag that's wet on the outside, avoid pouring water onto your dry gear. Open the bag so its mouth points down and allow water to run off.
- If your dry bag has a zipper, store with coil or plastic zippers completely shut; metal zippers should be stored in the open position.
- Clean and dry bags thoroughly after—or even during—each trip. (When Mary Gorman's elegant fruit salad fermented and exploded in her dry bag, the lining and contents were saturated with sticky goo.) Turn inside-out, rinse with fresh water, and sponge with a mild soap (Dr. Bronner's, Ivory Flakes) if necessary. Don't use solvents, which may damage coatings. Make sure there's no salt or sand trapped in seams or under fasteners.
- Make sure the bag is completely dry before folding and storing in a cool, dry place.
- Occasionally apply 303 Protectant to keep vinyl or coatings supple and to protect against UV.
- Don't keep your camera or other delicate gadgets in a dry bag,

which does not protect against impact (and is not usually completely watertight anyway). Condensation inside the dry bag can also cause damage to lenses or electronics. Use a hard dry box with O-ring seals.

Flotation Bag Tips

- Don't overinflate the bags, which stresses seams and coatings, making the bag more susceptible to abrasion or pinhole punctures. If you cannot depress the surface 3 or 4 inches, the bag is overinflated.
- Monitor bag pressure throughout the day. Sunlight can overheat float bags even through the deck of a kayak. Heating causes the air inside the bag to expand and can easily blow a seam. Excess pressure can also pop bags by forcing them against rough spots or protruding hull hardware.
- Release air and remove flotation bags from the boat for transporting. Not only is road grime hard on the material, but you're less likely to lose bags (basically giant balloons) along the highway.
- Rig your bags with a quick-release system so they're easier to remove for transport. Remember not to use cord stronger than 3,000-pound breaking strength for lashing, so the flotation

To Find a Leak in a Flotation or Dry Bag

Inflate the bag and close valve, or close air into empty dry bag and seal. Immerse in a tub of water and watch for telltale stream of bubbles. Another way to pinpoint leak is to spray inflated bag with mist of water and watch for bubbles on water-saturated fabric surface.

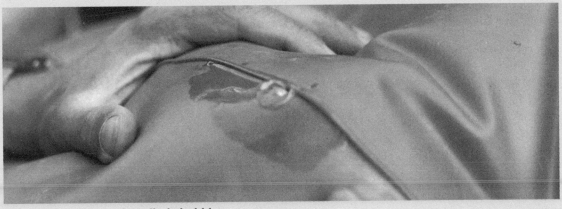

A little moisture, and a telltale bubble.

rigging is less likely to hang up your boat midstream.
- Clean with mild soap and water, but no solvents.
- Canoe flotation catches a lot more sun than kayak bags, so periodic use of 303 Protectant is a good idea.
- Flotation must be patched on the exterior, so it is especially important to use compatible adhesives. For vinyl, use VynaBond; for urethane coatings, use a urethane adhesive. As with dry bags, a fabric patch will last longer.
- If you absolutely can't find a slow leak, try a can of Fix-a-Flat, available at auto-parts stores. Fill the inflated bag and shake until the interior is well coated. This should seal any elusive pinholes. This is pretty much a last-resort solution.
- As with dry bags, most flotation is backed by a solid manufacturer warranty.

Dry Boxes

Though dry boxes are pretty simple, it's important to practice mindful use. When closing, always make sure carrying straps or other debris is not pinched in the lid or contaminating the O-ring seal. After each use, empty the box of its padding and use a water jet to clean the hinges of sand, salt and grit. If you notice the hinges or closures are stiff and hard to close, it means they're packed full of grime. If you don't irrigate these moving parts, they're likely to snap. O-rings should also be cleaned with soap and water. Use 303 Protectant or silicone to keep the O-ring supple and prevent cracking.

Appendix A

Adhesives

The Montreal Protocol

First signed in 1985, the Montreal Protocol is a treaty among developed nations that aims to reduce production of ozone-depleting chemicals. Many times expanded, ratified, amended, and sidestepped, the agreement requires participating countries to first eliminate production of chlorofluorocarbons (CFCs), then reduce halons and other chlorine-containing solvents like methyl chloroform, carbon tetrachloride and methyl bromide, all of which hasten global warming.

The response? Some of the more environmentally enlightened countries have aggressively begun essential research to create ozone-friendlier alternatives. Many big U.S. companies have yet to embrace "green" solutions and have focused on a stopgap use of hydrochlorofluorocarbons (HCFCs) to replace CFCs, which still contribute to our thinning atmosphere. Loopholes notwithstanding, HCFCs will be phased out, too, though probably not in this lifetime.

Non-developed nations, including India and China, are not bound by terms of the Montreal Protocol and use cheaper, more toxic chemicals to create foams, insulations, propellants, and other products that even-tually enter other markets as "cheap imports."

But what does the Montreal Protocol have to do with a book about outdoor gear repair?

Ask any maker of outdoor equipment and you'll hear a lot about how increased environmental regulations have decreased solvent options, particularly solvent-based adhesives, thereby affecting operations. In many cases a manufacturer would willingly switch to a less-toxic binder if there were one available.

"Until recently, nobody's really had to *try* to develop good, flexible, water-based adhesives," says Paul Hebert of Ascension Enterprises, a climbing-skin manufacturer. When his preferred adhesive was phased out of production, he was forced to switch to a highly flammable alternative. This unattractive situation in turn forced him to reconsider his manufacturing process, and he's now busy developing a heat applicator system for less-toxic and less-flammable bonds.

"The way footwear is made today, adhesives are everything" says Dave Page, a Seattle cobbler who gets his water-based glues from Germany. Since his shop runs 12 hours a day, six days a week, using solvent-based adhesives and inhaling their carcinogenic fumes would be just plain bad for business.

This gap between phasing-out solvent-based adhesives and developing environmentally friendly alternatives is beginning to touch the home user, too, as favorite standby products are quietly removed from the market. Unfortunately, most of the glues represented in this book are solvent-based, primarily because of their superior function and flexibility. Currently, the main drawbacks to water-based glues are that they're difficult to handle in cold weather and that good ones just aren't yet available to the average human. As restrictions increase, perhaps a powdered form (just add water!) will be developed.

Don't Know Much About Chemistry

Adhesives are pretty simple to understand, even for those who dozed through Chem 101. Adhesives cure in one of two ways: by evaporation of the solvent constituents, leaving the desired hardened material; or by a chemical reaction between two materials that when mixed together produce a third substance.

Set versus Cure

If you break a leg, first you set the bone, then allow time for it to heal. Adhesives work the same way: the bonded material must first set up, or harden, before it begins to cure and reach maximum strength. Even though many adhesives set up in minutes (like some epoxies), actual curing time may take days. Curing time is hugely affected by the external variables of temperature and humidity. Best adhesion occurs when there's little moisture and the ambient temperature is a consistent 55° to 70°F. Ideally, a glued repair should not be put to use until full curing has occurred.

Instant setup (as with Superglue or contact cement) is desirable if you can't clamp the two surfaces together and won't need to make adjustments. Instant setup does not necessarily mean instant cure—read the label.

Chemical versus Mechanical Bonding

Just like butlers, the best adhesive is invisible. That is, the bond created should be chemical rather than mechanical, penetrating surfaces rather than sitting on top and forming yet another layer of material. There are certainly situations where a mechanical bond is desirable; it's important to recognize the difference.

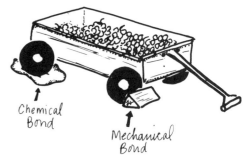

Chemical Bond

Mechanical Bond

General Glue Types

Contact Cement

Contact cement works well with foams and most plastics. Highly water-resistant, this is a favorite in the boatshop. Glue both surfaces with a thin layer and allow to sit until the material appears dry, and is tacky but not glossy. Solvent: acetone, nail polish remover. When contact cement has not fully evaporated before surfaces are joined, the leftover solvent trapped in the bond can cause damage to the original surface material. **CAUTION:** Like the name suggests, this stuff bonds upon contact—you only get *one* chance to position your repair.

Epoxy

Epoxy is a two-part structural adhesive mixed just before application. Different brands offer different viscosity and setting times. Putty-like consistency is most desirable for repairing small holes or binding nonsimilar materials because it sets up in as little as five minutes (curing overnight) to provide a bombproof, waterproof fill. Solvent: acetone while material is still soft. Epoxy is difficult to sand, so experienced users sand during the "green" phase when the material is set but not fully cured.

Hot-Melt

Normally used in special glue guns, hot glue is popular for its quick setting and curing capabilities, even though it is not nearly as strong as other types. A stick or cartridge of solid adhesive is ideal in the repair kit—melted with a candle, hot-melt glue sticks to fabric and leather, fills holes, and cures instantly. It is waterproof and fairly flexible. Solvent: acetone, nail polish remover.

Peanut Butter

P.B. is a particularly popular adhesive in the backcountry repair kit, and works well on porous surfaces like bread.

While excellent filling for belly holes, peanut butter has a long cure time and is difficult to work with in cold temperatures. Solvent: lemonade, whiskey, creek water.

Polyester Resin
This resin is activated with a small amount of liquid catalyst just before application and is normally used to bind fiberglass fabric layers to a fiberglass or Kevlar surface. Setup occurs within an hour; cure takes at least 24 hours. Hardened polyester is rigid and waterproof. Solvent: acetone while material is still soft, or Res-Away, a commercially available, more environmentally friendly alternative. Sanding is also very easy—wear a respirator mask and eye protection.

Silicone
Silicone is not really an adhesive but a sealant, producing a strictly mechanical yet waterproof bond. Removal: Hardened material can be peeled or scraped.

Superglue
Superglue and other cyanoacrylate adhesives work on nonporous materials. Superglue is very rigid, with no tensile strength or flexibility. It works well in cold weather and is water resistant. It is best suited to small repair jobs, like a stripped binding screw. Superglue sets instantly and cures in less than an hour under ideal conditions. Climbers use it on big walls to hold split fingers together, but this is not recommended. Create a Superglue filler by mixing with talcum powder (ideal for filling chips in a knife housing). Solvent: acetone, nail polish remover. Direct heat also loosens glue. **CAUTION:** Avoid use on polyethylene, and avoid contact with skin, face, or eyes.

Urethane
Urethane forms the base for the most-flexible adhesives, making this the repair material of choice for large and small fixes. Urethane rubber adhesives usually take about 24 hours to fully cure, but once hard, they are virtually indestructible. Many urethane adhesives will shrink as they dry, causing fabrics to pucker; a higher rubber-to-solvent ratio is desirable. To find out the content you'll have to contact manufacturer. Solvent: toluene, acetone while still soft. Direct heat for removal.

Vinyl
Used like contact cement, vinyl adhesive bonds PVC, vinyl, foam, and wood without clamping. Sets up in under 20 minutes; cures overnight. Solvent: methyl-ethyl-ketone (MEK). Nasty!

Vinylester
Like polyester, this is the most flexible thermoset resin used in boat layups. Due to a short shelf life and other mitigating factors, vinylester is rarely available in small quantities for home repair purposes.

Glue Rules
As Dave Page noted above, adhesives are everything to modern outdoor gear manufacture and repair, but they are usually toxic to living creatures. Many techniques in this book depend upon a successful chemical bond, from sealing seams to patching to filling gouges. No matter what material you use, the same general rules apply.

Safety Precautions
- Always work in a well-ventilated area. Generally, the toxic ingredients are heavier than air, so low-level ventilation is important (like a fan on the floor blowing away from the repair area).
- Work away from any heat source.
- Wear eye goggles and a mask to filter fumes. If you wear glasses, be aware that some solvents and adhesives can potentially alter plastic lenses and frames upon contact.
- Avoid working directly over, or with your face close to, the repair. If you're working with your head inside a kayak, come up for air every few minutes.
- Use gloves. If you do a fair amount of gluing or painting, spring for a pair of heavy-duty rubber gloves (not dishwashing or surgical gloves) for gunky jobs. For finer jobs you may want to use thinner gloves for more sensitivity (surgical type). Watch out! Thin gloves stick to many glues. Barrier creams are an option.
- Keep kids and pets away from the repair area until the adhesive has cured.
- Wash hands immediately after using any adhesive or solvent.
- Allow any unused, activated adhesives to fully harden before disposing of properly. Most community fire departments and transfer stations sponsor an annual household toxics roundup—call your town office to find out if there's one in your area.
- *NEVER* pour toxics down the drain.

Preparation Is Everything

- Remove any dirt, grease, or sticky residue with mild soap and water.
- Clean with alcohol or other solvent.
- Buff or roughen area with sandpaper, emery cloth, wire brush, beach sand, or a stone.
- Wipe again with alcohol or solvent.
- Apply adhesive.

Avoid Junk Bonds

A bad glue job is a hassle, particularly if you don't realize it until the material is hard. It's easy to create a permanent mess instead of a first-rate repair. Take every precaution and allow plenty of space and time when working with any adhesives.

- Use as little glue as possible—more is not better!
- Wait for ideal conditions before starting your repair. The two critical factors for a good bond are moderate temperature and low humidity. (If conditions are less than ideal, you can try to accelerate a cure by setting the object in direct sun or heating with a hair dryer or heat gun, using a circular motion to keep air moving.)
- After sanding large areas (as on a boat), vacuum, sweep, or wipe away any dust or shavings, then wait a few minutes before final prepping to allow airborne particles to settle.
- Carefully clean and prep the surfaces to be glued.
- After applying adhesives and joining surfaces, clean up any drips or slops with a lint-free cloth dipped in the appropriate solvent or alcohol.
- Contact cement or vinyl adhesive should be slightly tacky—not dry—to the touch. If you think your glue is too dry, swab a little of the appropriate solvent on both surfaces. Wait for the sheen to disappear, then mate.
- As you clean up the repair area, be careful not to stir up any dust that may stick to glues.

Appendix B

Low-Tox Cleaning Solutions

Is It Green to Be Clean?

Though keeping gear clean and cootie-free is the mainstay of preservation, there's no need to employ harsh chemical cleaners. Not only can these damage both natural and synthetic materials, average household cleaning products represent real environmental hazards on many levels—during manufacture, promotion, distribution, consumption, and storage—and, ultimately, during substance and container disposal.

Researchers estimate that more than 13 tons of liquid household cleaners are discharged into U.S. drains each month, not including the volume of hazardous waste discharged into septic systems or tossed into the backyard. Improper disposal stems not from malice but from ignorance. Most people simply don't realize that scouring the sink with an ammonia-based abrasive is both corrosive and toxic to creatures and ground water.

Most household paints, solvents, and cleaners affect humans and their ecosystems in one or more of the following ways:

Irritants can cause sore or inflamed tissue or mucous membranes.

Toxics can cause injury or death upon ingestion, inhalation, or absorption.

Flammables can be ignited under most temperature conditions.

Corrosives (substances or vapors) can irreversibly alter or deteriorate tissue or material at the contact site.

Home Brews

The following low-tox recipes and recommendations approximate the effectiveness of popular commercial mixes. Granted, there are times when you may resort to more potent measures, but as an everyday practice these simple solutions are easier on your health, environment, budget, and peace of mind, especially in a home with kids or pets. (Think of all the cupboard space you gain!)

Alternatives to . . .

Abrasive Cleaners—Use baking soda or borax instead. For tough spots, rub area with half a lemon dipped in borax, or presoak with citrus solvent.

Ammonia Cleaners—Substitute undiluted white vinegar in a spray bottle. My mother's personal favorite: 1 part vinegar, 1 part liquid soap, 1 part water.

Bleach Cleaners—Try ½ cup white vinegar, baking soda, or borax in the laundry. At the very least, seek out a non-chlorine bleach (basically hydrogen peroxide and water), available at natural food stores.

Disinfectants—Mix ½ cup borax with 1 gal. boiling water; try white vinegar or citrus solvent to kill mildew, pet odors, and other slimy stuff.

Metal Cleaner—For cleaning copper or brass, dissolve 1 tbsp. salt in ½ cup vinegar. Apply and allow to sit a few minutes before rubbing, rinsing and buffing.

Moth Balls—Use cedar blocks, chips, or essential oils in a pomander. Try other astringent herbal deterrents like tansy, rosemary, artemesia, lavender (also effective against fleas).

Oven Cleaner—Mix 2 tbsp. liquid Castile soap, 2 tbsp. borax, 2 cups water, and apply to desired area. Allow to set for about 30 minutes. Scrub with baking soda and salt.

Stain Remover—For greasy or oily stains, mix 1 tbsp. liquid Castile soap, 1 tbsp. glycerin (available from drugstore or natural food store), and 1 cup water. Apply to stain, work into spot, then launder or flush with water.

Stain Removal

There are two basic types of stains: protein (from food, plants, blood) and grease (from oil); to remove the stain you must use a like substance that will penetrate the material. However, the real secret to stain removal is to attack the spot as soon as possible. Don't expect to get a big glob of grease off your ski pants after storing them for the summer. Remember too, that you may scrub the material to death—sometimes it's better to accept the mark.

Protein Stains

Blood—Salt, milk, and 3 percent hydrogen peroxide are all common remedies. A commercial enzyme (as recommended for drain cleaning) is also effective (available at natural foods stores). My favorite secret weapon is a bar of seaweed soap (also from the natural foods store or kitchen shop), scrubbed directly on the stain with cool water. If the stain persists, bathe it in lemon juice and sunshine, then wash normally.

Food—For miscellaneous food stains like fruit juice, spritz with a vinegar/soap/water solution, then pour boiling water through the stretched fabric.

Grass—Try denatured alcohol or a vinegar/soap/water solution (ammonia substitute). An enzyme cleaner will also work.

Gum—Freeze the garment, then chip off the gum.

Slather remaining sticky stuff with peanut butter to remove as much as possible, then wash as usual. Peanut butter or cooking oil works well in the field.

Ink—Dab or soak in denatured alcohol, or try a short soak in citrus solvent at the recommended dilution.

Good Old Grease Stains

If the spot is fresh, dust with a little cornmeal or other absorbent material (talcum powder, cornstarch). Let it sit, then brush off and treat the grease spot with glycerin or clear glycerin soap. If the stain is persistent or has had time to set, apply citrus solvent, then rinse thoroughly before laundering. Another option is to soak in homemade oven cleaner (*described above*).

Paints and Thinners

Just about everyone knows by now that lead-based paints are bad juju, but oil-based paints are also flammable and toxic. Whenever possible, employ latex or water-based paints (which in turn contain their own hazards). Rustproof coatings are wicked, too, but as yet there are no viable alternatives. Purchase a handheld, refillable sprayer (at an auto-parts or hardware store) to reduce packaging waste.

Paint thinners and strippers are rife with acetone, esters, ketones, and other petroleum distillates—a case where the cure is worse than the disease. Use latex paint! Scrapers, heat guns, or sanders (used with a respirator mask) are the best paint-removal methods. If you use thinner, maximize it by storing used thinner in a tightly capped jar until contaminants settle out. Strain through a screen, store solid contaminants for later collection, and reuse the thinner.

Citrus Cleaners and Solvents

The best all-around alternative cleaners for household use are concentrated, citrus-based cleaners like CitraSolv, also sold as Citru-Solv-It (this and other brands are available at co-ops, auto parts, or hardware stores). Citrus solvents are made with D-limeone, a byproduct of the juice industry, instead of with petroleum distillates.

You can use varying strengths (dilute with water) of a citrus oil cleaner to penetrate and dissolve most sticky stuff like grease, tar, wax, gum, and adhesives, not to mention stains and general grime. While most citrus solvents are biodegradable and cruelty-free concoctions, they are still irritants and combustible to some degree, and are not recommended for use on silk, wool, or any styrene plastics. Contact: Citru-Solv-It, Chempoint Products, P.O. Box 2597, Danbury, CT 06813; 800-343-6588.

Harboring Household Hazards: A Few Good Rules of Thumb

Johnny was a chemist
but Johnny is no more
What he thought was H_2O
was H_2SO_4

- Keep substance in its original container.
- Store in a cool, dry place inaccessible to children or pets. A locked outbuilding is ideal.
- Keep incompatible chemical products separated.
- Periodically inspect containers for deterioration.
- Read product literature and instructions before each use, following manufacturers' recommendations.
- Use products at recommended strength, and do not mix different chemicals.

- Completely use all substances before disposing of containers. Buy what you need, or share the remainder with someone who will use it.
- Follow local disposal requirements—you may need to store spent containers for an annual toxics collection at your dump or recycling center.

air enters spout

Pour with spout at top to avoid splashing toxics.

Find Out More

Your library, town office, and local transfer station (that's p.c. for "dump") can provide you with more literature about toxics. Tell your family and friends about the alternatives highlighted here.

Environmental Hazards Management Institute, a nonprofit environmental organization, publishes unique "Waste Wheels," easy-to-use guides that help citizens and businesses identify and modify sources of toxics and waste in their daily lives. Contact: Environmental Hazards Management Institute, P.O. Box 932, Durham, NH 03824; 603-868-1496.

Appendix C

Kit Suggestions

There's a thin line between preparedness and retentiveness. If you tried to accommodate every possible emergency, you'd need a Sherpa just to carry your kit. In fact, most world travelers head confidently into the void with little more than a roll of duct tape and a Swiss Army knife. If you take exceptional care of your equipment or are of an innovative nature, the duct tape program should suffice.

However, during long, committing expeditions, cold-weather travel, or trips with large groups, you're likely to encounter many minor repairs, like a broken zipper or a clogged stove. And you'll need to be ready for catastrophes, like getting bumped by a whale or losing your sole 10 miles from the trailhead.

The following kit guidelines are culled from various resources and experiences, to be mixed and matched according to travel style.

Frita's Everyday Kit for Accruing Fabulous Favors

This is the lightweight contingency bag your author carries in her purse, engendering countless snide comments. The palm-sized packet slips into a pack or complements

other repair kits as needed. Remember Aesop's fable about the lion with the thorn in his paw? With this kit, one may accrue many favors.

- Swiss Army knife with corkscrew, screwdriver accessory, and scissors
- Old Chouinard sewing kit, including several sizes safety pins, needles, assorted thread, two buttons, heavy duty nylon thread, collapsible awl
- dental floss
- alcohol swab
- one 3-inch by 7-inch strip of self-adhesive nylon tape
- superfine nylon cord
- butane lighter (small)
- assorted rubber bands
- silk handkerchief
- box of wooden matches with several winds of duct tape wrapped around box

Essential Tent Repair Kit

Stash these items in your tent stake bag:
- large piece (about 1-foot square) of ripstop nylon cloth

- self-adhesive nylon repair tape
- alcohol swab
- pole splint wrapped with duct tape
- extra nylon cord

Stove Repair Kit

Depending on your preferred boiler, carry in your stove bag:
- jet cleaning tool
- spare jet
- scratchy cleaning pad (such as 3M Scotchbrite)
- spare O-rings
- spare pump cup
- operating instructions

Murphy's Law Backcountry Kit

Michael Jay Coe wanted to start a very small business that would fill a niche in the outdoor industry, provide a service, and remain affordable at his one-man level. After three summers as a wilderness ranger around Mount Hood, Coe saw more broken gear and heard more hikers' epic horror stories than he cared to count. *Murphy's Law Backcountry Repair Kit* is his answer to both self-employment and disaster deployment. With this 4-inch by 6-inch, 3.5-ounce kit you're completely covered. It contains 25-plus essentials, plus straightforward instructions to get you out of a jam. Commercially available at your favorite outdoor store for $14.95. Contact: Outdoor Essentials, 7276 SW Beaverton Highway, Suite 230, Portland, OR 97225; 503-233-1911.

David Goodman's Ski Repair Kit

Professional powder lunatic and backcountry luminary, David "The Doctor" Goodman is the author of *Classic Backcountry Skiing: A Guide to the Best Ski Tours in New England* (AMC Books, 1989). In his kit:
- ESSENTIAL: screwdriver (Pozi-Drive or No. 3 Phillips head)
- duct tape
- small sharpening stone
- predrilled scraper
- spare binding parts (cables, etc.)
- extra binding screws
- steel wool (for packing in binding screw holes)
- galvanized wire
- assorted hose clamps (to splint poles or skis)
- aluminum flashing or empty soda can (for splints)

- curved tent stake (for pole splint)
- small blister pack of quick-set epoxy sealed in a plastic bag
- Superglue (sticks better than epoxy in really cold conditions)
- spare pole basket
- wooden matches (for packing holes)
- small Vise-Grips
- small bungee cord
- nylon cord

Note: A multitool with adjustable heads (so you can place a No. 3 screwdriver or Pozi-Drive bit), knife, pliers, and awl is ideal for a backcountry ski kit.

Paddlers' Repair Kit

Depending on type of craft and materials, a group should have:
- duct tape, kept easily accessible in cockpit
- alcohol swab
- appropriate hull-repair material, e.g., epoxy, packaged in a resealable plastic bag with accouterments; e.g., rubber gloves, waxed paper mixing cup, squeegee or patch and rivets)
- small spool of galvanized wire
- knife with awl
- multitool, small Vise-Grips or pliers
- saw blade for wood (or hacksaw blade for metal if using a folding boat)—a "Pocket Chain Saw" is an excellent lightweight option
- 50 feet of nylon cord
- spare hardware or fittings
- rubber gaskets or one-size-larger screws to block enlarged fittings
- spare rudder cables and swages, and something to cut them with (multitool or pliers)
- tube of urethane adhesive or sealant
- large square of coated nylon
- bungee cord
- condom

Cascade Designs Therm-a-Rest Repair Kit

If you own a Therm-a-Rest or dry bag, you'll need this handy kit. Includes various pre-cut patches of compatible urethane-coated fabric, a tube of Seam Grip, and clear instructions for use. Available at your favorite outdoor store for under $5. Contact: Cascade Designs, 4000 1st Avenue South, Seattle, WA 98134; 206-583-0583.

The Ultimate Repair Kit

In the highlands of Guinea in the heart of West Africa a tent pole broke. A seemingly small matter in most places, but we were camped in suffocatingly dense sword grass with buzzing bugs blackening the air. All interstices were thick with carnivorie. To spend a night outside the tent (or with the mosquito netting flat against your body, allowing bugs to shove their proboscises through the nylon) was to wake up the next morning with malaria. But duct tape and a small aluminum sleeve put the tent right and possibly saved our lives.

In the high peaks of Tibet in the heart of Asia a stove stopped. No stove means no water, which means slow, thick blood and frostbite and hypothermia and death at altitude. Here every precious drop of water must be obtained by melting snow. A gasket in the stove's pump had to be replaced, but we didn't have a spare. With a tiny pair of scissors we fashioned a new one from a piece of leather clipped from the tongue of a hiking boot.

My grandmother used to say, "It's the little things in life that matter." In the backcountry, nothing could be more true. The backcountry is abusive; what is made in civilization will break in the wilderness. And it's always the little things that break. The only way to keep going, or sometimes simply to stay alive, is to fix those things yourself. In the wilderness you must be your own mechanic.

To do so, you need a bag of tricks. What follows are the contents of just such a bag. My bag. It's time-tested and has proved its worth on so many occasions I can't remember all the emergencies and all the continents. It weighs about 2 pounds, or 910 grams. (The weight of each item is in parentheses, for you gram counters.) And, like my grandmother used to say, "two pounds of cure are worth a ton of misadventure," or something like that.

- Spare AA batteries (2) for the flashlight (55 grams).
- Buckle, 1 inch, plastic, for ones that break on your pack (5 grams).
- Spare flashlight bulb (5 grams).
- Buttons (5), assorted sizes and colors (5 grams).
- Candle, a squatty one for melting the glue stick and ends of cord to prevent fraying when making repairs; also better than matches for fire-building in survival situations (35 grams).
- Tube of Barge Cement, a multi-purpose, heavy-duty glue strong enough to glue soles onto boots, available at shoe-repair stores (70 grams).
- Butane lighter, works better than matches (25 grams).
- Hose clamp, large enough to splint a broken frame pack (25 grams).
- Clevis pins (2) with wire rings, for external-frame pack repair (10 grams).
- Spare compass, very small, in case you lose your big one and your way at the same time (15 grams).
- Cord, 30 feet of the 2-mm thickness, for various duties like lashing pack parts together when zippers or straps fail (40 grams).
- Cordlocks, replacements for when those on your sleeping bag, pack, or jacket fail (10 grams).
- Duct tape, minimum of a half a roll of the highly adhesive, reinforced kind; uses are innumerable (60 grams).
- Glue, one stick of the heat-gun type which, when held over a candle, can be used for such things as sealing a tiny hole in a self-inflating sleeping pad, or a cracked water bottle (15 grams). You can opt for a tiny tube of Superglue.
- Mosquito netting, 5-inch by 5-inch piece, for patching holes in the tent's bug shield (5 grams).
- Paper and pencil, for emergency messages (20 grams).
- Nylon packcloth patch, 5-inch by 5-inch piece, for tent, pack or jacket repair (5 grams).
- Leather patch, 5-inch by 5-inch piece, for heavy-duty patching needs (wears better than nylon) (20 grams).
- Diaper pins (5), largest and strongest you can find (10 grams).
- Pliers, 4-inch, for zipper repair and removing teeth and stray bullets (150 grams).
- Pole sleeve, 3-inch aluminum tube that slips over broken tent poles (15 grams).
- Razor blades (2), single-edged (15 grams).
- Rubber bands, assortment, heavy gauge (15 grams).
- Sandpaper, 5-inch by 5-inch piece, medium grade (10 grams).
- Scissors, sturdy, high-quality, collapsible (40 grams). *(continued on page 235)*

(continued from page 234)

- Stove parts: filter, filter wire, plugs, stove wrench, gaskets, spare jet, and any other miscellaneous pieces your model might need (30 grams).
- Strap, 10 feet, 1-inch flat nylon with buckle, for replacing those that inevitably pop off your pack (100 grams).
- Thread, needle, and a metal thimble. Thread should be thin and waxed (or use dental floss). You'll need one large, one medium, and two leather needles (3-sided, that can penetrate thick material like leather and webbing). All should have large eyes (20 grams).
- Velcro, 5 inches of a 1-inch-wide strip with the sticky stuff on both sides, for jacket or sleeping bag repair when the zippers are shot (10 grams).
- Wire, 5 feet of high-quality braided steel, flexible and resistant to snapping (25 grams).
- Ziploc bags (5), assorted sizes (10 grams).
- Zipper heads and sliders, set each for tent, jacket, and pack zipper (20 grams).
- Small Swiss Army knife with bottle opener, blade, and screwdriver.

Carry it all in a well-stitched nylon stuffsack.

—Reprinted from *Backpacker* magazine, October 1992, with permission by author and adventurer Mark Jenkins.

Essential Miscellany

Aside from items mentioned in the above kits and throughout the book, you might wish you had:

- spare zipper slider
- extra nylon cord
- spare fasteners: hip-belt buckles, ladderlocks, and sliders in assorted widths
- spare cordlocks
- tweezers
- monofilament line
- hose clamps or Flex Clamps
- glue: Superglue or hot-glue stick
- urethane adhesive
- cork (fuel bottle cap, instant plug, good fire starter)
- alcohol swab
- butane lighter and matches
- webbing pack strap
- pair of 36-inch-long rawhide laces
- fishing swivel (fixes eyeglass hinges)
- 50-pound-test fishing leader (endlessly useful)

Zipper Rescue Kit

Any repair service will tell you that nearly a third of its income is zipper-related, and most of those jobs take about 15 minutes to fix. During his tenure in the canvas business, Mike McCabe of McCall, Idaho, realized that what most people didn't know about zippers would fill a book. Mike's superb booklet serves as a manual to his Zipper Rescue Kit, a complete zipper tackle box. The kit comes in two sizes, Basic ($12.50) or Deluxe ($25.50), and includes zipper sizes most commonly used in outdoor gear plus stops, thread and needle for home and field repair. Contact: Z.R.K. Enterprises, P.O. Box 1213, McCall, ID 83638, 208-634-4851.

Appendix D

Tools & Supplies for the Trail & Shop

Awl A punch for creating stitch holes in beefy materials, like leather or vinyl.

Bungee Elastic cord with hooked ends useful for temporary fastening; make your own from old inner tubes.

Caulk Urethane adhesive type or silicone comes in handy for filling holes or sealing joints.

C-clamp A size range of c-clamps are useful when gluing anything from boot soles to canoe rails. Vise-Grips also serve the purpose.

Chamois Ideal for cleaning optics or buffing glass boats.

Corrugator Small roller gives even distribution of adhesive or resin.

Dragonskin Cheese-grater-like sanding sheets originally designed for sheetrock; a popular sculpting tool for minicell foam blocks.

Drill Cordless is ideal for driving or removing screws, sanding, or buffing.

Fan May be required when working with flammable or toxic adhesives and resins to ventilate a space; usually placed low to blow away heavy toxic fumes.

File For sharpening skis and climbing hardware; a 10- to 12-inch mill bastard file gives best results. For field use, break the file in half to make it more compact.

mill bastard file

Flex clamp   This modern, lightweight alternative to lashing and hose clamps eliminates the need for tools, so is especially useful in the backcountry repair kit. Nylon flex clamps are reusable and don't rust. Contact: P.D.S. International, P.O. Box 381, New Milford, CT 06776

Gloves   Several types, including thin leather, heavy-duty rubber, and surgical rubber.

Grommet setter   Home users can purchase a small grommet kit, including setter, at a sewing supply or hardware store.

Hose clamps   Like the name implies, hose clamps are designed to secure auto hoses to ports; they come in zillions of sizes and adjust to fit any diameter with a screwdriver and wrench. Hose clamps are useful for splinting skis and poles of any type.

hose clamp

Inner tubes   Save old bicycle tubes for roof rack tie-downs or any job requiring elastic bungee action. For recycled straps rigged with Fastex buckles, contact: Tube Ties/Resource Revival, 2342 NW Marshall, Portland, OR 97210; 503-226-6001, 800-866-9923.

Lubricants   Various types for different tasks; i.e., silicone, dry graphite, waterproof bike grease, household oil.

Minicell foam   Super as padding, blocking, or filler—custom-shape with Dragonskin. Use as disposable applicator for adhesives, or as squeegee.

Multitool, a.k.a. Leatherman   Collapsible multitools are a pioneer's dream, with everything on a Swiss Army knife plus the torque of full-sized pliers. Definitely worth the price.

PakTowl   Cut up one of these viscose fiber camp towels to use like chamois cloth for a zillion tasks. Super-absorbent, easy to clean and dry.

Pozi-driver   An obscure but important tool for setting ski binding screws; may be purchased as a stout screwdriver or as drill bits (ask at a ski shop). A No. 3 Phillips head may be substituted.

Preval sprayer   Refillable cartridge sprayer for painting, sealing, or thin gelcoat applications.

Quick Grip   Mini clamp available at hardware or auto parts stores; like a ratcheting Vise-Grip for awkward jobs when you need an adjustable third hand.

Respirator mask   For use anytime you glue or sand to avoid inhaling fumes or particles.

Rivet gun   Basically a specialized stapler, a rivet gun saves a lot of extra dings and dents caused by hammering a rivet into position.

Safety goggles   Protect your eyes from metal, wood, or glass particles whenever filing, sanding, scraping, or cutting. Also essential safety measure when using adhesives or thermoset resins.

wear safety goggles

Scraper   The most versatile rectangular metal ski scraper gives you good control and is easily resharpened again and again. Useful for removing paint, applying wax, or smoothing a fill.

Seam sealer   Myriad uses, from filling to caulking to patching.

Sharpening stone   Palm-sized for a winter kit to smooth burrs on ski edges, and of course for sharpening.

Ski vises   Different from a regular bench vise, ski vises are sold by the pair and are designed to accommodate ski widths for efficient tuning.

Snap setter   Like a grommet setter, snap setters are usually procured as part of a kit at a sewing supply or hardware store.

Surform   A raspy file that looks like a cheese grater, this is the tool for trimming and shaping green epoxy, C4 rubber, and the like.

Sweater Stone   Square-cut pumice scrapes cooties and fuzz balls off wool and synthetic fabric. From Yarn shops or sweater boutiques. Contact: Sweater Stone, Box 467, Issaquah, WA 98027.

surform tool

Swiss Army knife   The original red essential can be all things to all people. Remember, a knife that's also a saw that's really a magnifying glass may be too cumbersome to actually carry.

Syringe   Irrigating type without needle (also used to dispense baby aspirin) is ideal for fine seamsealing work.

Tape   Duct tape, nylon repair tape, electrical tape, and white adhesive tape are all considered essentials.

Tool dip   Plastic grip material for recoating handles; useful for finishing raw edges and rope ends.

TriFlow   Penetrating lubricant with Teflon available at auto or bicycle shops.

Tweezers   A tiny precision tweezer will come in handy for stitch removal, splinter extraction, or when rebuilding watches. Use those on your Swiss Army knife or look for the superb handling pinpoint type manufactured by El Mar: 43 Cody Street, West Hartford, CT 06110.

Twist ties   Coated wire (gardener's tye), a litter nuisance cured by Ziplocs but very useful for eyeglass hinge, zipper pull, etc.

Utility knife   For cutting or trimming rubber, ABS, you name it.

utility knife

Vise-Grips   The third hand. Available in various sizes, adjustable, locking Vise-Grips are used as a clamp or pliers.

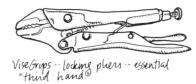

ViseGrips -- locking pliers -- essential "third hand"

Waxing iron   Usually a yard-sale score, a waxing iron is used to apply or remove waxes from ski bases, and occasionally to remove adhesives. Don't use an iron set higher than "wool" on any synthetic, or you risk altering the material. Commercial waxing irons (available at ski shops) allow you to control temperature settings more accurately.

Woodburning pencil   Useful when held in a vise to heat-seal edges of synthetic fabrics.

Appendix E

Useful Knots

Learning a few knots so well you can tie them upside down in the dark is an important aspect of repair. You may need to join two different-size lines or lash splintered parts together; with the basic knot repertoire suggested here, you're well equipped.

Bowline   Fast and super-secure, a bowline is favored for anchoring, hauling, and many other jobs because the knot is essentially slip-proof, making a fixed loop.

Clove hitch   Two stacked loops attach a line to a bar or post. A clove hitch is easily tied with one hand, is adjustable after tying, and is the start of most lashings.

Figure 8   Symmetrical and strong, the figure-8 is popular for fastening loops because it's easy to check for accuracy.

Figure 8 on a bight   One of the simplest methods to create a fastening link, an 'eight on a bight is fast and strong. Finish with an overhand knot.

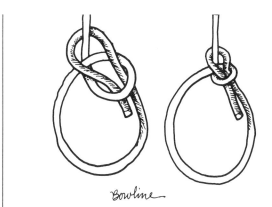

Bowline

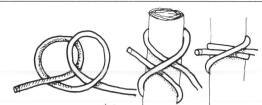

Clove hitch : 2 stacked loops

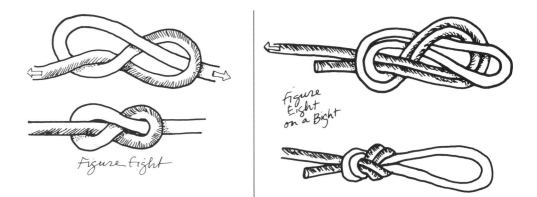

Figure Eight

Figure Eight on a Bight

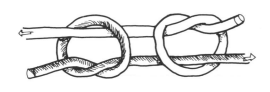

Fisherman's Knot

Fisherman's knot (grapevine)   Used to join two ropes of equal diameter, this knot is bombproof but difficult to untie. Basically formed by tying an overhand knot over another line, then repeating the step with the opposite line. A double grapevine is stronger than a single.

Lashing   Successful lashing relies on a secure start (the clove hitch) plus equal and opposite tension on the objects you are trying to lash.

Overhand knot   The simplest knot is most commonly used to finish another knot.

Sheet bend   Lines of unequal diameter are united with a sheet bend; use the larger-size line to form the bight. This is the classic jury-rigging knot and it's easy to untie.

Double Fisherman's Knot
aka a Grapevine

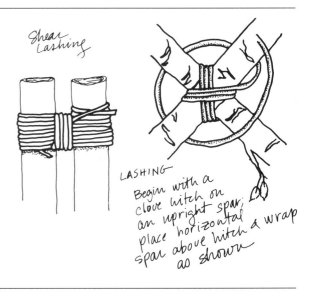

Shear Lashing

LASHING
Begin with a clove hitch on an upright spar; place horizontal spar above hitch & wrap as shown

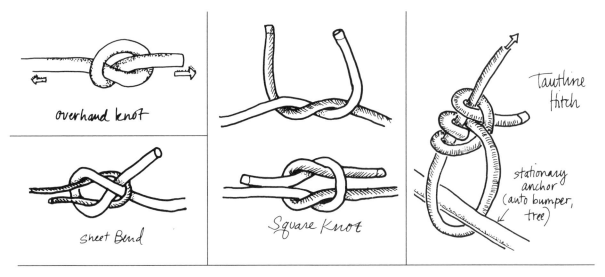

overhand knot

sheet Bend

Square Knot

Tautline Hitch

stationary anchor (auto bumper, tree)

Square knot   Join lines of equal diameter with a square knot. Be aware that this knot is a little *too* easy to untie.

Tautline hitch   Take up slack or maintain tension on a guyline with a tautline hitch; this knot works best with larger ropes (about ¼-inch diameter or greater).

Trucker's hitch   A must-know knot for roof racking, the truckers' hitch provides strong cinching power for tent guylines and boat tiedowns.

Whipping   Finish the end of a natural-fiber rope by tightly whipping with a length of string.

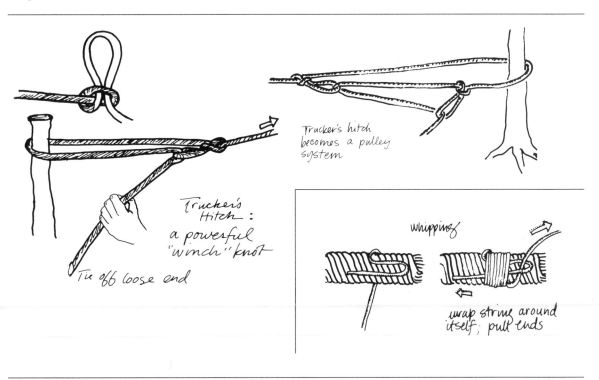

Trucker's hitch becomes a pulley system

Trucker's Hitch: a powerful "winch" knot

Tie off loose end

whipping

wrap string around itself; pull ends

Appendix F

Directory of Repair Services

There are always times when repair solutions are better left to an expert. Those listed here have long experience revitalizing worn equipment and know the ins and outs of fabric, boot, or stove construction better than anyone. Manufacturers, retailers, and consumers alike rely on the accumulated expertise of repair centers—many are actually factory-certified "outreach" clinics. For the best and most efficient service possible, it pays to follow a few simple rules of etiquette . . .

1. **Call first.** Find out the preferred method and exact location for shipping your gear, and what minimum charges and turnaround time may be. Do not expect a cost estimate over the telephone (although you can request one before any work is begun).
2. **Clean the gear prior to shipping.** Imagine the fumes in a cobbler shop with several dozen climbing boots waiting for resoles! If you do send in grungy gear, you'll be charged for cleaning—especially if you fail to remove a "temporary" duct tape patch. Remove laces from boots, check pockets, shake out tents, and detach any removable appendages.
3. **Clearly label your gear.** Provide a note with instruc-

tions or further information about the prospective repair.
4. **Send only the item to be repaired.** If a tent needs new zippers, don't send the fly and poles, too.
5. **Allow plenty of time** for repairs, or expect to pay a rush charge.

Soft Goods/Sewing Repair Services

Black's Camping – Sport Sewing Shop
Karen Abbot
100 Queen Street East
Toronto, Ontario M5C 1S6, CANADA
416-603-0744
Fabrics and notions supplier. General sewing/repair and alterations on packs, tents, bags, zippers, garments. Authorized Gore-Tex service, Suter waterproof testing, and factory-like finished repairs.

Cascade Designs
Warranty & Repair
4000 1st Avenue South
Seattle, WA 98134
206-583-0583

Warranty service on all Therm-a-Rest mattresses; field kits available.

Cyrex Accessories & Mountaineering Products
Andrew Mysyk
9 4412 Manilla Road SE
Calgary, Alberta T2G-4B7, CANADA
403-243-7086
Complete sewing repairs and cleaning of packs, garments, tents and bags, including zippers and tent poles. Custom design and modifications a specialty. Gore-Tex authorized.

Mountain Gear, Inc.
Paul Fish
2002 North Division
Spokane, WA 99207
509-325-9000/800-829-2009
General sewing and zipper repair to tents, packs, bags. Also provides general stove service and repairs to MSR and Optimus brands.

Needle Mountain Designs
Peggy Quinn & Laura Pierce
P.O. Box 3578 – 28261 Main Street
Evergreen, CO 80439
303-674-2941 / 800-795-2941
General sewing and repair of tents, bags, packs, zippers, including structural repairs, custom designs, and modifications for disabled athletes. Refilling of down bags and garments.

Rainy Pass Repair
Bob Upton
5307 Roosevelt Way NE
Seattle, WA 98105
206-523-8135/800-733-4340
Authorized Gore-Tex repair specialist. Repairs and alterations, custom sewing, down re-filling, zipper repairs, plus cleaning service. Also service on Coleman campstoves.

Ragged Mountain Equipment
P.O. Box 130/Rte 16 – 302
Intervale, NH 03845
603-356-3042
Fabrics, notions, and patterns available. General sewing and repair, plus custom packmaking. Climbing runners bartacked; also reslinging of cam units.

Seattle Fabrics
3876 Bridge Way North
Seattle, WA 98103
206-632-6022

Though not a repair service, this is fabric Mecca for outdoor enthusiasts. Fabrics, notions, patterns, accessories galore, plus sound advice. Call for listing of current inventory and prices.

Super Stitches
Terry Sheban
904 Tod Avenue
Youngstown, OH 44502
216-743-6865
Sewing and zipper repair to packs, tents, bags. No garments, please.

Stove Repair
Consult your local outfitter for parts, and ask if they'll service your stove.

A & H Enterprises
Clayton Abbot
Box 101
La Mirada, CA 90637
714-739-1788
Cleaning and repair of Optimus, Svea, Primus, Camping Gaz, Coleman campstoves. Spare parts available.

Coleman Products
Consumer Repair Information
800-835-3278
Don't expect to get through to an actual person when you call this national number. Instead, run down to your local outfitter and purchase the well-distributed replacement parts there.

Mountain Safety Research
Warranty & Repair
4225 2nd Avenue South
Seattle, WA 98134
206-624-7048/800-877-9MSR
If you simply can't work out the quirks on your stove, MSR's excellent service department can revive it.

Tent Pole Repair
Consult your local outfitter or tent manufacturer—your pole problem may be covered under warranty.

Ralph's Tent & Tarp
Ralph Powell
10253 Mississippi Blvd.
Coon Rapids, MN 55433
612-421-7053
General tent repairs including sewing, zippers and tent poles fixed or replaced. Also general sewing and zipper repairs to packs and bags.

TA Enterprises
 8212 NE 99th Circle
 Vancouver, WA 98662
 206-260-9527
Repair or replacement any tent poles using Easton aluminum tubes and accessories.

Tent Repair Services (formerly Moss Tent Repair)
 Pendra Legasse
 P.O. Box 577, 20½ Sea Street
 Camden, ME 04843
 207-236-0997
Besides waarranty repairs to Moss tents, repairs on tents, zippers, and other outdoor gear.

Boots

Most of these superb cobblers can provide you with factory-original replacement soles and several varieties of climbing rubber; just ask what brands they specialize in. Many also offer varying midsole stiffnesses for a custom fit. Not all have deep-cavity presses to rebuild molded-sole boots.

Cobbler & Cordwainer
 David Yulan
 73 Crescent Avenue
 New Rochelle, NY 10801
 914-632-8312
Resoling of hiking boots; telemark boots rebuilt, resoled; rock climbing shoes resoled. Can resole molded soles.

Dave Page, Cobbler
 3509 Evanston Avenue North
 Seattle, WA 98103
 206-632-8686/800-252-1229
Repairs and resoles for climbing, hiking, telemark boots. Besides restoring to original quality "every moutain or hiking boot sold in North America for the last 25 years," including plastic mountain boots and supergaiters, Dave Page is also the place to get your Birken-stocks or sport sandals attended to. Deep-cavity presses for molded soles.

Komito Boots
 Steve Komito
 P.O. Box 2106/235 West Riverside
 Estes Park, CO 80517
 303-586-5391/800-422-2668
General repairs and resoles of climbing, hiking, and telemark boots. Custom fitting a specialty; also conversion of leather hiking boots or old leather downhill boots to telemark.

L.L. Bean Boot Repair Center
 Casco Street
 Freeport, ME 04032
 800-341-4341
Reconditioning and rebottoming of the classic gum rubber and leather boots.

Mekan Boot
 Gary Mekan
 2070 E. 3900 South
 Salt Lake City, UT 84124
 800-657-2884
General repairs and resoles on hiking, climbing, and telemark boots. Birkenstock and sport sandal resoles. Custom boots made to order.

Morin Custom Boots & Repair
 P.O. Box 3277/1446 Miner Street
 Idaho Springs, CO 80452
 303-567-4686/800-228-BOOT
Custom boot construction plus repair and resoling to all types of boots, featuring a proprietary "Morin" midsole. Custom footbeds and orthotics fitted. Molded soles resoled.

Mountain Soles
 Bill McKinney
 P.O. Box 28
 Trout Lake, WA 98650
 509-395-2844
Call for shipping address. Climbing, mountain, and telemark repair and resoles, including leatherwork on telemark boots. Conversion of hiking/ski boots to telemark a specialty. Birkenstocks and sport sandal resoles.

Progressive Outdoor Footwear Repair
 John Southward
 8235 La Mesa Blvd
 La Mesa, CA 91941
 619-469-0567/800-783-7764
General repairs and resoles of climbing, hiking, and telemark boots; sport sandals and Birkenstocks a specialty.

Wilson's Eastside Sports
 206 N. Main Street
 Bishop, CA 93514
 619-873-7520
Full boot service: resoling rock, hiking, telemark, and double boots. Supergaiter rands rebuilt. Also pack, tent, and stove repair.

Canoes and Kayaks

Consult your manufacturer for the recommended repair resource closest to you. The manufacturer is also your best source for repair kits and parts suited to your exact hull.

Jack's Plastic Welding
Jack Kloepfer
115 South Main
Aztec, NM 87410
505-334-8748

Although Jack's is a wholesale supplier of plastic welding supplies, they do offer a kayak repair video that demonstrates the process. Additionally, they may be able to refer you to someone in your area who is experienced and equipped for welding polyethylene hulls.

Klepper Service Center – North America
Mark Eckhart
2526 South Adams
Denver, CO 80210
303-782-9743

Full repair service for Kleppers of all vintages. Replacement parts available.

*(See also **Appendix G, Materials Resources, Canoe and Kayak Outfitting and Supplies**, page 247.)*

Appendix G

Materials Resources

This listing groups suppliers of materials referenced in the text—some are manufacturers/distributors, others are mail-order retailers. Consult your nearest outfitter first and buy locally if possible (especially when purchasing adhesives, often hazardous to ship). Manufacturers or distributors may choose to refer you to a dealer in your area.

Seamsealers, Fabric Treatments, and Repair Adhesives

*(See also: **Appendix F** for purveyors of fabrics and notions)*

Kenyon Consumer Products
P.O. Box 3715
Peace Dale, RI 02883
800-537-0024
Manufacturer of the ubiquitous K-Tape nylon repair tape available at most outfitters; K-Kote seamsealer and recoating products; some waterbased formulas also available. Spray and wash-cycle fabric treatments and cleaners for down. Compact sewing kit.

McNett Corporation
1405 Fraser Street
P.O. Box 996
Bellingham, WA 98227
800-221-7325
*Superior urethane adhesive products designed for watersports but transcending to any outdoor fabrics that require waterproofing—Seam Grip, Freesole, etc. (See also: **Essential Techniques: Seamsealing and Patching**.)*

Nikwax USA
P.O. Box 1572
Everett, WA 98206
206-335-0260
Ask your local outfitter to carry these fine waterbased fabric and leather treatments. High-performance and long-wearing DWR treatments are state-of-the-industry, with formulations for leathers, cotton, down, waterproof-breathable, and coated fabrics.

Trondak, Inc.
11710 Airport Road, Suite 300
Everett, WA 98204
206-290-7530

Manufacturer of waterbased Aquaseal-brand products for cleaning, seamsealing & coating fabrics, maps, boots.

Rock Shoe Resole Kits

Five Ten
P.O. Box 1185
Redlands, CA 92373
909-798-4222
Various types of sticky rubber for do-it-yourself resoles.

Alpine and Winter Gear Resources

Ascension Enterprises
Box 159
Ridgway, CO 81432
303-626-5612
Climbing skin manufacturer provides re-gluing service and proprietary adhesive for at-home repairs. Custom tip and tail kits available. Skin regluing service using proprietary hot-melt process.

Mountain Tools
140 Calle del Oaks
Monterey, CA 93940
408-393-1000
Excellent catalog offeres top-quality mountain gear and care accessories, including boot-fitting supplies, resole kits, rope cleansers, webbing, more.

Ramer Products
1803 S. Foothills Hwy.
Boulder, CO 80403
303-499-4466
State-of-the-art backcountry ski technology includes climbing skin accessories and adhesives, plus high-tech adhesive laminate process for skins that have not seen silicone. Ask about the unique Ramer Pole Patch, ideal for any aluminum tube repair.

Stowe Canoe & Snowshoe Company
Box 207 River Road
Stowe, VT 05672
802-253-7398
Repair parts, accessories, and terrific step-by-step instructions for reweaving traditional wooden snowshoes with rawhide or neoprene lacing.

Canoe and Kayak Outfitting and Supplies

H.H. Perkins Company
10 South Bridge Street
Woodbridge, CT 06525
800-462-6600
Since 1917. Caning supplies and instructions for repairing canoe seats. Small quantities available.

Headwaters
P.O. Box 1356
Route 8, Box 204
Harriman, TN 37748
615-882-8757
Canoe and kayak outfitting supplies and accessories. Check out their E-Z UV Cure fiberglass patch kit, a wilderness tripper's dream.

Mad River Canoe
P.O. Box 610
Waitsfield, VT 05673
802-496-3127
Mad River spends about as much time educating about care and repair of their fine boats as they do designing and paddling them. Repair kits plus a full range of outfitting adhesives and supplies available, including the sometimes-hard-to-find 303 Protectant.

Nantahala Outdoor Center
41 Hwy. 19 West
Bryson City, NC 28713
800-367-3521
If you're stumped for a boat-fixing solution, chances are somebody at NOC has already been there, done that. Great catalog with full range of adhesives, foams, outfitting supplies, and ideas.

Northwoods Canoe Company
RFD #3 Box 118-A2
Dover-Foxcroft, ME 04426
207-564-3667
Home of wood-and-canvas gurus Stelmok and Thurlow. Find literature, supplies, and a l-o-o-ong waiting list for one of their signature canoes.

Northwest River Supply
2009 South Main Street
Moscow, ID 83843
800-635-5202
Another fine regional resource for watersports outfitting and repair accessories and adhesives.

OS Systems
33550 SE Santosh
Scappoose, OR 97056
503-543-3126
Drysuit seals par excellence, including proprietary adhesive and suggestions for home repair. Gasket replacement service.

Appendix H

Recommended Reading

Books

Avalanche Safety for Skiers & Climbers, by Tony Daffern (Seattle, WA: Cloudcap, 1983).

The Backpacker's Handbook, by Chris Townsend (Camden, ME: Ragged Mountain Press, 1992).

The Backpacker's Photography Handbook, by Charles Campbell (New York: Amphoto, Watson-Guptill Publications, 1994).

Canoeing Wild Rivers, 2nd ed., by Cliff Jacobson, (Merrillville, IN: ICS Books, 1989).

Classic Backcountry Skiing: A Guide to the Best Ski Tours in New England, by David Goodman (Boston, MA: AMC Books, 1989).

The Coastal Kayaker's Manual: A Complete Guide to Skills, Gear & Sea Sense, by Randel Washburne (Old Saybrook, CT: Globe Pequot, 1989).

Complete Folding Kayaker, by Ralph Diaz, (Camden, ME: Ragged Mountain Press, 1994).

Complete Wilderness Paddler, by James W. Davidson and John Rugge (New York: Random House, 1982).

Cross-Country Skiing, 3rd ed., by Ned Gillette and John Dostal (Seattle, WA: The Mountaineers, 1988).

Field Manual for the U.S. Antarctic Program, ed. Melanie Haban (Englewood, CO: Antarctic Support Associates, 1994).

Free-Heel Skiing: The Secrets of Telemark & Parallel Techniques—In All Conditions, by Paul Parker (Post Mills, VT: Chelsea Green, 1988).

The L. L. Bean Guide to the Outdoors, by William Riviere and the staff of L. L. Bean (New York: Random House, 1981).

Making the Attikamek Snowshoe, by Henri Vaillancourt (Greenville, NH: Trust for Native American Cultures & Crafts, c.1987).

Mountaineering: Freedom of the Hills, 5th ed., ed. Don Graydon (Seattle, WA: The Mountaineers, 1992).

Murphy's Law, And Other Reasons Why Things Go Wrong, by Arthur Bloch (Los Angeles, CA: Price/Stern/Sloan, 1977).

No Picnic on Mount Kenya, by Felice Benuzzi (Layton, UT: Peregrine Smith, 1989).

Outdoorsman's Fix-It Book, by Monte Burch (New York: Harper & Row, 1971).

Sea Kayaking, A Manual for Long-Distance Touring,

3rd Ed., by John Dowd (Seattle WA: University of Washington Press, 1988)

Sew & Repair Your Own Outdoor Gear, by Louise L. Sumner (Seattle, WA: The Mountaineers, 1988).

Snow and Ice Climbing, by John Barry (Seattle, WA: Cloudcap, 1987).

Sports Afield *Outdoor Skills: An Almanac with Thousands of Helpful Ideas for Better Hiking, Fishing, Camping, & Other Outdoor Activities*, by the editors of *Sports Afield* (New York: Hearst Books, 1991).

The Snowshoe Book, by William E. Osgood and Leslie J. Hurley (New York: Viking Penguin, 1983).

A Snow Walker's Companion, by Garrett and Alexandra Conover (Camden, ME: Ragged Mountain Press, 1995).

Taking Care of Outdoor Gear, by Rich Kline and the editors of Stackpole Books (Harrisburg, PA: Stackpole, 1983).

Winterwise, A Backpacker's Guide, by John M. Dunn (Lake George, NY: Adirondack Mountain Club, 1989).

The Wood & Canvas Canoe: A Complete Guide to its History, Construction, Restoration & Maintenance, by Jerry Stelmok and Rollin Thurlow (Gardiner, ME: Tilbury House, 1987).

Wood & Canvas Kayak Building, by George Putz (Camden, ME: International Marine, 1990).

Periodicals

Backpacker, 33 E. Minor Street, Emmaus, PA 18098.

Canoe & Kayak, P.O. Box 3146, Kirkland, WA 98083

Climbing, P.O. Box 339, Carbondale, CO 81623

Sea Kayaker, P.O. Box 17170, Seattle, WA 98107

Index

ABS. *See* canoes and kayaks, ABS/Royalex
acetone (solvent), 172, 174, 226–27, 230
adhesive-backed nylon repair tapes: 8–9, 36, 39–40, 51; Iron Mend, 39–40, 212
adhesives/coatings: curing and bonding, 8, 36, 67, 90, 95, 145, 226, 228; disposal, 227, 231; inhibited by silicone, 82, 155, 156, 211; safety precautions, 227; solvent- vs. water-based, 155, 225–26. *See also* ambroid glue; caulk; contact cement; epoxy; hot-melt glue; resins, thermoset; Superglue; urethane adhesives/coatings/ sealers; vinyl adhesive
air transport of outdoor gear, 73–74
alcohol, denatured, use: preparation for patching/gluing/caulking, 8,

36, 67, 90, 95, 145, 208, 228; removing stains/sticky stuff, 36, 230; solvent, 172, 174
aluminum: canoes and kayaks, 167, 179–82, 202; snowshoes and crampons, 157–58, 159–60
aluminum poles/frames, splinting and repair: folding boat frames, 184; pack frames, 74–75; pole sleeve (Ramer Pole Patch), 56, 152, 234, 247; ski poles, 152; tent poles, 56, 234
ambroid glue, 200
animals: damage to packs, 73, 74
Aquaseal (McNett): urethane adhesive, 10, 39–40, 44, 94, 97, 158, 246–47
Ascension Enterprises: Gold Label glue, 156; tip and tail kits for climbing skins, 156, 247

awls, 6–7, 90, 236

backpacking: recommended reading, 248, 249. *See also* packs
backpacks. *See* packs and luggage
baking soda, 36, 48, 229, 230
batteries: camera, 120, 124, 125, 126; disposal, 128–29; flashlight, 128–31; head-lamp, 130; lithium, 130–31; rechargeable (nicad), 129–30; solar chargers, 130; spare, 3, 234; storage, 128, 129
bear bags. *See* food bags
beeswax, uses: candles, 128–29; leather treatment, 81; zipper lubricant, 16
Bibler Tents, 23, 49
bicycle tube patch kit, 42, 67
binoculars, 119–20; alignment/focusing, 122–23; inspection and cleaning,

120–21; service/repairs, 122; storage, 122; waterlogged/ condensation, 121–22

bleach: flushing water filter, 113; low-tox alternatives (non-chlorine), 230

Blue Water Ropes, 136; rope marker, 138

boats. *See* canoes and kayaks

boots, hiking, 79–89; breaking in, 85–86; cleaning, 83, 90; custom fitting, 85–88; drying/ temperature, 79, 83–84; fabric-and-leather, 9–10, 79, 83; fabric patching, 9–10; fastenings/hardware, 87; laces/lacing, 87–88; leather, 79, 81–83, 85–86; liners and insoles, 83–84, 86; outer- soles, 86–87, 90; preventing chafe/blisters, 9, 86, 87; preventing mildew, 83–84, 85; preventive maintenance, 79, 80–84; repairs, 89–90; repair services (cobblers), 79, 90, 91, 92, 93, 96, 244; seams and seamsealing, 21, 81, 85–86, 90; storage, 84; vapor barrier liners (VBLs), 80, 84, 91; waterproofing treatments, 80–84, 85, 89

boots, rubber, 96–97; L.L. Bean, repair service, 96; repairing, 96–97

boots, telemark and ski touring, 90, 91–92; plastic, 92; repairs, 91; repair services, 244; seams and seamsealing, 21, 91; soles, 91–92; "Stein Comp" conversion, 149; storage, 92

borax, 36, 48, 60, 229, 230

buckles, 18–19; field fixes, 18, 71–72; ladderlock, 18, 71; Quik-Attach Tensionlock, 72; spares (repair kit), 72,

234, 235; types, 18–19

bungee cord, 236; alternative to (inner tubes), 236; trimming (kayak rigging), 213

buttons and buttonholes, 5, 17

cameras, 119–20; batteries, 120, 124, 125, 126; cleaning, 124, 125–26; cold-weather tips, 124–25, 126; condensation and temperature, 124–25, 223; dessicant/silica gel, 122; lens protection (filter/cap), 123, 124, 125; storage, 123, 124, 125, 126–27, 222–23

candles, 128–29, 234

canoeing: recommended reading, 248, 249

canoes, 201, 206; cartopping/ transport, 165, 176, 196, 205; gunwales/rails, main- tenance and repair, 202–03; rigging and hardware, 205; seats and thwarts, 203–04; storage, 166–67, 199. *See also* canoes and kayaks, *specific hull materials*

canoes and kayaks: adhesives, 166–67, 171; caned seats, repairs/supplies, 204, 247; D-rings, 165, 175, 205; duct tape patches, 9, 180, 184; field fixes, 170, 171, 176, 180–81, 187–88; furniture and seats, 203–04, 210–11; gunwales/coaming, 175, 202–03, 209–10; hull mate- rials compared, 166–67; pre- packaged repair kits, 169, 171, 176, 200, 247; outfitting and supplies, 166–67, 175, 205, 247; repair services, 244–45; rigging and hardware, 205, 207–09, 212–15; roof- racking/transport cautions, 165, 176, 196, 205, 220;

skid plates (grunch pads), 176–78, 186–87; UV protec- tion, 166–167, 170, 175, 185, 195, 196. *See also* canoes and kayaks, *specific hull materials*; resins, thermoset

canoes and kayaks, ABS/Royalex, 166, 173–74; adhesives/fillers, 166, 171, 174–75, 205; creases and tears, 176; delamination, 175, 176; dents, 175; gouges, 176; gunwales, 203; outfitting, 175; preventive maintenance and storage, 166, 174–75, 176, 215; quickie patch, 177; repair overview, 166, 171– 72; scratches, 175; skid plates, 176–78; structural patches, 175, 176, 178

canoes and kayaks, aluminum, 167, 179; adhesives/fillers, 167, 171, 179; creases, cracks, tears, 180–81; dents, 180; glass patch, 181; gunwales, 202; preventive maintenance and storage, 167, 179; repair overview, 167; riveted patch, 181–82; scratches, 180; setting rivets, 179–80

canoes and kayaks, fiberglass, 166, 171, 184–85; abrasion, 187; adhesives/resins/fillers, 166, 171, 186–87, 193; fiber- glass cloth, 184–85; field fixes, 187–88; filling old screw/ hardware holes, 193–94; gel- coat patching, 190, 191–94; gunwales, 202; preventive maintenance and storage, 166, 192; punctures, cracks, creases, 187–88; repair kits, 188; repair overview, 166, 169, 171–72; stem repair/ reinforcement, 185–87; structural patch (cloth-and-resin), 189–91; waxing/ protection, 192

canoes and kayaks, Kevlar, 167, 170, 171, 184–85; abrasion, 187; adhesives/resins/fillers, 167, 171, 185, 186, 193; fabric characteristics, 185; field fixes, 187–88; filling old screw and hardware holes, 193–94; gelcoat patching, 190, 191–94; gunwales, 202; preventive maintenance and storage, 167; punctures, cracks, creases, 187–88; repair kits, 188; repair overview, 167, 169, 171–72; stem repair/reinforcement, 185–87; structural patch (cloth-and-resin), 187, 189–91

canoes and kayaks, polyethylene, 166, 194–95; adhesives/fillers, 197, 198; bends and wrinkles, 196; cartopping/transport, 165, 196, 205; coamings, 210; cracks, 197; field fixes, 198; gunwales, 202; hull deformities (twists, hogging), 195, 196; patching, 197–99; plastic welding, 198, 245; preventive maintenance and storage, 194–95, 195–96, 215; repair overview, 166; scratches and gouges, 196–98; when to retire, 197

canoes and kayaks, skin-on-frame/folding (Hypalon): cleaning, 182–84; fabric patching, 9; field fixes, 183, 184; frame care, 183–84; Klepper repair services, 245; patch kits, 183; preventive maintenance and storage, 182, 183

canoes and kayaks, wood-and-canvas, 167, 171, 199–200; adhesives/fillers, 169, 171;

field fixes, 200; gunwales, 202–03; outfitting and supplies, 247; preventive maintenance and storage, 167, 199; recommended reading, 249; repair kit, 200; repair overview, 167, 199–200; seats, 247

canvas, cotton: filler (for canoes), 167, 169; mildew prevention, 167, 203

carabiners: types of, 133; inspection and maintenance, 134

carbon fiber: composite paddles, 218

Cascade Designs, 64, 233, 242–43; Slip Fix, 65; Therm-a-Rest mattresses, 9, 10, 64–69, 233, 242–43

caulk: caulking technique, foam bulkheads (kayak), 208; polyurethane, 197; silicone, 212, 236; urethane adhesive, 197, 212, 236

chemicals: disposal, 227, 231; fabric degradation, 52; ozone depletion/environmental considerations, 225–26, 225–26, 229, 231; protection from (303 Protectant treatment), 42. See also soaps and cleaners; solvents

citrus solvent/cleaner, 146, 147, 155, 182, 208, 229, 230; CitraSolv (Citru-Solv-It), 146, 147, 182, 208; Kwik Citra-Clean, 155

clamps: C-, 236; hose, 145, 157, 234; Flex, 237; Quik-Grip, 237

climbing gear, care and repair: carabiners, 133–34; crampons, 141, 157, 159–60; harnesses, 139; ice tools, 139–40; Kevlar cord, 138; rock shoes, 92–97, 244;

ropes, 135–38; SLDCs, 134–35; slings, 138

climbing skins: adhesives and solvents, 153–54, 155–56, 247; care and storage, 153–54; cleaning, 155; custom fit, 154–55; lubricants, 155; regluing service, 247; tip and tail kits, 156, 247

clothing. See outerwear

coatings. See adhesives/coatings; seam sealers; waterproof coatings/treatments

Cocoon sleeping bag liners, 59

Coe, Michael Jay (Outdoor Essentials), 233

cold-weather tips: batteries, 125, 126, 130–31; binoculars, 121–22; cameras, 124–25, 126; canoes and kayaks (winter storage), 175; glues/resins/adhesives, 150, 155, 188, 226, 227; stoves/fuel, 107–08

condensation, minimizing: in binoculars, 121–22; in cameras, 124–25, 223; in kayak cockpit, 210; in tents, 49

condoms: field uses, 162

contact cement: Barge, 90, 96, 234; cautions (ABS/Royalex), 174–75, 205; solvents for, 174, 226; uses, 90, 96, 166–67, 183, 226, 228, 234

cookware: blackening pots (to conserve fuel), 107, 109; care/cleaning, 109–10; cast-iron, 109–10; double boiler technique, 107; heat exchangers, 107; packing for air transport, 73; plaque radiant (metal spacer), 107. See also stoves, liquid fuel

cord, 20, 234. See also bungee; shock cord

cord locks, 19, 234
cotton garments/tents: care and storage, 27–28; mildew treatment, 28, 230
crampons, 141, 157, 159–60
cross-country skiing. See ski touring

D-rings, 19, 165, 175, 205
Daly, Malcolm, 139–40
darning technique, 5–6
DEET, effects of: on climbing rope, 137; on rubber, 42; on synthetic fabrics, 30, 52, 64–65, 222
dental floss, uses: thread, 5, 99, 162
dessicant/silica gel, 122, 125, 127
Dolliver, Tom (Swallow's Nest), 143
down-filled garments/bags, 33–34, 36, 58–60; care/laundering, 34, 35, 58–62; removing stitches from seams, 15, 34, 60; storage, 34, 61–62; wash-in treatments/conditioners, 34, 58, 246
drawstrings: cord locks, 19; rethreading, 8
dry bag: care, 222–23; cleaning, 222; fabrics/coatings, 221–22; patching, 222; repair kit, 233; seam leakage, 222, 223; storage, 222
dry boxes, 125, 223, 224
drysuits, 40; care, 40–42; gaskets (seals) and replacement, 41–44, 247; zippers, 16, 41
duct tape, used for repairs, ix, 9, 232, 234; beauty and perils of, 9, 66–67; chafe prevention (boots), 9, 86, 87; dry bags, 222; fabric patching, 8–9, 36, 51; hull repairs/prevention

patches, 170, 183, 184, 187, 198, 207; pack buckles, 71; packing/storage, 131, 151, 232; paddle, 217; sleds, 160; snowshoe laces, 157, 158
Durable Water Repellency (DWR), 32–34

E-Z UV Cure fiberglass patch kit, 188, 247
egg white, 36
Eken, Diana (Cascade Designs), 64
Ellis, Win, 99, 129
environmental impact/ considerations, xi–xii; adhesives/solvents, 225–26; hazard updates ("Waste Wheels"), 231; repairing/recycling gear, xi, 63; synthetic fabrics, 29–31, 225–26
environmentally friendly alternatives: sealers, 23, 24; solvents, 146, 147, 225–26, 230; stain removers, 229–30
epoxy: five-minute (Sea Goin'), 176; Marine-Tex, 186, 187; metal (aluminum)-proved, 167, 181; putty, uses, 166–67, 171, 179, 180, 181, 186, 187, 210, 226; resin/adhesive, uses, 145, 217, 219, 226; solvent for, 226; WEST System, 186
eyeglasses: antifog treatments (lens solution), 127; cautions in using solvents, 227; cleaning, 127; field fixes, 127, 162; frame adjustment, 127

fabrics. See patching techniques, fabric; seams; sewing techniques
fabrics, natural, 27, 30; cotton, 27–28; cures for pilling, 29; hemp, 29; laundering tips, 28, 29, 30, 35; silk, 28, 35;

wool, 29, 35. See also mildew; stains, preventing/removing
fabrics, synthetic, 27, 30–31; adhesives/solvents for, 10, 23, 64–65, 226–27 (see also urethane adhesives/sealers/coatings); appropriate thread for, 5; coated, 31–33; coating/recoating, 37; cures for pilling, 30–31; DEET and fabric breakdown, 30, 64–65, 137, 222; fleece (acrylic/polyester), 30–31, 36; laundering, 30–33, 35–36; nylon (taffeta, ripstop), 5, 8, 12, 31, 36, 212; packcloth, 5, 12, 22, 31, 72, 76; polyester (Thermax/Capilene), 30; polypropylene, 30, 31; recycled, 31; sources for, 242–43; stinky, cure for, 31; UV degradation, 11, 47, 51, 52, 72, 185, 220; waterproof, 31–33. See also mildew; stains, preventing/removing
fabrics, waterproof, 31–33; Gore-Tex, 32, 242; Helly-Tech, 32; laundering, 32–33; recoating, 37; sources for, 242–43; Ultrex, 32; water-repellent coatings/treatments, 28, 31–33, 35
fasteners and hardware: boot eyelets and hooks, 87; buckles, 18–19, 71–72, 234, 235; buttons, 17, 71; clevis pins/rings, 74–75, 234; cord, 20, 234; cord locks, 19, 234; D-rings, 19; grommets, 18, 74–75, 237; Quik-Attach Tensionlock, 72; reinforcement patches for, 12, 17–18; sliders, 19, 71; snaps, 17, 237; Velcro, 17, 20, 35–36, 45

fasteners and hardware, for boats, 211, 212–13; avoiding galvanic corrosion, 211; D-rings, 165, 205; filling old holes, 193–94; reseating, 213
fiberglass. *See* canoes and kayaks, fiberglass
file, mill bastard, 139, 236
fillers/putties: epoxy putty, 166–67, 171, 179, 180, 181, 186, 187, 226; gelcoat, 192–93; polyester-based fairing putty (Bondo), 193–94, 200; Superglue, 227
Finn, Brad (Indian Island Canoe Company), 187, 214
flashlights and headlamps, 119; batteries, 128–31; operating tips, 130–31; switches, 130–31
fleece garments (acrylic/polyester), 30–31, 36; cures for pilling, 30–31
flotation bags: care, 223; cleaning, 224; fabrics/coatings, 221–22; patching, 222, 224; seam leakage, 222, 223–24
foam: adhesive for, 226; closed-cell polyurethane, 63; minicell, 177, 207–08, 237; open-cell, 63–69
folding boats. *See* canoes and kayaks, skin-on-frame/folding
food bags, 73
footwear: cobblers/repair services, 79, 90, 91, 92, 93, 96, 244; evolution of, 79; orthopedic inserts, 86–87; preventing chafe/blisters, 9, 86, 87; resoling kits, 247; seamsealing, 21. *See also* boots, hiking; boots, rubber; boots, telemark/ski touring; rock shoes
fuels, for camp stoves: alcohol, 101, 108; auto gas, 102; bottled gas (butanes), 101, 108; cautions, 52, 107–08; conservation, 106–07, 108, 109; effect on coated fabrics, 52, 65; impurities/filtering, 102, 105, 106, 108, 109; kerosene, 102, 108; storage, 72, 109; temperature/insulation, 107–08; white gas (Coleman/MSR), 101, 106, 107

gaiters, 80, 91; care and repair, 44–45; prevention patches, 8; Supergaiters, 91–92, 244
gelcoat, 170, 171, 185, 186; color matching, 186, 192, 193; cracks, 191, 194; fading, 191, 192; forms and characteristics, 191, 192; patching chips and gouges, 186, 187, 190, 191–94; scratches, 191, 192; sprayer, 194; UV protection, 191, 192
gloves, protective (rubber), 27, 172, 237
gloves, shelled: seamsealing, 21, 44
glues. *See* adhesives/sealers/coatings
glycerin, 230
goggles, 127; safety, 172
Goodman, David, 150, 233
Gore-Tex garments, 32, 40; care, 32, 40–41
graphite: lubricant, 16, 184; stem reinforcement plates, 186–87
grommets, 18; replacing, 74–75; setting, 18, 237
gum, chewing: removing, 36
gum, spruce: for patching hull, 169, 170, 180, 181; removing, 36

harnesses, climbing, 139

headlamps, 130–31
Headwaters, 188, 247; E-Z UV Cure fiberglass patch kit, 188, 247
Hebert, Paul, 155–156
hemp, 29
hose clamps, 145, 157, 234, 237
hot-melt glue: solvent for, 226; use, 226, 234
Hutchinson, Derek, 207
Hypalon, 157; care and repair (folding boats), 182, 183; patching (snowshoe decking), 9, 158; patch kits, 183. *See also* canoes and kayaks, skin-on-frame/folding

ice tools, 139–40; packing, 74; sharpening, 139–40
inner tubes: recycling uses, 237
insect repellents: "alternative," 50; DEET and synthetic fabrics/fibers/coatings, 30, 50, 64–65, 137, 222
insulations. *See* down-filled garments/bags; neoprene; synthetic-filled garments/bags

jackets. *See* parkas/anoraks
Jenkins, Mark, ix, 31, 234–235

kayaks, 206–07; bulkheads and recaulking, 207, 208; cockpit coaming, 210; condensation in cockpit, 210; deck rigging, 213–15; finding leaks, 212–14; footbraces, 211; hanging seats, 210–11; hardware, 211, 212–13; hatches, 209–10, 215; rudder assembly, 207–09; seams, 213; spray-skirts, 212; storage, 209–10, 212, 215; transport, 212, 214. *See also* canoes and kayaks
kayaks, folding: recommended reading, 248

kayaks, sea: hull repairs, 190; suggested reading, 248, 249
Kenyon Consumer Products: down conditioner, 34, 246; K-Tape nylon repair tape, 36, 246. *See also* adhesive-backed nylon repair tapes
kerosene, 23, 60, 102, 108, 135, 147
Kesselheim, Alan, 176
Kevlar: fabric characteristics, 185; skid plates/stem reinforcement, 176–78, 186–87; used for structural hull patch, 175, 178, 185. *See also* canoes and kayaks, Kevlar
Kevlar cord, 138
kits, repair. *See* repair kits, prepackaged; repair/survival kits
Klepper: on preventive maintenance, 183; repair services, 245. *See also* canoes and kayaks, skin-on-frame/ folding
knives and multitools: cleaning, 115–16; filling chips in housing, 227; lockbacks, opening, 116; multitool (Leatherman), 237; Opinel, 116; rust and stains, 115–16; sheaths, 115–16; stones and sharpening, 117–18, 237; storage, 116; Swiss Army, 3, 6, 114–15, 120, 150, 162, 232, 235, 237–38; utility, 238
knots and ropework: bowline, 239; clove hitch, 157, 238, 239; figure 8, 239–40; fisherman's (grapevine), 240; lacing tips for boots, 87–88; 99, 156–57; sheet bind, 240–41; square knot, 241; tautline hitch, 241; trucker's hitch, 205, 241; whipping, 241
Komito, Steve (cobbler), 79, 91, 244

lashing, 240; pack frame, 71, 99; snowshoes, 156–57
latex: paint, 230; rubber, 169. *See also* rubber/latex
laundering methods, for outerwear/tents/bags: drycleaning, 34, 61; drying, 35; hand-washing, 35, 61; machine-washing, 35–36, 61; removing stains, 35, 36, 48, 60–61, 229–30; removing sticky stuff, 36, 60, 230. *See also* soaps and cleaners
lead, white, 169
leather, care and repair: adhesives for, 226; conditioners/ treatments for, 81–83, 92; patching (boot repairs), 89–90; sewing technique, 6, 90; snowshoe bindings, 158–59; splicing technique (rawhide snowshoe laces), 157
lemon juice, 28, 229, 230
life raft, vinyl: repair, 43
life vests. *See* PFDs
liners, for sleeping bags, 59; Cocoon, 59
L.L. Bean: gum boot repair service, 96, 244
lock-stitchers, 6–7; Speedy Stitcher, 6, 70
long underwear: silk, 28, 30
lubricants and uses, 237; beeswax, 16, 81; graphite (LocTite), 16, 184; paraffin wax, 16; silicone, 16, 42, 121, 150, 155, 158, 159, 160, 184, 209, 211, 220, 224; soap, 16; 303 Protectant, 97, 121, 174, 192, 202, 211, 224, 247; Tri-Flow (Teflon), 16, 18, 121, 135, 150, 184, 209, 211, 220, 238
Lysol: mildew remover, 28

Mad River Canoe, 175, 247; Kevlar patch kit, 176; repair

kits, 247
Martin, Sandy (Lincoln Canoes), 194
McCabe, Mike: Zipper Rescue Kit, 16, 235
McNett Corporation, glues/sealers, 10, 23–24, 246; adhesive patches, 9–10; Aquaseal, 10, 39–40, 44, 94, 97, 158, 246; Freesole, 10, 50, 91, 94, 96, 246; Iron Mend nylon adhesive tape, 39–40, 212; Sea Drops, 127; Seam Grip, 10, 25, 39, 44, 50, 64, 67, 68, 91, 246
MEK, 23, 227
metal cleaner, 230
mildew: prevention (tents, garments, mattresses, footwear), 28, 64, 72, 83–84, 85; prevention (canoes), 167, 204; removal, 28, 48
mitts/mittens: darning technique, 5–7; seamsealing, 21
MSR (Mountain Safety Research), 243; Heat Exchanger, 107; stove fuel, 101, 106; stove repairs, 243; stoves/operating tips, 101, 107;
Murphy's Law, 161, 190

nail polish remover (solvent), 36, 226–27
needles and thread, 1, 5, 99. *See also* dental floss
neoprene, care and repair: kayak hatch covers, 209; kayak sprayskirts, 212; patching, 39–40, 212; snowshoe laces/decking, 157–58; wetsuits, 38–39
Nikwax, 246; Down Proof down conditioner, 34, 58, 246; TX-Direct, 33, 246;

water-repellent treatments, 246

Northwoods Canoe Company, 200, 247

nylon (taffeta, ripstop, rope), 5, 8, 12, 31, 40; DEET and, 50, 52, 64–65, 137, 222; self-adhesive repair tape, 8–9, 36, 39–40, 51, 212; waterproof coatings, 31–32

O-rings, care and repair: dry boxes, 224; stoves, 102, 104

oil: as lubricant, 135; effect on coated fabric, 65; leather treatment, 82; mink, 82; Watco Oil (substitutes for), 203; wood treatment (canoe paddles, gunwales), 203, 217

Old Town Canoe Company: canoe repair supplies, 198

outerwear, 26; cleaning methods, 34–36; insulations, 33–34; making custom garments, 4, 248; natural-fiber, 27–29, 30; parkas and anoraks, 28, 33–34; patching, 36–37; raingear, 31–33; removing sticky stuff, 36; repair services, 242–43; seamsealing, 23, 25; synthetic-fiber, 27, 30–31; vests, 33–34, 36

packs and luggage, care and repair: buckles, 18–19; cleaning, 71, 72, 73, 76; external-frame, 74–75; fabric and coating, 72, 76; fasteners and hardware, 71–72; field fixes, 71–72, 75; food storage, 72; frames, 74–75, 99; fuel storage, 72; inspections, 70–72, 74–75; internal-frame, 70–74, 76–77; pack cover, 72; packing for air transport, 73–74; patching, 74; preventive maintenance, 16; recoating, 76; repair kit, 72, 74, 234–35; repair services/factory repairs, xi, 16, 70–71, 74, 242–43; seams and seamsealing, 16, 21, 22, 72, 76; straps/shoulder harness, 70, 71, 74–76, 77; stuff sacks, use of, 72, 73; tumpline, 77; zippers, 16, 70–71

paddles: composite, 218–20; preventive maintenance, 216–17, 218–20; repairs, 216–17, 219; take-apart, 219–20

Page, Dave, 79, 82, 95, 225

Page, Harvey, 90

paints: environmental impact, 229, 230; thinners (water- vs. oil-based), 230

PakTowl, 237

parkas/anoraks: cotton (waxing), 28; down–filled, 33–34; synthetic-filled, 34; zippers, 13, 15

patching techniques, fabric: basic tips, 12; duct tape, 8–9, 74; for heavy/multiple layers, 5–7, 74; for laminates (e.g., Gore-Tex), 5, 41; for nylon (taffeta, ripstop), 5, 8, 12; for packcloth, 5, 74; heat-sealing, 12, 76, 238; nylon tape/adhesive, 8–9, 36, 39–40, 51, 74; panel patches (large areas), 10–12; prevention/reinforcement patches, 8, 12, 51; professional approaches, 11; punctures/holes, 8–10, 72, 74, 90; sewn patches, 10–12, 52, 74; taped patches, 8–9, 36, 51, 74; tears, 8, 36; temporary (field fixes), 8–9, 36, 74; urethane adhesive patches, 9–10, 36–37. *See also* Hypalon; leather; Neoprene; plastic/vinyl/polyethylene

PFDs (personal flotation devices): test for, 220

pine tar, uses: for canoe and kayak hull repairs, 169; for touring skis (*grundvalla*), 144

pitch: removing, 36, 60; use, 1

plastic/vinyl/polyethylene, patching and repairs: adhesives for, 226–27, 228; basic tips, 12, 160; filling gouges (P-Tex candle), 146, 147, 160; mountain boots, 92; plastic welding, 147, 244–45; sleds, 160; touring skis, 147. *See also* canoes and kayaks, polyethylene

plastic welding, 147, 198, 199; service and supplies, 244–45

Pocket Chain Saw, 184, 233

poles, aluminum: pole sleeve (Ramer Pole Patch), 56, 152, 234, 247; repair services, 243; splinting, 56, 152

polyester (Thermax/Capilene) garments, 30; waterproof coating, 31–32

polyester resin: solvents/removal, 172, 227; uses, 166–67, 177, 186, 187–88, 192, 227

polyethylene/P-Tex: filling gouges (P-Tex candle), 146, 147, 160, 198. *See also* canoes and kayaks, polyethylene

polypropylene garments, 30, 31

pots, cooking. *See* cookware

Pozi-Driver/Pozi-Drive screws, 149–50, 233, 237

Preval sprayer. *See* sprayer, handheld

puttees, 44–45

putty. *See* fillers

P-Tex (plastic filler), 146, 147, 160, 198
PVC plastic: adhesive for, 227

Quinn, Peggy (Needle Mountain Designs), 9, 243

raft, vinyl: repair, 43
raingear, 31–33; fabric patching, 36–37; seams and seamsealing, 21, 22, 25; water-repellency treatments, 28, 32–33, 36–37
Ramer Products: "hot-melt" laminating process for climbing skins, 156, 247; Pole Patch, 56, 152, 247
repair kits, prepackaged: bicycle tube patch kit, 42, 67; for hull repair, 169, 171, 176, 183, 188, 247; for Hypalon, 183; for patching Therm-a-Rest, 67, 233; for resoling rock shoes, 93, 247; for snowshoes, 156–57; Murphy's Law Backcountry Repair Kit, 233; sewing, 7, 246; skid plates, 176–78; Zipper Rescue Kit, 235
repair kits, prepackaged, for canoes and kayaks, 169, 171, 176, 247; E-Z UV Cure fiberglass patch kit, 188, 247; Hypalon/raft patch, 183
repair services, directory of, 242–45
repair/survival kits: author's everyday, 232; first-aid, 3; for canoes and kayaks (hull repair), 165, 176, 180, 181, 187–88, 207, 233; for dry bags, 233; for packs, 72, 74, 234–35; for self-inflating sleeping pads, 67, 233; for stoves, 104, 233, 235; for tents, 56, 232–33, 234; for

touring skis, 144, 145, 149, 233; for zippers, 16, 235; "possibles" bag, 2–3; sewing, 7, 232, 235; ultimate, 234–35; using everyday objects, 162
resins, light (photo) curing: E-Z UV Cure patch, 188, 247
resins, thermoset, 169–72; bond compatibility, 186, 192; epoxy, 166–67, 171, 179, 180, 181, 187–88, 192, 226; gelcoat, 170, 171, 185, 186, 191–94; how they work, 170, 226; mixing/curing, 170, 171–72, 188, 226–27; polyester, 166–67, 177, 186, 187–88, 192, 227; safety precautions in using, 171–72; solvents for, 172, 227; vinylester, 171, 185, 227
Ridout, Mike (Mountain Safety Research), 101
rivets (pop-rivets): aluminum hull repair, 181–82; avalanche shovel repair, 160; polyethylene hull repair, 198–99; rivet gun, 237; setting, 179–80; sled repair, 160
rock shoes, 92–97; custom fitting, 92; home resoling/kits, 93–96, 247; repairs, 93–96; repair services, 244; soles, 92–96
roof-racking/cartopping, of canoes and kayaks, 205; cautions, 165, 176, 196, 223; tiedowns from recycled inner tubes, 237; trucker's hitch, 205, 241
rope and lines: canoe and kayak painters, 205, 214; hemp, 29. See also bungee; cord; Kevlar cord; knots and ropework; shock cord
rope sealer, vinyl: Tool Dip, 138, 213, 238

ropes, climbing: cleaning/care, 136–37; coiling, 136–37; dry, 136; marking, 138; sealer (Tool Dip), 138, 238; trimming, 138; when to retire, 135–36, 137
Royalex. See canoes and kayaks, ABS/Royalex
rubber/latex: drysuit gaskets, care and replacement, 41–44

safety gear, for home repairs: fan, 236; gloves, 237; goggles, 237; respirator mask, 237
sailmaker's palm, 6, 90
sanding: power buffers, 191, 192; wet-sanding (gelcoat), 191–92
sandpaper: Dragonskin, 198, 236, 237
saw, 233; Pocket Chain Saw, 184, 233
sea kayaks. See kayaks, sea
seams, 21; bound, 22, 72; double-needle stitched, 22; heat-sealing, 12, 22, 76, 238; lap-felled, 22, 25; machine-stitching techniques, 11–12, 22–23; mock-felled, 11; removing stitching, 5, 12, 15, 34, 51, 60; taped, 22–23, 72; unfinished/fraying (trimming/sealing), 16, 22, 76
seam sealers/coatings, 237, 246; basic tips, 24–25; silicone, 227; urethane, 23, 44, 246; water-based vs. solvent-based, 23–24
seamsealing: footgear, 21, 81, 85–86, 90, 91; mitts, 21; packs, 21, 22, 72; raingear, 21, 22, 25; syringe for, 24–25, 238; tents, 21, 22–23, 25, 49–50
sewing: making custom garments, 4, 248; repair

services, 9. *See also* patching techniques, fabric; seams; seamsealing; sewing techniques

sewing, equipment for: awls, 6, 7, 90; lock-stitchers, 7, 70; needles and thread, 1, 5; sailmaker's palm, 6, 90; sewing kits, 6–7, 232, 235;

sewing techniques: backstitching, 5; basic hand-sewing, 5–6; bar-tacking (stopper stitches), 5, 8, 12, 17; buttons/buttonholes, 5, 17; darning, 5–6; hemming (whipping), 5; lock-stitching, 7; machine sewing, 12; mock-felled seam, 11; removing stitches, 5, 12, 15, 60; rethreading drawstrings, 8; running stitch, 6; Velcro, 17, 20, 35–36, 45; webbing/pack straps, 20, 71. *See also* patching techniques, fabric; seams; seamsealing

sharpening stones, 117–18, 237

shock cord, elastic: restringing tent poles, 55

shovel, collapsible (avalanche), 160

silicone: caulk, 212, 236; cautions (poor adhesive bonds), 82, 155, 156, 184, 211; lubricant, 16, 42, 155, 158, 159, 160, 209, 220; removal, 227; waterproof treatment/sealer, 33, 53, 82, 227

silk garments, 28

ski bindings: boot pinholes, trouble with, 91; cable, 91, 150–51; field fixes, 91, 151; lubricants, 146, 150; Pozi-Drive screws, 149–50; replacing screws, 149–50; safety straps, 151; system,

151; three-pin, 150

ski poles: adjustable, 152–53; field fixes, 152; Ramer's Pole Patch, 152

ski touring: recommended reading, 248

skid plates (grunch pads), 176–78, 186–87

skins. *See* climbing skins

skis, touring, care and repair: base, preparing/restoring, 143, 144, 145, 146, 238; bindings, 149–51; camber, 143–44; climbing skins, 153–56; delamination, 145, 149; field fixes, 144, 145, 149; filling gouges, 147; metal-edged, sharpening, 145; packing, 147; pine tar (*grundvalla*), 144; poles, 152–53; repair kit, 144, 145, 149, 233; storage, 143, 144; tuning and filing, 147–49, 237; waxable polyethylene, 143; waxes and waxing, 144–45, 146–47, 238; wax-less, 143, 144–45; wooden, 143–44

sleds and pulks, 160

sleeping bags, care and repair, 33–34, 57–62; baffles and shingles, 58–59; down-filled, 5, 12, 15, 33–34, 58–62; drying methods, 58, 61–62; laundering, 34–35, 58–61; liners, 59–60; shell and lining, 59–60; stains, 60–61; storage, 34, 58, 61–62; synthetic-filled, 34, 57–62; vapor barrier liners, 59; zippers, 13, 15, 60

sleeping pads: closed-cell poly-urethane foam (Evazote, Ensolite), 63; detecting leaks, 67; fabric patching, 9, 10, 64–65, 66–69; open-cell

foam, 63–69; preventive maintenance, 64–65; recycling, 63; repair services, 242–43; self-inflating mattress (Therm-a-Rest), 9, 10, 64–69, 233; Slip Fix, 65; storage, 64, 66; valve replacement, 66

sliders, 19

Smith, Patrick, 2–3, 7

snaps, 17; snapsetting, 17, 237

snow and ice climbing: avalanche shovel, 160; crampons, 141, 157, 159–60; recommended reading, 249

snowshoeing: recommended reading, 248, 249

snowshoes, care and repair: aluminum, 157–58; bindings, 157, 158–60; crampons, 157, 159–60; field fixes, 156–57; laces/webbing, 156–57, 247; patching decking, 9; repair kits, 156–57, 247; wooden, 156–57

soaps and cleaners, 229–31; citrus cleaner, 31, 36, 65, 155, 229, 230; low-tox alternatives, 229–31; mildew remover, 28; non-detergent, 35, 48. *See also* solvents

soaps and cleaners, recommended, 35; for camera lens, 124; for climbing ropes, 136–37; for climbing skins, 155; for eyeglasses, 127; for folding boats (Hypalon), 182, 184; for footwear, 83; for kayak interior, 208; for metals, 230; for sleeping bag shells, 60; for stinky synthetics, 31; for tents, 48; for wetsuits, 39

socks: darning technique, 5–6; silk, 28

soldering iron, 22

solvents, 225–28, 229–31; acetone, 172, 174, 226–27, 230; alcohol, denatured, 8, 36, 67, 90, 95, 145, 172, 174; CitraSolv (Citru-Solv-It), 146, 147, 182, 208; citrus, 146, 147, 155, 182, 208, 229, 230; disposal, 227, 231; effect on coated synthetic fabrics, 65; environmental impact/low-tox alternatives, 146, 147, 225–26, 229–31; gasoline, 23; kerosene, 23, 60, 135, 147; Kwik Citra-Clean, 155; MEK, 23, 227; nail polish remover, 36, 226–27; paint thinner, 146, 147; Res-Away, 227; toluene, 23–24, 227; which to use (glue types) 226–27

sprayer, handheld, Preval, 194, 237; for coating/recoating synthetic fabrics, 37, 76; for painting/sealing/gelcoating, 194, 230

spring-loaded camming devices (SLDCs), 134–35

squeegee: minicell foam, 177

stains, preventing/removing, 229–30; clothing, 35–36; packs, 72; sleeping bags, 35–36, 60–61; tents, 48

Stelmok, Jerry, 199–200, 247

stoves, liquid fuel: alcohol, 101, 108; anatomy of, 102–03; bottled gas (butanes), 101, 108; cleaning/maintenance, 103–05; cold-weather/high altitude operation, 107–08; fuel cautions, 52, 107–08; fuel conservation, 106–07, 108, 109; fuel impurities/filtering, 102, 105, 106, 108, 109; heat exchangers, 107; leaks, checking for, 105, 106, 108; multifuel, 101–02;

packing up/storage, 109; priming, 103, 105, 106; repair kit, 104, 233, 235; repair services, 243; simmering hints, 107; troubleshooting/repairs, 104–06, 234; windscreens, 106, 108; white gas (Coleman/MSR), 101, 106, 107

stuff sacks, 72

sunscreens: damage to coated fabrics, 65

Supergaiters, 91–92; repair service, 244

Superglue: solvent/removal, 227; use, 150, 226

Surform planing tool, 94, 171, 196–97, 198, 237

Sutherland, Audrey, 162–63

Sweater Stone, 29, 30–31, 237

Swiss Army knife, 3, 6, 114–15, 120, 150, 232, 235, 237–38; cleaning, 115, 162

synthetic-filled garments/bags (fiberfill): care/laundering, 34, 58–62

syringe, 24–25, 238; use: seamsealing, 24–25

tapes, repair. See adhesive-backed nylon repair tape; duct tape

Teflon: coating, 136; Fabric Protector, 33; lubricant, 135

tents, care and repair: cleaning, 48–49; cooking in vestibule, 107–08; fabric patching, 9, 11, 51–52; groundcloth, 48, 49; leaks/condensation, 49; mildew, 27–28, 48, 52; mosquito netting care and repair, 9, 11, 50–51, 234; pitching/siting, 47, 48, 49, 57, 241; poles, 53–56, 73, 234, 243; preventive maintenance, 8, 28, 46–48,

50–51; recoating, 52–53; repair kit, 56, 232–33, 234; repair services, 242–43; seams and seamsealing, 21, 22–23, 25, 49–50; stakes and guylines, 56–57, 241; storage, 28, 47–48; taped repairs, 51; UV degradation/protection, 11, 47, 51, 52; waxing (cotton canvas), 28; zippers, 14–15

Therm-a-Rest, self-inflated sleeping pad: inflating/deflating, 66; patching/field fixes, 9, 10, 66–68; preventive maintenance, 64–65; repair kit, 67, 233, 242–43; repair services, 242–43; valve replacement, 65

Thurlow, Rollin, 199–200, 247

toluene, 23–24, 227

Townsend, Chris, 105

Trondak, Inc., 246–47. See also Aquaseal

Tubbs: snowshoe repair kits, 157

tumpline, 77

tweezers, 238

twist ties, 238

Upton, Bob (Rainy Pass Repair), 10, 34, 243

urethane (polyurethane) adhesives/sealers/coatings, uses, 10, 23, 39–40, 43–44, 65, 89–90, 95, 182–83, 224, 227, 246; Aquaseal, 10, 39–40, 44, 94, 97, 158; Freesole, 10, 50, 67, 91, 94, 96, 246; Seam Grip, 10, 25, 39, 44, 50, 64, 67, 68, 91, 246; Shoo Goo, 67; solvents for/removal, 67, 227; Sta-Bond, 43; Urebond, 64. See also urethane adhesive caulk; urethane structural adhesive;

waterproof treatments/ coatings

urethane structural adhesive (hull repairs), 166, 167, 175; 3M 3552, 175; urethane adhesive caulk, 166–67, 182

UV damage/protection: canoe and kayak hulls, 166, 167, 174, 182, 183, 196, 202; climbing ropes, 136, 137; gelcoat, 185; kayak spray-skirts, 212; neoprene, 212; packs, 72; PFDs, 220; tents, 11, 47, 51, 52; 303 Protectant, 42, 47, 166, 167, 174, 182–83, 192, 196, 202, 247

Valley Canoes, 209

vapor barrier liners (VBLs), 59, 80, 84, 91

varnish/varnishing, 183, 216–17

Velcro, 17, 20, 45; laundering tips, 35–36

vests, down, 33–34, 36

vinegar, white, 31, 36, 60, 65, 182, 229, 230

vinyl: adhesive for, 166–67, 175, 224, 227, 228; gunwales, care of, 202; raft repair, 43

vinyl adhesive: solvent for, 227; Tool Dip rope sealer, 138, 213, 238; use, 166–67, 227, 228; Vynabond, 166–67, 175, 224

vinylester resin, 171, 185, 227

Vise-Grips, 54, 238

Vynabond, 166–67, 175

Washburne, Randel, 188

water bag bladder: wine bladder as, 162

water filters: bleach flush, 113; care/maintenance, 113; operating tips, 112

Water Pik: used for cleaning knife, stove, etc., 162

waterproof coatings/conditioners, for down, 34

waterproof coatings/treatments, for fabrics/fibers: Aquaseal (Trondak) Poly Coat, 37; finish spray, 53; fluoropolymers, 32–33; Kenyon Recoat 3, 37; liquid polymer, 37, 52–53; Nikwax TX-Direct, 33; polyurethane, 32; recoating synthetic weaves, 37, 52–53, 76; Scotchguard, 33, 36; silicone spray, 33, 53; Teflon, 33, 136; tent wax (cotton canvas), 28; Thompson's Water Seal, 37, 53, 76, 183; urethane, 31–32. See also adhesives/ coatings; seam sealers

waterproof coatings/treatments, for footwear, 80–84; cautions, 82; grease, 81–82; liquid polymer coatings, 82–83; oils, 82; silicone, 82; waxes, 81, 82

wax: beeswax, 16, 81; paraffin, 16, 155; removing from fabric, 36, 147; used as fabric coating, 28; used as lubricant, 16, 81, 155; used on boat hulls, 166, 192

wax, for touring skis, 144–45, 146–47; Maxi-Glide, 144–45; solvents/removal, 146, 147

webbing, nylon: canoe seats,

204; fasteners for (buckles, sliders, D-rings), 18–19, 71–72; flat, 20; patching/ reinforcing loops, 12, **52**, 71; tubular, 20

wetsuits, 38–40; care, 39; patching, 9, 10, 39–40; prevention patches, 39–40; zippers, 16

winter gear, care and repair, 142–60. See also cold-weather tips

wood, maintenance and repair: canoes, 167, 199–200, 202–03; oil treatment, 202–03; paddles, 216–17; snowshoe frames, 156–57, 158–59; varnishing, 183, 204, 216–17; wood-framed folding boat, 183–84

woodburning pencil, 22, 238

wool garments: boiled, 29; care, 29; cure for pilling, 29; moth protection, 230

zippers: dry bags, 222; laundering tips, 35; lubricants, 16; parts of, 13–14; preventive maintenance, 16; repair kits, 16, 235; repair services, 242–43; replacing, 4, 16, 34; replacing slider, 15; sizes, 14; sleeping bags, 13, 15, 60; tents, 50; troubleshooting, 14–15; types of, 13; wetsuits, 16; Zipper Rescue Kit, 16, 235